THE POWER OF
THE PRESS

THE ANTEROOM OF THE REPORTERS' GALLERY DURING A STUPID SPEECH.

THE POWER OF THE PRESS

The Birth of American Political Reporting

Thomas C. Leonard

OXFORD UNIVERSITY PRESS
New York   Oxford

Oxford University Press

Oxford   New York   Toronto
Delhi   Bombay   Calcutta   Madras   Karachi
Petaling   Jaya   Singapore   Hong Kong   Tokyo
Nairobi   Dar es Salaam   Cape Town
Melbourne   Auckland

and associated companies in
Beirut   Berlin   Ibadan   Nicosia

First published in 1986 by Oxford University Press, Inc.,
200 Madison Avenue, New York, New York 10016

First issued as an Oxford University Press paperback, 1987

Oxford is a registered trademark of Oxford University Press

Library of Congress Catalogine-in-Publication Data
Leonard, Thomas C., 1944–
The power of the press.
Bibliography: p.
Includes index.
1. Press and politics—United States—History.
I. Title.
PN4888.P6L46   1986   071'.3   85–21621
ISBN 0-19-503719-7
ISBN 0-19-505184-X(pbk.)

2   4   6   8   10   9   7   5   3

Printed in the United States of America

For Carol, Peter, and Anne

Contents

THE POWER OF
THE PRESS

INTRODUCTION

The Press Vernacular and American Politics

America's first lawmakers got letters like this one, sent to Washington in 1832 from a voter whose address was "about the land" of the Duck River in Tennessee: "I have this moment concluded . . . to write this very letter to you first to say 'how de y do' and therefore, *how are you* and in the next, in place of instructions upon great political subjects to ask a favour: to wit, I want to read the news this winter and therefore want you send me . . . papers on both sides of questions." This "virgin in politicks" said nothing about what was at stake for him in Washington. He apparently had no more need for advice from an editor than from the congressman (and he worried that a journalist "might beget me with bastard opinions"). This man said, simply, that political news suited his taste.[1] We do not know what this citizen made of the controversies he followed in the newspapers that reached the Duck River, but if we can understand how reporting drew him into political life we will learn something about how Americans made their experiment in government work.

The point of this inquiry is to help answer questions on a simple theme. What led Americans to pay so much attention to their government . . . to welcome debate . . . and to vote? In other words, how did Americans come to find politics *interesting*? This, "one of the least studied important themes in political history,"[2] can be better understood by paying attention to political reporting.

There is no argument here that all of American political culture

3

is thrown open by a reevaluation of its journalism. Much careful work on the press has been weakened by claiming too much and asking readers to look at too little. Rarely is the press the ultimate source of political interest, so a full account of what directed attention to politics would have to encompass everything from reference groups and religious ideals to the mechanics of electioneering. What I hope to show is how the press provided a vernacular—a common language in both words and pictures—for political interests to be expressed and shared.

"Vernacular" suggests a means of expression whose appeal and meaning can be taken for granted. Often the press has invented the seemingly natural ways of making sense of political life. Catchwords come from political reporting: "the system," "the interests," even "graft" and "bunk." To think about the American political process is to sort through an archive of dramatic devices and pictures fashioned by journalists. This book is about how the press and the public together learned this storytelling.

"Vernacular" also suggests the unplanned and the adaptable, and it is certainly true that political reporting has had a vernacular tradition in this sense. Reporting grew and changed with the flexibility of a living language. No one set down standards at the outset, and few conventions have proved lasting. Devices for telling political stories often had no sanction stronger than the popular culture of the day. The "lead" that every reporter today prizes held little interest for journalists of the eighteenth and nineteenth centuries. The syntax for pictures of political leaders has changed in astonishing ways. When this nation was formed, few knew how to take down what a leader said and many citizens believed the words of government should be embargoed. The man from the Duck River, in asking for the news of politics, was asking for information swirling by in new forms. The papers he requested were novel in their focus on the talk of legislative chambers. This book is about the shifts in taste of precisely this sort.

The birth of political reporting is part of the creation of those values that made politics, as America knows it, legitimate: the notions that competing points of view benefit a community and that the press exists to offer varied perspectives. It is worth emphasizing—as recent scholarship has shown—that this was not the common wisdom at America's beginning.

The first communities in the New World had no sturdy institutions to circulate political discussion and few habits of respect for disagreement. The printing press was tightly controlled where it was allowed into a colony. New York had no press under the Dutch, and the English kept the machine out during the first decades of their ascendancy. Virginia, one royal governor thanked God, had no press in its first century of government. Churches in the colonies did not welcome debate on public questions. Whether in the austere "peaceable kingdoms" of the New England Puritans or amidst the show of wealth and power in Anglican Virginia, religious communities rarely tolerated dissent. Each denomination tried to speak with a single voice. Villages argued about public questions, sometimes quite democratically, but serious disagreement usually meant separation and the creation of a new community of the like-minded. Colonial legislatures often did ring with a clash of views. But the elected representatives muffled this. All the assemblies restricted the publication of proceedings, and before 1766 not one was regularly open to the public.

In the eighteenth century, the idea of party and faction was universally hated. Each city had its own web of family and business interests, ready to trap an advocate who took a wrong step. Candidates for office did not campaign in the modern sense of announcing what they stood for. Parades and banquets were common in political life, but compared with Europe, colonial Americans were poor in rituals and settings for competing ideas to be dramatized. During the French Revolution, Paris had more than 200 theaters. During the American Revolution there were only a handful of theater companies in the thirteen colonies.

(Most theater people passed the crisis in Jamaica; those that remained were encouraged by the Continental Congress not to perform.)

The invention of a republic was not the same thing as the creation of meaningful forums for argument. The Anti-Feder-alists viewed the Constitutional Convention as a dangerous and illegitimate gathering (many opponents of the Constitution were barred from the work in Philadelphia). The statesmanship of 1787 was a good deal easier to celebrate than Congress in its first decade. Like the congresses of the Confederation period, this was an itinerant assembly, often arguing in secret when it stayed put in a town and rarely able to fix the public's attention.

Many American institutions and arts grew shy of politics in the early republic. The dozen or so propaganda plays written to inspire Patriots against Great Britain did not lead to a theater much interested in how the republic was run. Melodrama, for example, had almost nothing to say about government. En-graving and the stunning new art of lithography drifted away from early political uses (Paul Revere's illustrations set a different agenda than the shipwrecks and winning horses that dominated the Currier & Ives catalogue). "Art of the Revolution" is a useful category for the fine arts, but terms like "Jacksonian" or "Whig" or even "anti-slavery" fit surprisingly little of the nation's visual arts. Even public address kept political ideas at bay. Early in the nineteenth century Americans rushed to lecture programs that ignored electoral politics and admitted political gadflies only on condition that they cease their buzzing. Nearly a half-century after America won its independence, Alexis de Tocqueville found a society that was oblivious to debate on fundamental issues and poor in ways to dramatize serious public questions. Amer-icans, the Frenchman thought, were deeply suspicious of com-peting ideas.

Democratic and egalitarian forces in American society did not *uniformly* build forums for controversy. In a society where stage managers and picture merchants found politics a plague, how did journalists do so well with public controversy? Certainly the commercial press had slim success with political debate before the nineteenth century. The first newspapers of the eighteenth century stepped around the angry factional disputes in their communities as one would dodge recruiters for an unpleasant voyage. Few of the men who drafted the Constitution suspected that newspapers would play a central role in the republic. Thomas Jefferson's remark in favor of newspapers without government rather than a government without newspapers was a *bon mot*, not a commitment. In office he speculated that citizens were better informed if they never looked at a paper. Well after 1789 many leaders found the entire enterprise of reporting an annoyance, at best. Largely without tradition, often without welcome, the commercial press found itself at the center of government in the young republic.

In the second quarter of the nineteenth century both the jockeying for public office and the substantive debate about government captured the attention of even the most isolated citizens. The dizzy growth of voluntary organizations and new political parties is only the most obvious sign of this popularization of politics. Americans liked to talk politics. Candidates were expected to thrust and parry Constitutional questions throughout the campaign. The inability to make a good three-hour speech on the tariff was as damaging to careers as an inept thirty-second spot on television today. Citizens turned out for speeches and, like the man from Tennessee, they sought out the merciless, narrow columns that spread the debates across the nation. Journalists and politicians used newspapers to tell readers, in no uncertain terms, how to vote. Election days were climaxes of public excitement with turnouts which were often 50 per cent above those in recent American history. Measured by voter turnout, (which was above 95 per cent of those eligible in several states), this broad appeal of politics continued with the rise of populism, socialism and the beginnings of the progressive movement. In the first decade of the twentieth century, however, elections lost their magnetism, and apathy became a potent new factor in national politics. How can we explain the relish for political news and debate in the nineteenth century? Why did politics become less engaging for the general public at the very time journalists were better able to record and dramatize how America was governed?

The press has not been looked at closely enough in addressing these questions. Many researchers have given a detailed record of how papers were linked to parties and candidates. The "stands" of important (and not very important) editors have been set down in many books. There is no reason simply to continue on this path. Scholarship set so firmly in the institutional development of press and party cannot say enough about how journalists came to write stories that made politics compelling and so drew readers into political wrangles. This is not, then, a history that always stays close to the familiar sweep of national politics and its famous battles.

Our concern will be the episodes in political reporting that have given form and weight to new attitudes about government. Some of these changes in journalism, such as the rise of muckraking at the beginning of this century, are staples of American political history. I take the matter up again because there are new lessons to learn. Other developments, such as the simple act of reporting what a politician says, have received remarkably little attention. Perhaps the rapid changes in political coverage in the last decades of the twentieth century make it easier to ask questions about what an earlier society lived through.

These case studies take us close to current worries about the media in politics. The inadequacies of reporting today are rarely a simple matter of ideology or special interest getting in the way of the facts. The main limitations of political journalism are built into the ways most of us, inside and outside the profession, think political stories should be told. We prize certain forms in political narratives. We expect drama and conflict. We want simplifications and pictures that are easy to grasp. Since the narrative forms are a large part of the trouble with political reporting, it is important to see how they arose. What sorts of truth about government is journalism prepared to tell? What does the press give up to meet its imperative to reach and hold its public? The study of how the press helped Americans to become interested in politics in the first place suggests reasons why some of the public today has tuned out.

I

NEW PRACTICES AND
NEW IDEALS OF THE
EIGHTEENTH-CENTURY PRESS

1

"The Wicked Printer"

The first American to publish dissent, week after week, was James Franklin. Before the first issue of the *New-England Courant* in the summer of 1721, Boston's newspapers contained what the town's religious leaders and magistrates found agreeable. In 1690 a printer had scorned the government and found his paper suppressed after one issue. The lesson was not lost on the publishers of the first successful papers after the turn of the century. Franklin competed with two newspapers that bore the legend, "Published by Authority" on the masthead.

There were no prosperous merchants of news in the New World at this time and James Franklin had no reason to think he would be the first. He was a twenty-four-year-old printer starting up his shop on a back street. His front door faced the prison. He proposed to criticize the very figures in church and government he needed for the additional printing jobs that would pay his bills. Independence was not a practical ideal for printers, especially when they risked bringing out a newspaper. The public had to be lured into a habit that was new in the English-speaking world outside of London and a few country towns in Great Britain. Readers had to be attracted to the shop with a sixpence in hand. Subscriptions through the post riders were so seldom paid in full that eighteenth-century newspapers frequently carried appeals and threats to the customers. Delinquent subscribers often settled with produce or any other goods that could be spared, making the printer a perplexed warehouseman. Paid or unpaid, the circulation of a Boston newspaper had never been more than five hundred.

All else was to this scale. A colonial print shop was often one press in a single room. Visitors to the restored shops in Colonial Williamsburg or Sturbridge Village see the tight accommodation between artisan and tools. A printer could span the flatbed press with an arm; an extra step back while pulling the platen down on the sheet carried the operator to the end of the machine. Racks to dry the paper and braces for the press were just over-head. Close by, a work table or case flanked every window. No news could pass quickly from this cell. It took sixteen hours to set the type for two pages of a newspaper. Two artisans working smoothly together on the thirteen operations required to bring inked type down upon paper were expected to print 240 sheets an hour. Each page must dry before the process could begin again to print the other side. Through most of the eighteenth century, the four-page weekly paper was not far from the limits of the resources at hand.

Putting out the news in this way was the direct ancestral line to the modern world's "journalist" (a term not in common use until the end of the eighteenth century). In so far as journalism suggests gathering information and catching attention with a point of view, few of the people who brought out the first news-papers were journalists. They were mostly artisans with no spe-cial training in collecting information. Legend did not yet credit them with special knowledge of their community but only with stigmata: ink stains and an uneven gait from the straining at the press. Some who conducted newspapers were entrepreneurs removed from manual labor— a bookseller or, more commonly, a post-master (a prized position because the editor could dis-creetly read mail and see incoming newspapers ahead of com-petitors). The talent, leisure, and vanity of the first editors were not great enough to tempt them to fill their papers with their own writing. They were citizens who waited for news to be brought by others. Failing to receive such gifts, the first journalists simply reprinted what they already found published in European papers.

James Franklin had wider experience and a stronger interest in news than his competitors. He had practiced his trade in London and there contracted a taste for Augustan wit. If Boston was not yet capable of its own *Tatler* or *Spectator*, Franklin meant at least to test the limits of what a printer could do with a newspaper. Inevitably, Franklin stands in history as a fumbler who missed his main chance. His chief asset in 1721 was his brother Benjamin, the fifteen-year-old apprentice on the *Courant*. Benjamin was the only man in the print shops of the first half of the century with both a ready pen and a golden touch on the ledger books. James beat his brother, so the ambitious boy broke free of the apprenticeship after the first year of newspaper crusading. Benjamin's *Autobiography* describes his brother with little sign of affection. Benjamin, though, did not forget his brother's dissent and left an archive to mark it. Convention and prudence led most contributors to the eighteenth-century press to write anonymously. Benjamin's file of the *Courant* is in the British Museum with his notations of the major contributors in his brother's political battle. From Benjamin Franklin's hand we have a rare chance to see how social criticism entered American journalism.

Death was the news of Boston in 1721. In April the *H. M. S. Seahorse* docked in the harbor, carrying the smallpox. The disease spread before the town's selectmen could order a quarantine. That summer brought an epidemic; more than half of the population was infected, and of these one in seven citizens died. In the year after the *Seahorse* arrived, the funeral bell upset the peace of the city so frequently that the authorities restricted the tolling.

Boston was not, as in the epidemics of the seventeenth century, helpless before the calamity. Leading ministers and doctors believed that inoculation might save the town. In the Rev. Mr. Cotton Mather, the will to lead burned as strongly as in his Puritan forefathers who had founded the colony. Mather read, in scientific literature from Europe, of inoculation in the Near East. He was also impressed by the stories told by illiterate slaves (North Africans used inoculation successfully earlier than Europeans). As was Mather's habit, he rushed into print with his discoveries and enlisted other godly men to help the community. The Latin reports of doctors and the folk traditions of blacks led to the same procedure. Healthy citizens were to be lanced, twice, and after the blood was wiped away, the pus from a victim of smallpox was placed in the cuts. A mild case of discrete smallpox was expected, but the patient recovered (it was said) with immunity to the virulent forms. To a society without a germ theory of disease (and not accustomed to looking to Asia or to Africa for wisdom) this procedure was open to attack. There were important medical figures on the other side of the question. By the late summer of 1721 the medical treatment had set off a political campaign between inoculators and anti-inoculators. The *Courant* rose to the argument.

No one who took up the pen was ignorant of the literary forms that had long guided discussions of public questions in New England. This was not a culture likely to allow calamity to pass without a meticulous self-examination. Every Protestant community had its careful accounting of martyrdom during the past century. The wilderness of America was thought of as a new stage for this drama of survival. Puritans expected adversity and studied the lessons it taught. From the earliest days of the colony, "God's Controversy with New England" had been a theme of sermons and personal devotions. The presses of Boston and Cambridge were kept busy with tracts that took the measure of disasters as well as less tangible signs of God's displeasure: worldliness and a dulling of the religious spirit. More than watchmen and stewards, the ministers assumed the role of Jeremiah, beseeching citizens to return to God's way. Civil authority followed, pointing with alarm, declaring fast days, and punishing iniquity as it was detected.

New England's energy for self-examination extended far beyond the jeremiad. Few cultures have taken the personal journal more seriously. The founding governors, William Bradford of the Plymouth colony and John Winthrop of Massachusetts Bay, both kept journals of the voyage, the desperate early years, and their travail in office. Like the ministers—and citizens of lower status—they wrote to collect evidence of God's plan, and no event was too trivial, or too appalling, to be set down. The journal of Samuel Sewall, a merchant and benefactor of the Franklin family, covers half a century in several volumes. Sewall showed equal determination to chart the commercial life around him and to decide on the evidence against witches. For some in New England these broad interests and stern habits of attention led directly to the cosmopolitan lure of science. Cotton Mather had showered the Royal Society with his observations and had been elected a fellow for his efforts. From the provincial darkness of seventeenth-century Harvard, a few men did work that even Sir Isaac Newton found valuable. This much, then, could be expected of Boston's calamity: a run of jeremiads; careful accounts of death in journals; and scientific papers addressed to Europe.

Not one of these models could easily serve the weekly press. Much of what was searching and exhortatory in New England culture simply ran aground in the first newspapers. Printers were town boosters, eager to foster trade by hiding bad news. Epidemics were often hushed up in the eighteenth century.[1] Already by the 1720s, proprietors had learned not to go looking for trouble close at hand. The information and instruction they admitted to their papers was usually distant. Scourges happened in rival cities. Brief notes of foreign affairs—mostly royal affairs—marched down the columns, stopping at reprints of improving essays taken from British publications. Political announcements appeared as authorities wished them to reach the public. In Westminster, or even the Boston town hall, governors got little information about what citizens thought by reading newspapers of Boston. Happily, from their point of view, the men in authority also got little advice. Other than polite essays on manners, neither did anyone else. Notes of ships in the harbor and of goods for sale were the only local stories sure to be in a newspaper.

Beyond boosting commercial life, the principle behind news selection was that of readable indifference: fresh notices of matters that had no bearing on public questions. Royalty in Poland was one dependable well for such items in the eighteenth century. The first newspapers were museums filled with curiosities from around the world. The editors were not eccentric, they were careful. Exotic items were almost always safe. There was almost no change in the technology of printing in the eighteenth century; and in the first newspapers that came from the flatbed press, there were no signs that the shape of news would change either.[2]

James Franklin's step into the smallpox controversy was as bold as the act of any printer before the Revolution. His bid to lead his community went beyond the trade practices of most printers until the political storms of the 1760s. The comment and news supplied by James Franklin have not lost the power to shock. There was no sentimentality and little empathy for fellow citizens in Franklin's crusading. The *Courant* stood against the powerful New England traditions of close observation and meditation on the suffering. The *Courant* ridiculed the ministers' remedy for the smallpox, prodded the government to stop it, and, while frightening fellow citizens, tried hard to amuse them.

Boston's most distinguished physician, William Douglass, made a strong case against inoculation in the weekly press. Trained in Edinburgh, Leyden, and Paris, Douglass was the only person in the colony to hold a doctorate in medicine. At the time of the epidemic he had been a resident of Boston for only three years and he had certainly not gotten over the sense of living among gullible provincials. Douglass used his training to pick apart the rationale of the inoculators. He was not, first of all, impressed by the reports of inoculation in the Near East. He had read those case histories, indeed, it was his copy of the Royal Society of London's *Philosophical Transactions* that Mather had studied. The doctor believed that Boston's divines, and the physicians who supported them, had missed the point. In the first issue of the *Courant*, Douglass called his chief medical rival, Zabdiel Boylston, an "illiterate" who fumbled with the Latin reports and "Quack Advertisements." Douglass said that the Rev. Mr. Mather, too, had not understood what he had read. To this doctor's trained mind, inoculation was "not in the least vouched or recommended (being meerly published, in the Philosophick Transactions by way of Amusement). . . ."

Douglass claimed that "discouraging Evidences" of inoculation had been overlooked by certain "*Gentlemen of Piety and Learning, profoundly ignorant of the Matter.*" The doctor said there were "dismal Consequences" of inoculation in three cases he had heard about. He feared a greater danger from the "*mischievous propagating the Infection* in the most Publick Trading Place of the Town then entirely free of the same." That is, the inoculated would carry the infection through the town and into the country, even if they survived their exposure to the disease, because Boylston simply lanced patients and let them go. Douglass found that his enemies would not face these facts and were content to gamble with lives to please their vanity. He dared to say in Franklin's paper that this was a crime and impiety.[3]

Douglass, with this opening charge, marked the two lines of attack in the *Courant*'s long war against inoculation. More cases would keep the danger before readers. A deeper look into the character of inoculators would reveal the arrogance and folly of their experiment.

This line of argument carried a great many people along, some in the twentieth century. After a first call for contributors on both sides of the question, James Franklin gave his paper over to the anti-inoculators. Perry Miller, in his magisterial work on the Puritans, credited Mather and the inoculators with only "a lucky shot." "Douglass and the *Courant*," Miller argued, "had reason, caution, sobriety, and scientific authority (as well as all the wit) on their side."[4] How can this newspaper's view of its world be judged? The hindsight of modern preventive medicine is unfair. The standard of judgment cannot be modern reporting practices nor even what was possible in a literary capital (where Daniel Defoe was preparing his *Journal of the Plague Year*). Boston must be taken in its own time and on its own terms and judged only by those ways of presenting information that were available in this culture. There is no need to strip the laurels Perry Miller awarded to this first struggle over public policy in a newspaper. But there is good reason to look more closely at the course the *Courant* set for newspapers to follow in the eighteenth century.

The *Courant* stood, as newspapers were for so long to stand, against the great tradition of exact observation that had obsessed New England. In this newspaper the marshaling of facts was casual and almost incidental to argument. Douglass, so skeptical of reports to the Royal Society, did not accept his chance to examine the inoculated. At the beginning of Boylston's experiment Douglass refused an offer to examine his colleague's patients and simply announced that inoculation had *"proved to be of fatal & dangerous Consequence."* It is likely that this primitive form of inoculation did spread the disease, but the *Courant* in the next six months never looked to confirm Douglass's hunch. The paper ignored the careful reports of successful inoculation that the ministers circulated in the fall of 1721. Franklin did not make contact with that "Army of Witnesses" to the safety of inoculation that a rival paper found in Boston. According to one minister, none of the critics visited the inoculated "as they might easily have done" to see the success of the procedure. Even the public display of successful inoculation was not reported in the *Courant.*[5]

Douglass gave a dark prognosis of patients he had chosen not to see and countered reports of joyful inoculations with speculations of how closely these people had cheated death. Rumor was indeed the doctor's main authority: "The Town knows the violence of B—'s Son's Inoculation-Fever, the narrow Escape of old Mr. W—b, the height of C—'s Fever, the great Degree of Despair in Mr. H— while ill. . . ." This was a strange way for Douglass to proceed. He was a skilled observer, not normally ready to draw conclusions without information he could verify.

In the next decade his accounts of a scarlet fever epidemic were the first adequate description in medical history. Douglass chose a point of view for newspaper controversy that was at variance with his training and his talents. Boston's weekly press offered less acute reporting than the pamphlets published that fall by the less talented men on the other side of the question.[6]

James Franklin promised readers news of the victims of inoculation, but the *Courant* could not improve on Douglass' hearsay. Another practitioner, George Steward, was given space to gossip about the sad fate of the inoculated. Franklin published the report of fourteen deaths, but admitted that the man who told this story to Steward would not stand behind it. Franklin adopted the solution of many fearful printers and deleted most of the letters in the names of people mentioned in reports. Only once did the *Courant* print the full name of a citizen of the town "who receiv'd the Infection by Inoculation." (And the paper did not tell readers that in this case the man was infirm before he was inoculated and that he received the treatment over Boylston's protest.) Most victims were found just out of sight of townsmen, to the south in Roxbury. In the first half-year of this newspaper, Roxbury served as a moral example. Readers learned nothing of the village except that citizens were inoculated there and, regularly died of the smallpox.[7]

In Boston, as one citizen in thirteen died, the *Courant* reported not the course of the disease, but rather the insults of the survivors. In this town of fewer than 11,000—with the total number of doctors, ministers, and contributors to the press fewer than 100—much of the inoculation controversy inevitably was colored by personal animosities. Like Douglass, many in the debate were attempting to redress slights to their authority. James Franklin did much to encourage fractures along status lines. Franklin was the only one to publish (and he did this twice) the curse he received from Cotton Mather. When they met on a Boston street the Rev. Mr. Mather had reminded the young man of the Biblical threat to *"Smite thro' the loins"* those critics of men who served God.[8]

The printer answered with his own charges of a reckless clergy. The *Courant* saw an exercise of illegitimate power. Dismissing the ministers' reasoned case for inoculation, Douglass saw a simple issue: "viz. their Character, should prevail with the Populace. . . . " The *Courant* went further and laughed at the *"naked Merits"* of clerics as physicians—

> Who like faithful Shepherds take care of their *Flocks*,
> By teaching and practicing what's Orthodox,
> Pray hard against *Sickness*, yet preach up the *POX!*

And it was not the laymen of Boston alone who would suffer. John Eyre, three years out of Harvard College, lectured the ministers about their proper place. He warned that when a divine falls "from a Star in the Firmament of Heaven, he becomes a sooty Coal in the blackest Hell, and receiveth the greatest Damnation."[9]

This was the *Courant*'s cruelest act, to perform the ministers' job of watching and warning the community. James Franklin's own verses seem written for a pulpit:

> But cursed Sin with rapid Feet
> And quicker Flight spread thro' the Town,
> Taints every Soul in every Street,
> And calls the hov'ring Vengeance down.

Readers learned, *from a newspaper*, that the "crying Abominations" of Boston were profaneness, debauchery, pride, idleness, luxury, and contempt of the gospel. Then the *Courant* added to the list *"Injustice* and *Oppression"* and the *"irregular Conduct"* of ministers bent on inoculation. The paper concluded, "we might justly expect that God would *visit for these Things*, and that his Soul would be avenged on such a people as this."[10]

The journalist had taken over the role of Jeremiah. It was, of course, presumptuous for a young artisan such as Franklin to think that he could guide the community as wisely as the learned gentlemen of the church. But nothing seemed beyond the reach of the contributors to this new publishing enterprise if, as the *Courant* judged, many citizens "are disposed to give a fairer hearing to what they find in a *News-Paper* than in a *Sermon*."[11]

The Massachusetts colony had probably never been free of men and women who scoffed at the Puritan leaders. But before these issues of the *Courant*, the abuse was shouted in taverns or scrawled on buildings at night, not dignified by print. It had been impossible for even the best organized critics (such as Anglicans or Quakers) to remain within this society and publish their dissent. In 1721 the *Courant* was, to the ministers, one of the most galling signs that times had changed. "I can well remember," the patriarch of the Mather family thundered, "when the Civil Government would have taken an effectual Course to suppress such a *Cursed Libel*!"[12]

But this journalism was not simply a continuation of angry gossip about men in authority. The *Courant* focused and directed abuse, it made personal insults add up to an explicit social grievance. Before Franklin published, Cotton Mather found the enemies of inoculation to be incoherent. "They rave, they rail, they blaspheme; they talk not only like Ideots but also like *Franticks*," he noted in his diary in July. After August, with the *Courant* in the town, Mather and his friends knew their enemy and what he wanted:

Warnings are to be given unto the wicked Printer, and his Accomplices, who every week publish a vile Paper to lessen and blacken the Ministers of the Town, and render their Ministry ineffectual.

A Wickedness never parallel'd any where upon the Face of the Earth![13]

The Rev. Mr. Mather was quite capable of imagining attacks on the ministers, but in this case the assault was real. The upstart newspaper challenged the clergy's special role of steward for New England.

Public health was not a peripheral issue for the ministers. The body as well as the soul had long been their business. In the first decades of settlement the clergy often practiced medicine; though ministers welcomed an independent medical profession by the eighteenth century, men like Mather assumed they still had the duty to supervise. It was this stewardship itself that James Franklin and his newspaper ridiculed.

Journalists took on some of the ministers' duties but rejected others. The press did not comfort the bereaved during the epidemic and did nothing to add meaning or dignity to the deaths. The Puritan clergy, so suspicious of church rites, accepted the elegy and kept printers busy with their compositions. Even the stern Calvinist who took the occasion to remind sinners of the horrors of predestined hell, sanctified death with this poetic form. A minister who told bereaved parents that their child might be in hell was at least facing the terror of death head on and putting it in a divine scheme. Theorists of modernization who see an extension of empathy as a hallmark of secular society miss this point about a key network of communication. Newspapers had a narrower conception of benevolence than the elite groups whose power they challenged.[14]

The *Courant* has often been read as a harbinger of a changing colony, announcing the respectability of anti-ministerial sentiment and the insouciance of polite letters. This it was, but the news of Boston's dead in the *Courant* should halt any simple scheme to see the paper as a prospectus for a modern society. In two respects newspapers turned back the clock.

Death is always marked by ritual and, in many cultures, by elegy and meditation on the loss. The discovery of the dramatic shifts in these habits has been an impressive achievement of cultural historians. In his classic study, *The Waning of the Middle Ages*, Johan Huizinga noted, "the elegiac note is wanting altogether" in that era. He found that the horrible had become so familiar in fifteenth-century Paris that the funeral rituals became mixed with pleasure. Pictures of the 'Dance of Death' entertained the public. Feasts were held on the burying ground. Prostitutes lurked by the charnel house. In the folklore and the high art of early modern Europe it is not hard to find a similar antic quality in marking death. The riotous wake and the absurdist or erotic presentation of death itself were common among both the worldly and the pious. This was, of course, a world far different from the austere experiment in New England, but that is the point. The secular press of the eighteenth century put an antic quality back into death that the Puritans had done much to excise. The *Courant* offered an opportunity to escape the tolling bells and the constant fear of the pox by opening windows on sinful pleasures.[15]

In his second issue James Franklin pledged his good manners but called for contributions "Sarcastick, Ludicrous, or otherways amusing," and this set his course for the plague year. In the next issue the *Courant*'s resident wit, John Checkley, gossiped about Cotton Mather's nephew—an inoculation man who "with another *Debauchee*, at a Lodging with Two Sisters, of not the best Reputation in the World, upon the Bed with them several Hours, and this Spark sent for *Punch* to treat them with, and would have had *the Candle put out*, but they not having a Conveniency to light it again, it was *lock'd in a Closet*, and ————&c." Supporters of the inoculating ministers described the *Courant* as Boston's Hell-Fire Club, a wicked gathering of blasphemers and the debauched. Franklin, with an eye to readers, filled more space with prurient description of that London establishment than with indignant denial that he and his friends held a franchise.

In another respect, the *Courant* was recapturing a tradition of facing death that Cotton Mather's generation had lost. The first settlers of Massachusetts Bay had rarely brought their dead to public attention and if we may judge by the diaries that have survived, death was marked stoically. These Puritans had few services at funerals and did little to decorate graves. But by the end of the seventeenth century, death became an elaborate ritual in the colony. Funeral sermons were a major part of the work of ministers (and printers), while engravers were kept busy doing ever-more intricate designs for the gravestone and the printed page. Beautiful gloves were sent out as invitations to funerals

and members of the procession were often given commemora-
tive rings. In some journals, such as Samuel Sewall's, it appears
that funeral-going had become the center of social life. The quiet
funeral of the first decades of the colony gave way to meetings
for talk and music.[16] The din of the bells in Boston in 1721 was
not only testimony to the number of dead, but also to the number
of living who insisted that death be brought to the attention of
the town.

The young newspapers of Boston, especially the *Courant*, took
little notice of the dead. They seemed to care only for the living.
In October 1721 and then in January, at the end of the epidemic,
the *Courant* published the town's count of the deaths due to the
smallpox. (An equivalent loss today in Boston would be more
than 250 dead each day for six months.) But the paper gave
readers little more than these short columns of figures. In this
respect, too, Franklin was not "modern" for he stood as if trans-
ported back to the silent churchyards of early New England.
Journalism made death once again private, neither describing it
nor wrapping it in ritual. There were no last words, no elegies,
no testimonies from relatives.

What was new in the colony was the idea that, in addition to
the ritual, the meditative tradition could be dispensed with altogether. In the terrible month of October 1721, when nearly
half the deaths occurred, the *Courant* gave more space to verses
about nymphs than to obituary notices. Week after week, the
few victims who were noticed were not sanctified, as with "John
Rogers the Baptist, who while he lived said more than was
desired, and when he came to die said less than was expected. . . .[17] The ability to notice and dramatize the suffering
of fellow citizens has been the bedrock of most journalists' efforts
for reform in America. But at the birth of social criticism in the
media, this empathy is hard to detect. The notion of reform
rested on a different foundation.

Defiance was the soul of the *Courant*, the spirited cry of newcomers bumping against an old elite, of artisans mocking the

more respectable classes, of provincials picking up the language of London coffee houses, and of eighteenth-century men recovering the nerve to mock and amuse in the face of the grave. All of these impulses grew in the next generation, especially in the newspapers of the colonies. It is not possible to find a creative period of the press that was neatly bounded by principle or free of the ideas of a much earlier age. Sober and altruistic reporting was always admixed with the sort of defiance and ridicule of cherished institutions that James Franklin dared to make.

The Revolution (we shall see) best illustrates this rugged course of political journalism, but recurring crises such as the smallpox make the point almost as well. The greatest urban calamity of the eighteenth century, Philadelphia's yellow fever epidemic of 1793, was reported to the public in far greater detail than in the newspapers of James Franklin's day. But these newspapers in the capital city of the new nation quickly politicized the disease. Federalist and Republican papers blamed ideological enemies and found in public health a way to stretch their own claims for leadership. With some 15 per cent of citizens dead, the most talented journalists reached for the same antic notes that had come from Franklin's print shop. Newspapers offered the wretched survivors of Philadelphia ribald stories and Philip Freneau's poems to mock the epidemic.[18]

Already in James Franklin's Boston, newspapers were making the arguments for factions— but the political importance of the press was more than this. Readers found in these sheets the unexpected and the inappropriate at times of grave decision. These printers released the bottled thoughts of their readers, allowed old ideas and new ideas to drift together, and then claimed honor for the news let loose. Newspapers did nothing more important than to legitimize this wide sweep of argument in political life. The caution and even indifference of so much editing meant that voices, once raised, carried far. Since there was so little in the way of a routine for dissent in the newspapers, criticism meant a flailing about in which all sorts of tender interests were likely to be hit. A press secure in its role as a political observer might well have been more predictable and so easier for authorities to tame.

Beyond what they published, we have very little information on the motives and philosophy of individual printers as they stepped into controversy. These journalists did not set down their principles or goals before they plunged ahead. The silence speaks for them. Principles had little to do with the enterprise at first. Grievances that had not been articulated before, the excitement of a new role before the public, and the pleasure of defying convention were the sparks for social criticism. James Franklin showed what was on his mind a week after the first issue of the paper when he printed up an "Anti-Courant" broadside in hopes that the notoriety might increase sales of the *Courant*. Franklin was a man selling curses (his own and the ones he earned), strutting before the specter of death as he sought, seriously, to lead his fellow citizens.

Dignity was an afterthought, but a most important one. In the course of getting into trouble, Franklin acquired serious purpose. During the fall of 1721 the *Courant* reprinted three of "Cato's Letters" that had appeared in the London *Journal* early that summer. This was the first American publication for two Whig pamphleteers, John Trenchard and Thomas Gordon, and no editor has ever discovered authorities better able to pull their publication onto high moral ground. The complaints of these radical Whigs seemed to many Americans to be their own: Britain abused her long-suffering colonies and magistrates placed a yoke on the people's liberties. In the next decades Cato's Letters were quoted in every colonial newspaper, and editions of Trenchard and Gordon were a staple of American libraries. In the half-century before the Revolution, these English writers were probably as famous as Locke and certainly better known than Montesquieu, Rousseau, or Voltaire.[19] James Franklin showed the way to make Cato's Letters sound more radical than Trenchard and Gordon meant them to be. (The printer deleted praise of

George I when he printed generalized criticism of arbitrary, princely authority.) But in 1721 Franklin was not looking abroad for inequity; he had found it in Boston and used Cato to steady his course as he fought.

"Cato" offered an apologia for printers and made even their indiscretions seem noble. It is true that Trenchard and Gordon condemned personal libels and calumny and found "there are some truths not fit to be told. . . . " But when the evil affects the "Publick," then they said that blunt, even offensive criticism must be heard. "The exposing therefore of publick Wickedness, as it is a Duty which every Man owes to his Country, can never be a Libel in the Nature of Things. . . . Whoever calls publick and necessary Truths, Libels, does but apprize us of his own Character, and arm us with Caution against his Designs." Critics of inoculation who read Cato were not led to worry about an excess of zeal, nor were they taught to regret hot words about ministers. Historically, the blame of calumny rested with the unjust authorities who forced critics to be abusive. Today, the critic could not hold back: "the best Defence which we can have against their being Knaves, is to make it terrible to them to be Knaves." New tyrants might show themselves whenever critics failed to challenge them: "It is nothing strange, that men who think themselves unaccountable, should act unaccountably. . . . " Men in power who abused citizens thus stood unprotected against the press and Cato left these authorities cold comfort: "The best Way to escape the Virulence of Libels, is not to deserve them. . . . "[20]

In the continual reprinting and paraphrasing of this argument, printers came to believe these things. They idealized a role of scourge to their community that they had assumed without much thought. Fairness was another virtue, rarely practiced, but discovered and cherished in the course of getting into trouble. In the only piece he signed in the *Courant*, James Franklin claimed the dignity of "Impartiality" in working toward Cato's goal of saving citizens from " 'the same Standard of thinking'." He claimed that "those that have read the Courants must know that

I have not only publish'd Pieces wrote among ourselves in favour of Inoculation, but have given as full an Account of the Success of it in England, as the other Papers have done. . . . What my own Sentiments of things are, is of no Consequence, or any matter to any Body."[21]

As he publicized ideals that would guide the American press, Franklin overlooked what the *Courant* had done. In fact the paper dragged out the inoculation controversy and did not publish the facts that helped to resolve it. During the epidemic in Boston the paper carried twenty-one major pieces that condemned inoculation or inoculators and only two items favorable to the experiment (and one of these, to the knowing reader, was a parody of the inoculators' claims).[22] No matter, in the pages of the *Courant* Americans first found the exposure of "publick Wickedness" practiced actively and stated defiantly. The self-righteous conception of the crusading journalist as an "impartial" servant of the community was born.

The fire of controversy did not suddenly purify these ideals, but civic responsibility and fairness were bonded to the eighteenth-century printer. In the Mathers' Boston, in the worldly seaports of the Revolution, in the capitals of the new nation, journalists proved unable to explain themselves without clinging to these ideals. The press was, of course, often engaging in lip service and hypocrisy, but that was not all. The notion of civic impartiality made the press something more than a commodity shaped by the market or the mouthpiece for a client. James Franklin set the terms of debate about the press as he illustrated that a kept press would be difficult to achieve in the new world. Artisans given to lofty and cantankerous moods were not a comfort to government.[23]

It seemed, in the *Courant*'s first year, that the inoculators were routed, and not simply by words. During the epidemic it was unlucky to be ridiculed in this newspaper. A grenade (with a curse on inoculation attached) was thrown into Cotton Mather's house. The bomb landed near the bed (if not near the punch or women) of Mather's supposedly debauched nephew. In the spring of 1722, the epidemic past, William Douglass gloated that inoculation, "like the Serpents in Summer," had been crushed.[24] However, the grenade thrown at Mather was a dud, and newspapers did not resolve the issue of inoculation or prove that journalists could defy authority with impunity.

In the 1720s, town gossip and pamphlets written by inoculators showed Boston how to escape the smallpox. Boylston had inoculated more than 200 townsfolk, and, as stories circulated among neighbors, the experiment gained a good reputation. Careful reporting of cases by Boylston and one of the "inoculating ministers" in pamphlets provided the information about the course of the disease that the *Courant* had showed no interest in gathering. This reporting convinced the most skeptical guardians of the public health. The *Courant* played no role in setting the record straight.

The Mather curse on printers echoed through all the colonies in the half-century before the Revolution. The Common Law did not bend for Cato, and journalists risked libel actions, even if they printed the truth, on the grounds that criticism disturbed the public peace. Royal governors and colonial assemblies agreed that disrespectful printers should suffer and that simple inquisitiveness was grounds for discipline.

The men of the *Courant* were some of the first to learn just how many readers held the keys that could put writers in jail. John Checkley, the man Franklin prized for his wit, was fined when he renewed his attacks on the religious establishment in Massachusetts. The colony's General Court indicted another contributor to the *Courant* for daring, in the next decade, to publish his own newspaper that was a "sink of sedition, error and heresy."[25] James Franklin was caught in the summer of 1722 when he chided the government for waiting on the wind and weather to chase pirates. The authorities put him in the prison across the lane from his print shop. Now the civil arm was ready

to return slaps at the ministers, as James Franklin learned the
following January when the Massachusetts assembly banned his
paper.

In this dangerous world printers learned to defend themselves. They did not adopt a sweeping libertarian theory (reprinting Trenchard and Gordon was as far as they went in
philosophy). Business guided sentiment, especially toward the
dead. Editors did not open up their columns to unpaid mem-
orials to their fellow citizens. The obituary and the elegy had
small place in the eighteenth-century newspaper. Sentiment and
civic responsibility did not lead journalists to take serious notice
of death until the very end of the century when Boston papers
came together to grant free coverage to "eminently public characters."[26] Franklin had seen that a newspaper might be steward
to the community and know better than ministers or magistrates.
Mather was justified in using strong language, for much was at
stake. Upstarts were using the printed word to take on the government. What he could not foresee was that "wicked" printers
would carry their sense of moral authority almost as far as he
did.

2

News for a Revolution

With the American Revolution taking shape about him, a Boston shopkeeper built a file of newspapers. Harbottle Dorr was one member of that radical group, the Sons of Liberty, who put more energy into collecting than direct action. He numbered some 3500 pages, bound them into four folios, constructed indexes, and then, through a complex code of numbers and letters, led the reader back and forth through a decade of news. Dorr scribbled praise of patriots and insults for Crown officials in the margins. He hoped that all of this "very GREAT Trouble" would contribute to the political history of his country. Dorr saved pamphlets too, and a few engravings, but their place—crushed beneath the thick layers of newsprint—is a reminder of how much more available newspapers were to those who followed political developments.[1]

One type of report during one period of resistance to the Crown is especially significant. Newspaper exposés—the dramatic revelation of hidden information—show how revolutionary ideology was translated into a language ordinary citizens could use to make sense of daily events. General ideas of republican virtue and royal corruption were, indeed, ancient and sprang to life outside newspapers. But the task of making evidence fit such notions was taken up by the weekly press. Political exposés were particularly important between 1768 and 1773, after the Stamp Act crisis and before the Tea Party in Boston harbor quickened the pace. Most of Harbottle Dorr's collection is a record of the many months when British power seemed overwhelming and political theorists hung on current events, producing letters for the newspapers. Here one has the chance to see how ideas entered the lives of citizens who followed the news.[2]

Political news itself still was novel enough in Dorr's colonial society to be worth collecting. Before the protests of the mid–1760s, few American newspapers had taken broad and sustained interest in the political disputes of the New World. There were plenty of entrepreneurs with presses in the colonies. The growth of newspapers, especially in seaports, kept pace with the spread of printing in England. There were about two dozen American weekly papers in the mid-60s, and since James Franklin's day nearly that many new papers had been born and died. The colonies lacked the intellectual resources for a political press.

The schooling for political controversy in the press was poor: disconnected wrangles in different cities, conducted by factions that shut down for long periods, then resumed arguments with much switching of sides. The colonies did not have the patrons for writers and traditions in quarrels that could nurture political advocacy. In this respect, the remoteness from the central political community in London was important. There was not the concentration of talent and patronage to make an American Grub Street. Political journalism did exist in several towns. Elections in New York, Philadelphia, and Charleston, for example, saw factions push their appeals and screeds into newspapers, past the worried printers. Advertisements for votes were common in newspapers by 1750. Political reporting did not yet bring disputes in other communities into view or sustain interest at home much beyond the crisis of the moment. There was little of the clarity and pride in argument that one finds so easily in Georgian Britain or in the press of the Revolution. It is revealing that much political matter in the press of the early eighteenth century is so veiled and elliptical that specialists cannot be sure they understand the references. The newspaper did not yet reach out to insist that the general reader attend to the disputes. Often, newspapers stuck by the tradition of passing over conflict, especially if it was close at hand, and serving readers with reports of distant intrigues, wars, and good manners. Printers and readers alike celebrated "indifferent" news that could be peacefully received by the community.[3]

This seemed a prudent course to journalists who had seen bolder editors jailed. The cheerful memoirs of the printer's life written by Benjamin Franklin and Isaiah Thomas as old men should not mislead us about the dangers of gathering news. Before these famous memoirs were published, the most detailed narrative of the trade was *A Total Eclipse of Liberty* (1755) by Daniel Fowle. This printer was thrown in a cell without trial for publishing criticism of the Massachusetts assembly. Fowle wrote about political reporting on the floor of his damp cell in the company of large rats. Benjamin Franklin published nothing to support Fowle's cry for justice. Benjamin conducted his successful *Pennsylvania Gazette* with far more caution than his brother had shown. Nor had Franklin spoken out during the ten months John Peter Zenger of New York was imprisoned for publishing criticism of the royal governor. Zenger's harassment and trial seemed to impress journalists more deeply than the not guilty verdict he finally won in his celebrated trial of 1735. "I once thought a little *Politics* now and then thrown out among our Readers might wet their Appetites," a New York printer mused, addressing "Brother Zenger," "but upon Second thoughts (Brother) we had as good let that alone." The advice was sound, even in the comparatively open political atmosphere of New York. Zenger himself left court a tame publisher, ready to accept government patronage.[4]

At the beginning of a folio, Harbottle Dorr noted what no American of his generation could take for granted: "News Papers in General contain, not only the News of the Day, often Intelligence of the greatest Moment. . . . " Never before had the colonial press carried so much heated talk about the public good, and most of the arguments began or were amplified in Boston's newspapers. There is an abundance of "propaganda" and "partisanship" here, as many observers have noted.[5] There are also new turns in the talk of politics that have not been clearly recognized. Political exposés brought a commitment to investigation and a common language deploring misrepresentation in the press.

The first work of newspapers in the Revolution was not the planning of a new society but rather the exposure of injustice in the old. The criticism was rarely straightforward or even focused on the largest abuses as the patriots saw them. Because the insurgents were artful, because they were discovering where they wished to go, and because political debate proceeded from a stream of confusing events, the press charted a meandering path for resistance to the Crown. This process throws as much light on American politics as the eventual settlement with its mature republican philosophy and constitutional documents. The press was showing citizens how to think about politics, not just what to think.

John Dickinson's anonymous newspaper articles against British legislation, "Letters from a Farmer in Pennsylvania," owed much to his ability to fascinate Americans with disguises. The Farmer (as patriots insisted on calling this urbane politician even after his name was revealed) addressed two bold measures from London: an act suspending the New York assembly and the Townshend Revenue Acts which taxed tea, lead, paper, and paint imported into the colonies. News of the British measures did not stir the colonies in 1767. The ever-vigilant Boston patriots met to protest the Townshend duties, but even they did not think this was a crisis. It was the way information was presented, not the news itself, that moved the public. Dickinson used newspapers to show Americans the disguise that hid the menace.

The Farmer told Americans that he spent his days in a library and that research was his harvest. Works on history and political economy graced these letters and readers could well believe that "*every statute* relating to these colonies" had been parsed. The scholarship made British policy seem like a rationale for lawlessness. London had announced that the punishment of New York for failing to grant supplies to the king's troops was not a tax question at all. The Townshend Revenue Acts were called "external" levies—simple customs duties that would defray the administrative costs of the empire. Throughout the colonies, in nineteen of the twenty-three English language papers, the Farmer unmasked the deception: "UNLESS THE MOST WATCHFUL ATTENTION BE EXERTED, A NEW SERVITUDE MAY BE SLIPPED UPON US, UNDER THE SANCTION OF USUAL AND RESPECTABLE TERMS."[6] In New York, as the Farmer saw it, the British were extorting a tax, not simply quartering troops. The Townshend Acts were not the "external" duties regulating trade that Americans expected from Parliament but rather the same sort of taxation without consent that the colonies had fought in the Stamp Act during the mid–1760s. "External" was the camouflage of an administration bent on imposing a tyrannical British establishment on the New World.

The danger, the Farmer admitted, was hard to see because the tax burden, even in New York, was small. "*That* is the very circumstance most alarming to me. For I am convinced, that the authors of this [Townshend] law would never have obtained an act to raise so trifling a sum as it must do, had they not intended by it to establish a *precedent* for future use. To console ourselves with the *smallness* of the duties, is to walk deliberately into the snare that is set for us, praising the *neatness* of the workmanship." Here are striking features of Dickinson's political reporting and of the Farmer's appeal. The real political condition of America is disguised but stands revealed by small signs. Words with cunning double meanings are the clues to tyranny. Small injustices, because they *are* small, are signs of a larger conspiracy against liberty.[7]

Dickinson was far from alone in 1768 when he discovered a conspiracy. An Anglo-American political tradition predisposed most Whigs (and Tories) to conclude, by this time, that they faced conspirators. Yet that predisposition left open the question of precisely how citizens could recognize the enemy and his designs. This is the question that patriots blessed the Farmer for answering. He acknowledged that it was difficult to judge a government 3000 miles away. "But surely," the Farmer wrote, "the conduct of the crown or of the house, would in time sufficiently explain itself."[8] Dickinson told readers that by following the news of the day they would learn the truth. He implied that no matter how hidden or small the impositions, Americans could now see the trap—by opening their newspapers.

The newspaper format was in fact essential to his appeal. It was not simply that newspapers quickly built a public much larger than the later pamphlet sale. The "Letters from a Farmer" sought to draw the reader into the exposé—to answer doubts and make the reader an investigator of corruption. The illusion of a weekly exchange with readers made this possible. The twelve letters were written before the first was published, but Dickinson made it seem that readers shaped and encouraged the inquiry. "I rejoice to find that my two former letters to you, have been generally received with so much favour. . . ." Letter III reports, "Sorry I am to learn, that there are some few persons, who shake their heads, with solemn motion, and pretend to wonder, what can be the meaning of these letters." Dickinson frequently posed as a good listener ("An objection, I hear, has been made against my second letter"); then supplied patient answers. No single pamphlet could have so easily led readers to hunger for more revelations. "As you have already raised our expectations," a (real) reader insisted early in the series, "it is become a duty in you to gratify them." The exposé, for Dickinson, was a democratic art. Corruption, he believed, took concrete forms that citizens would not mistake even in the midst of crisis: "Ought not the PEOPLE therefore to watch? to observe facts? to search into causes? to investigate designs?"[9]

"The Farmer's Letters opened the eyes of all America," Harbottle Dorr scrawled on his copy. A Boston town meeting declared that the Farmer had "AWAKENED the most indolent and inactive to a Sense of Danger." A delegation of citizens of Pennsylvania, on orders from the governor, presented Dickinson with a box made from the heart of an oak and expressed the gratitude for an almost magical revelation that lay at the center of the Farmer's appeal. Dickinson was praised for showing "that destructive Project of *Taxation* . . . under a *Disguise so artfully contrived* as to delude Millions, YOU, Sir . . . ALONE detected the Monster concealed from others by an altered Appearance, exposed it, stripped of its insidious covering, in its own horrid Shape. . . ."[10]

As the Farmer's first letter was published, Dickinson himself departed from the calm tone of the essays. He wrote to a leader of the Boston Sons of Liberty calling attention "to the most imminent Danger." "I look towards the Province of Massachusetts Bay. She must, as she has hitherto done, first kindle the Sacred Flame, that on such occasions must warm and illuminate the Continent."[11]

The threat to American liberty in 1768 turned out to be unmistakable in the eyes of patriots.. Redcoats occupied Boston that fall. In response, Sam Adams and other Sons of Liberty clandestinely published in newspapers a serial "Journal of Occurrences." Boston's *Evening Post* spread the stories in the garrisoned town and every week stories of Boston under military rule appeared in papers from Salem, Massachusetts Bay, to Savannah, Georgia.

Set against the Farmer's letters of the previous year, these stories were notes from the underground. There was no show of law books or linguistic analysis in the "Journal of Occurrences." The news from Boston was that "violences are in the midst of us; and the sun as well as the moon and stars, witnesseth to the shameful prostitutions, that are daily committed in our streets and commons."[12] According to these reports, the troops left a trail of blood. The army made a spectacle of its cruelty by lashing deserters on Boston Common, and the men of the king's army and navy mauled each other when they met: "Several of the parties have lost thumbs and fingers," readers learned. The peaceful citizens of Boston suffered just as cruelly and precisely in these reports (the "Journal" measured a quart of American blood on the ground after one incident).[13]

An accounting of the crimes was, the "Journal" said, "as tedious, as it is painful," but the reporters stuck to the job. Consider this busy day:

> A married lady of this town was the other evening, when passing from one house to another, taken hold of by a soldier; who otherways behaved to her with great rudeness; a woman near Long Land was stopped by several soldiers, one of whom cried out seize her and carry her off; she was much surprised, but luckily got shelter in a house near by; Another woman was pursued by a soldier into a house near the north end, who dared to enter the same, and behave with great insolence: Several inhabitants while quietly passing the streets in the evening have been knocked down by soldiers . . .

This systematic effort to present "all the riots, outrages, robberies, &c. that are daily perpetrated among us" was something new in American newspapers. Scattered notes of crime had been common enough, but these reports from Boston placed crime and vice in a different light. Now the detail built a picture of a hidden city that journalists had the duty to reveal to citizens in need of political enlightenment. The "Journal" did not hesitate to enter a bedroom to locate the political danger:

> A worthy old gentlemen, the other morning discovered a soldier in bed with a favourite grand-daughter: The aged parent, in the height of his astonishment, ordered the soldier immediately to quit the room; but he absolutely refused; saying she was his wife, and he had an undoubted right to her, and that if he went out of the house he was determined to carry her with him: Upon examining further in to the matter, it was found that the soldier had found means to ingratiate himself with one of the family, and had by her aid seduced the girl with the promise of marriage; that accordingly, one evening as the girl informs, he carried her to a house in town, where as she thought, they were married by a person drest as a priest.

The "Journal" saw at once that "enemies of the Constitution" were behind the ingenious seducer.[14]

Patriots had long assumed that liberty was impossible without stern virtue in private life and that the vices of men in power were a contagion that could make citizens incapable of self-government. These values of civic humanism stem from the Renaissance and can be found in many political treatises available to colonial Americans. As early as John Peter Zenger's *New York Weekly Journal* of 1733, a royal governor was cited as an "overgrown criminal." But it was a new departure to fit actual crime reports into this mental scheme. Traditionally, crime had raised questions about the devil, not the government. "To the colonists," one scholar has concluded, "the presence of crime . . . was not symptomatic of social breakdown." Patriot journalists were doing what newspapers—and what their culture—had rarely done before: agonizing over political power as they watched crime in the streets. The lurid reports brought political issues into view.[15]

Corruption in Boston was as indefinite as it was pervasive. The redcoats' victims were everywhere, yet nowhere, for in these reports of daily outrages there was rarely a name or address to verify the story. Dates for the incidents gave a false appearance of documentation. The "Journal" was first published outside of Boston, where readers had no way to check the accounts, and in the garrisoned town patriots usually held back publication for two months, until memories of what really happened in the street had grown vague and rumors had had a chance to grow. The source was usually hearsay—"a report is current" or "we are told." In Boston the print medium slowed down the communication of information and made it difficult for citizens to evaluate what they were told. The "Journal" offered a highly literate society the opportunity to cling to the oral tradition, not to shake loose from it.[16]

The two royal governors of Massachusetts during the occupation watched this treatment of news with a fury tempered only by respect for the patriots' skill and gall. The "Journal,"

Thomas Hutchinson said, "was managed with great art, and little truth," but it had, he noted sadly, "a very great effect." "If the Devil himself were one of the party," Governor Francis Bernard wrote, "as he virtually is, there could not have been got together a greater Collection of impudent virulent and seditious Lies, perversions of truth and misrepresentation than are to be found in this publication."[17]

If the devil spoke in the "Journal," he sounded like Governor Francis Bernard. The most heated charge in the "Journal" was not that royal authorities were tyrants but rather that men in power enlarged upon trivial incidents and placed events in a false perspective. Patriots searched for false reports about Boston and found them in the private letters that royal officials wrote to London. When Bernard's secret letters were officially "exposed to the view of y^e. Public" in the summer of 1769, the "Journal" crowed: "the man is now held up to public view in his true colors." The governor had been publicly insulting the sensibilities of patriots for a long time and the "Journal" did not find words in the correspondence surprising enough to quote. But the governor's reporting habits about events in the streets of Boston drove the patriots to a frenzy: "such a budget of little malicious stories, of inflammatory details, and gross misrepresentations . . . [Bernard] has heap'd up and disguised little incidents to irritate and inflame: He has reported as facts, what never existed: He has given a malevolent turn to what is true. . . ." This, the "Journal" concluded, was the work of an "infamous pimp."[18]

By 1770 the passion for exposure was at the center of Boston political life. Leaders of resistance had no stomach for a renewal of the mob violence that had proven effective during the Stamp Act crisis. Patriots now did little to advance political or legal theories. The marshaling of secrets and the illumination of deception was the patriots' work. Crown officials met this protest on its own terms. Like the patriots, loyalists saw opponents as secretive conspirators who prospered by deception and who could be destroyed by exposure. On taking up the powers of governor in the fall of 1769, Hutchinson identified his enemy as contributors to the press "who if they would sign their names need do nothing more to blast the credit of everything they say."[19]

The nonimportation movement, the main protest against the Townshend duties, was a battle of newspaper exposés. Colonists had boycotted British goods during the Stamp Act protest of 1765. When the movement was renewed in 1769, importers were again shunned, cursed, and shown tar and feathers. But patriots now held out a new humiliation, "That a true List of their Names be published in the News-Papers." "May this," the "Journal" said, " . . . lead them to reflect on the baseness of their crime." The press thus provided the functional equivalent of the shaming punishments administered by the legal system. The Boston *Gazette*, the chief newspaper of the patriots, published the first list soon after the first threat, and the exposé now became a standard part of revolutionary action. In the summer of 1769 the patriot press also began to accept the "Acknowledgments" by importers: "I do now declare that I am sensible of and sorry for my Misbehavior. . . ." Exposure in the newspapers thus mimicked the eighteenth-century legal process, a "status degradation ceremony."[20]

Perhaps the prime candidate for punishment in the patriot view was the printer and bookseller John Mein. This Scot had lived in the town less than five years, and he was not a man of settled political philosophy. He made friends and enemies easily. Not pleased by an article in the Boston *Gazette*, Mein beat up the patriot who published it. He then welcomed help from Crown officials in carrying on his fight.

Mein's name was a fixture near the masthead of the Boston *Gazette* in lists "of those who *audaciously* continue" to import despite warnings. In his own paper, the Boston *Chronicle*, Mein gave as well as he got: he published fifty-five lists of importers that friends on the customs board allowed him to see. These manifests of ships in Boston harbor during the boycott seemed to reveal that New England was filled with merchants who prof-

ited by sneaking in forbidden goods; many of them were hyp-
ocrites who signed a pledge to boycott. Mein's lists of importers
and cargoes made his paper look like a ledger book. He distributed thousands of copies of this "precious record" through the
colonies. Patriot newspapers of 1769 were filled with evidence
to "undeceive" readers.[21]

Mein, for instance, found prohibited British linens on the man-
ifest of a ship owned by John Hancock. Patriots countered with
an affidavit from Hancock's clerk that the bales of cloth were
really the allowable "Russian duck." Mein called for invoices,
and patriots told readers where the documents could be found.
Tory and Whig addressed the most compelling question of the
day, "What did the Box really contain?"[22]

Tempers did not cool as the newspapers patiently described
the unloading of ships. As the antagonists hurled insults, they
boasted of their fidelity to facts. Now, reporting practices, no
less than political principles, were the battleground. Mein was
proud to "present facts, not offer conjectures," and he saw himself exposing "the vale of artifice and subterfuge" and battling
"the partiality" of the nonimporters. Patriots thought that Mein
belonged in a "sink of filth and rottenness" because of his "fal-
lacy and misrepresentation . . . studied evasion and numerous
artifices." Here was "as perverse a Misrepresentation as ever
[Governor Bernard] himself was guilty of." The merchants who
had pledged not to import proclaimed that their "fair, just and
impartial Account" of trade that they had published in patriot
newspapers disposed of "the fallacious and scandalous Assertions of one John Mein." Here again, the passions of Boston
politics were expressed in a great show of investigation to reveal
that the enemy alone twisted the facts.[23]

The shootings on King Street of March 5, 1770, produced a
monument to the stylization of information and fascination with
secret criminal acts: the famous illustration of the "Bloody Massacre" by Paul Revere. This silversmith and engraver had been
in town on the night of the shooting and apparently saw patriot
bodies in the snow. Twenty days later he offered an engraving

for sale that embellished what he had seen and improved upon the public testimony of other witnesses.

Like most pictorial reporting of the eighteenth century, there was much borrowing from other artists. The Yankees in the square act out the descent from the cross as well as the pieta. Revere took a free hand with both small and large points. The town clock gave the wrong time. The number of soldiers was wrong. The list of mortally wounded was wrong. One martyr, Crispus Attucks, was transformed into a white man in this colored engraving. Revere hid facts that even the survivors acknowledged in their testimony a few days after the shooting. Citizens were depicted without the clubs they had used to worry the soldiers. The patriots claimed only that the redcoats fired at will; Revere had them shooting simultaneously, with Captain Thomas Preston apparently in control. Few eyewitnesses maintained that shots had come from the Custom House. Revere found the idea of secret assassins too good to resist and put a smoking rifle in a second-story window, trained on the street. The Custom House, that symbol of hated legislation and vile importers, was labeled "Butchers Hall."

Below this scene Revere challenged the legitimacy of the courts, delivered a verdict of murder, and gave the patriots a dream of punishment:

> Should venal c—ts the scandal of the Land,
> Snatch the relentless Villain from his Hand,
> Keen Execrations on this Plate inscribed,
> Shall reach a JUDGE who never can be brib'd.

In sum, this was an icon for consolation. Revere's first prints, in fact, seem to have been issued glazed and framed, ready for the patriot's wall. The "Bloody Massacre" was of a piece with the news columns of the Revolution (the print also appeared in broadsides furnishing news accounts).[24]

The exposé required grievances that could easily be dramatized, and Britain took many of these away from the patriot press soon after the deaths in Boston. London removed all Townshend duties save the one on tea. That favorite villain, John Mein, fled from the mobs who had been enraged by his exposés. The Crown's assumption of salaries for executives and judges in Massachusetts Bay was not easy to turn into a compelling tale of corruption. Having won a larger circulation in the 1760s, patriot printers had trouble keeping up interest in resistance. Their solution was to turn away from the events of the day and, in 1773, to relive the British occupation.

A packet of Governor Hutchinson's letters, along with the letters of other Tories, made Boston feel old wounds. Benjamin Franklin, an agent for the province in London, had come across the seventeen letters and shipped them to the patriots who controlled the assembly. This private correspondence of 1767–69 was discussed secretly in Boston early in 1773 and then spread across the pages of Massachusetts newspapers for several months.

The papers that took up the purloined letters held fixed opinions on the governor. Hutchinson's lone ally, the *Massachusetts Gazette*, edited by Richard Draper, was in large part written by members of the administration. The attorney general, writing as "Philalethes," defended the government. Hutchinson's critics had old scores to settle. Isaiah Thomas nearly lost his *Massachusetts Spy* in 1771 when the governor ruined his credit in a heavy-handed effort to still this patriot voice. Hutchinson had long endured the "dirty stuff" in the Boston *Gazette*, and behind the patriot press he saw "the most Profligate abandoned fellows that ever lived." The governor feared the *Gazette* because "seven eights of the People," he judged, "read none but this infamous paper and so are never undeceived."[25]

Hutchinson marveled at the "infinite art" of his enemies, and this judgment was well-founded. Although the patriot press announced that "the hidden things of many of the most subtle, crafty and designing men have been laid before the Sun," these discoveries were not simply put in patriot newspapers. The Boston papers did not at first fill their "supplements extraordinary" with the documents. Instead readers found debate about the discovery and authenticity of the letters, denunciations and paraphrases, and the assembly's own exposé of "the Paragraphs, that appeared the most exceptionable." The *Massachusetts Spy* quickly sounded the alert that the letters were "foot-steps *stained with blood*" but waited several weeks before reporting in full what the Tories said. The Boston *Gazette* made "the subtle malignant genius of a Hutchinson" notorious, but never printed the six brief letters he had written.[26]

There was a great need for an airing of the constitutional issues raised by the letters of the governor, Lieutenant-Governor Andrew Oliver, and four other Tories that had fallen into the collection. Here was succinct commentary on the main issues of Massachusetts politics. The correspondents foresaw a lessening of colonial autonomy, asked London to take a firmer hand with the colonies, and suggested possible interventions. Hutchinson, in words that would haunt him, declared that in America "there must be an abridgement of what are called English liberties."[27] In New England these letters encouraged patriots to clarify the political theories they wished to live by. John Adams, for example, used Hutchinson's letters as a foil in the sophisticated legal arguments of his "Novanglus" essays in 1775. But in patriot newspapers during the summer of 1773 writers rarely sharpened their theories of government or proposed any action beyond sacking the letter writers. This press became a nostalgic chronicle of deceptions, a record of secret crimes.[28]

The patriot papers detected a scheme to bring on the occupation of their town in virtually every remark that Hutchinson made before the fatal autumn of 1768. When he wrote in August that "with all the aid you can give to the officers of the crown they will have enough to do to maintain the authority of government and to carry the laws into executions," the *Massachusetts Spy* asked, "Is not this as loud a call for ships, troops, &c, as the most virulent enemy of our rights could utter?" The Boston *Gazette* made ingenious computations with the calendar for the summer of 1768 to show that such remarks sent troops sailing.

"May Heaven send a prosperous gale to the fleet," the paper could hear Hutchinson saying. Less concerned with the exact moment of the conspiracy, the *Massachusetts Spy* caught the "infernal fiend" calling for the troops in a letter written two months after all the redcoats had come ashore.[29]

This exposure of an alleged 1768 plot to bring troops to Boston affected some patriots more strongly than what they had seen during the occupation. One sign of this can be found scribbled in the margins of Dorr's newspapers. The pattern of his comments is revealing. During the occupation his annotations are restrained. He simply identified enemies, cited the legislation he opposed, but did not go further to vilify the agents of the crown. The revelation of Hutchinson's letters in 1773 brought Dorr back to these years with an angry pen. His scholarly apparatus grew luxuriantly (the index has twenty-six references following "Hutchinson, Governor, his original traitorous Letters"). Dorr pasted in a woodcut, "The Wicked Statesman, or the Traitor to his Country, at the Hour of DEATH," then wrote in the governor's name. The devil in this print holds a tablet marked "List of Crimes," and lest there be any doubt what these were, Dorr instructed the reader to look up extracts from the Hutchinson letters. When Dorr added the correspondence to his file he footnoted the letters with curses: "a vile Lie!" "a vile Traitor," and "oh the villain!"[30]

For John Adams, too, the exposé of 1773 was the bursting of a dam. He had been distracted by concern for his family on the night of the Boston Massacre; that evening, after he heard of the killings, he looked on the redcoats in the street as if "they had been marble Statues." Adams accepted his duty as a lawyer and defended the soldiers who had fired on his countrymen. Three years later the Hutchinson letters brought from Adams a long-delayed patriotic outcry. "You will hear from US with Astonishment," he addressed the governor. "You ought to hear from Us with Horror. You are chargeable before God and Man, with our Blood." Adams, speaking now for the men who had died on King Street, laid out the charge of murder and signed this letter for a newspaper with the name of the martyr Crispus Attucks.[31]

The growing hints that men in authority belonged to a criminal class and that street crime revealed the corruption of the state were not the only ways newspaper exposés took colonists beyond traditional political ideas. To watch patriots thrown into a rage by these letters, to see them dissect every sentence, is to sense that it was the enemy's falsification of the patriots' personal experience of political life that filled newspapers with angry replies. "Aggravated Accounts of Facts, and Misrepresentations," were denounced by Boston's political leaders as well as by humble protesters like Dorr. The reporting habits of Tories were as maddening as their philosophy of government and in fact received more attention.[32]

Hutchinson's "exaggerated accounts of the turbulence" drove newspapers into detailed and patient inquiries. The sentence from his correspondence that received the most attention in the press was not his dark thought on English liberty. It was this sentence, describing Boston shortly before the troops arrived: "The minds of people were more and more agitated, broad hints were given that the troops should never land, a barrel of tar was placed upon the beacon, in the night to be fired to bring in the country when the troops appeared, and all the authority of the government was not strong enough to remove it." Patriots and Tories assembled a treatise on the barrel. The patriots acknowledged that a barrel had rested on top of Beacon Hill for several days, but it was, they insisted, an empty nail barrel. Far from a signaling device, it was "put there as a scarecrow, or more probably put there by some wanton lads to make for themselves diversion." "No man in Boston," said the *Massachusetts Spy*, "believes a child would have been hindered to have removed the old nail cask, at what time they pleased, while it remained there."[33]

This was only the opening salvo in the barrel controversy. "Philalethes" gave a lawyer-like defense of the governor in the *Massachusetts Gazette*. Hutchinson did not mean to fill the barrel—he surely meant "tar barrel" instead of "barrel of tar." In any case he was closer to the truth than the patriots. This Tory newspaper printed affidavits to show that turpentine, not nails, had once been in the barrel, making it an excellent beacon. The sheriff told how five years earlier the barrel had been thrown down to him and he had seen "some Patches of dry hard Turpentine which adhered to the inside of the Staves." Further, two employees of the newspaper had handled fragments of the barrel in 1768; both found the staves to be flammable pitch pine, while one man scraped off the dried turpentine, rolled it into a ball, and kept it as a souvenir. To counter this, the patriots rushed their documents into print. The housewright the sheriff took with him to seize the barrel declared it "had neither Tar, Pitch, nor Turpentine sticking to it." A merchant who had crossed Beacon Hill that day recalled that he had taken hold of the barrel, looked inside, and found it empty and clean. The Boston *Gazette* dismissed references to turpentine as part of the Tories' "knack at exaggeration."[34]

The tempest of detail and insult in political reporting was important. News was helping to shift attention in ways that were crucial to political change. The simplest accomplishment of the patriot press was the purchase of time. While the nonimportation campaign seemed ineffective, even hypocritical, the protesters staged a spectacle to divert the public. The maze of inquiries and answers kept patriots busy. When protest itself lapsed, the insurgents filled their newspapers with nostalgic accounts of resistance. The protesters had a larger purpose: to make the display of British power appear lawless and feeble. This is what the exposés helped to bring about. The troops sent to demonstrate the might of the empire were transformed by the patriot press into an armed force without discipline. Epithets such as "pimp" were part of a rhetorical strategy to turn society upside down, making legitimate authority assume the place of criminals in the streets. Like the ritualistic smearing of tar, feathers, and manure over the men who governed, news worked a magical transformation, symbolically taking away power by changing appearances.[35]

Like much of the ritual of this revolution, the exposé helped to bring order to the political process as much as to disrupt it. The mobs and desecrations before the war with Britain did not take the life of a single Tory. There was little anarchistic spirit in this decade of political activism. Much of the protest had a quasi-legal character that mocked royal justice as it prepared the way for a new authority. When patriots hung effigies, issued the "confessions" of men in power, and cursed or pelted the outcasts, they behaved as the eighteenth-century criminal justice system had taught them to act. Newspaper exposés that turned political enemies into criminals fit this ritual perfectly and inflicted the shaming punishments that the patriots could not yet control through the courts. News of this type was itself a way of governing. Boston, New York, and, soon, all of the colonies through the Continental Congress, ran an economic boycott by relying on newspaper publishers to expose violators.[36]

Simply to total up the distortions and lies, the manipulation and abuse in the press, is to miss much. Never before had printers taken so much testimony or rushed so many affidavits and lists to the public. A network took shape, spreading news to each colony. For the first time in America, a governor's blunt words, a merchant's dealings, or a soldier's curses might come to the attention of all who cared about liberty and who wished to fit their local grievance into the conspiratorial picture.[37]

An immersion in "facts" is not, perhaps, what the press sought, and it is likely that only political passion could have led so many journalists to become investigators. Convinced that corruption was hidden and that enemies lived by deception, the press set about to detect it and unmask enemies. Here the political antagonists were trapped by their inquiry. "Facts," now became each side's ammunition and "misrepresentation," the strategy of the enemy camp. Legal historians have celebrated the steady growth of legal forms and a "language of facts" in this political struggle. Journalists too seem to have learned forensic skills.[38] They took care to gather evidence, narrowed disputes to specific cases, and mimicked the charges as well as the punishments of the criminal law. Sifting, checking, indexing it all, Harbottle Dorr meant to document the Revolution, and he left a record of something just as momentous—the passion for news.

A half-decade of news—mainly from Boston—hardly gives the full picture of how Americans made their revolution or a press adequate for self-government. Modest claims are in order. It is worth a great deal to see how journalism casts information into dramatic forms and in that way builds expectations and sustains actions.[39] We can better understand familiar artifacts of the Revolution such as the Farmer's letters and Revere's engravings when we restore them to their place in the ongoing news of corruption in the press, for this is how they reached the eighteenth-century public. Newspaper exposés add to our picture of how the notions of corruption and virtue became compelling for the many colonists who never entered an assembly hall and had only partial knowledge of the treatises and sermons that defined American grievances. No one can argue that such formal texts were incidental to protest. Through them, for example, many patriots were inspired by an international struggle for liberty when American protests faltered. What has remained most puzzling is how the actual course of the dispute with Britain—the sequence of mundane as well as melodramatic conflicts—fit this frame of mind. The political reporting in newspapers, more clearly than the pamphlet literature, shows how abstractions and remote events were connected to daily occurrences. One sees nothing less than how interest in the political realm was nurtured.[40]

The exposés of the Revolution mark a fundamental change in the press. The habit of searching for political secrets in the community became fixed and the citizens who conducted the press gained confidence that their discoveries were true. These ideas had been exceptional before the 1760s, now they became common, almost an unthinking assumption around print shops.

Before the Revolution printers were modest about claiming their news was true.[41] American newspapers had made less of an effort to record political news from London than provincial English papers. Harbottle Dorr's folios show a new world of political discourse, where local news was joined to momentous issues and self-righteous assertions that these things really happened in the way they were reported. The political passions of the Revolution forced journalists to turn inward on their community and to stretch their claims about what they knew, and the dramatic devices of the exposé were an important tool.

By stylizing gossip and information the patriot press gave readers a sense of discovery. In the exposé the newspapers of the eighteenth century found a way to compete successfully with the oral tradition of local news. Indeed, for some, newspaper reading was becoming a way of life. Weekly journalism now required investigation at least thorough enough not to make readers in the town incredulous or bored. Promising discoveries of great importance encouraged printers (whatever they in fact delivered) to take on the role of stewards to the community.

The historian Bernard Bailyn, in publishing the modern edition of the pamphlets of the struggle, observed that "frequently as one reads through the pamphlet and newspaper polemics that accompanied the factional battles, one has the sense that the sheer explosiveness of the controversies are propelling men's minds beyond the frontiers of eighteenth-century political culture, toward a mode of understanding altogether new, altogether modern." This seems true of political reporting itself. The new critical and self-righteous stance of the press could not be confined to its narrow partisan purposes. The extensive talk about the reliability of the press turned out to be much like the loose talk about the freedom of the press during the Revolution. It was deeply felt, not well thought out, and certainly not consistent. Once the language was used by factions who had to live together, many would come to ask precisely what it meant, to take the argument further, and to hold the press to ideals newspapers were only dimly aware of during the Revolution.[42]

TOWARDS THE
NINETEENTH CENTURY

Few newspapers won their own independent life in the Revolution. Editors printed only what the king's army or the patriot militia allowed. The peace was brutally selective. The taint of loyalism was fatal. The *Massachusetts Gazette* shut down when the redcoats left Boston. In New York, Hugh Gaine and James Rivington gave up their important print shops when the British forces sailed. Most newspapers were not strong enough to survive the death of a proprietor or the decline of the town. Patriot newspapers that were built on the skill of one or two entrepreneurs faded as old men (or their widows) were unable to find worthy successors. (This was the fate of the Boston *Gazette*.) A town by-passed by commerce or government could pull printers down with it. Williamsburg, Virginia, had three newspapers in 1776, one when the capital was moved to Richmond in 1780, and no paper for the next 44 years. In 1800 there was no good reason to suppose that a newspaper could support a young proprietor even into middle age. America had about 200 papers yet not more than a dozen had a clear pedigree to the Revolution. No state south of Maryland had a newspaper that was even twenty years old at the turn of the century.

In this republic, journalism was the business of upstarts. And worried ones at that. Boom towns on the frontier could make a printer rich, but if this happened it was after years of anxiety about the pace of settlement and many stories about communities that had gone bust. The only certainty at the beginning of the nineteenth century was that this was a rural society—only one citizen in twenty lived in a city—and that newspapers needed a concentration of population to thrive. There is no evidence that journalists were endowed with unusual patience or stoicism. "Subsisting by a country newspaper is generally little better than starving," a New Jersey editor complained in 1802. Thurlow Weed put his family on a diet of bread, butter, and water when he started a paper in New York state. The newspaper failed, and only by weeping in front of the editor of an established paper did Weed get a second chance. Proprietors kept anxious watch. As late as the middle of the nineteenth century, a leading paper in New York City was run by an editor who slept each night outside the printing room. Ledger books were a constant worry. Cajoling readers to pay up was the editor's duty, a literary form that tended toward sarcasm. "When a person subscribes," a Jeffersonian editor told readers, "he should always calculate on sometime paying."[1]

Perhaps the most terrifying fact about bringing out a paper was that nerve and talent did not guarantee survival. James Thomson Callender, an effective scandal-monger first for the Jeffersonians and then for the Federalists, died destitute. William Cobbett, who as "Peter Porcupine" was the best writer to attempt a career in political journalism, failed in America. "If I wielded the pen of Burke or of Junius, it would be of no profit," a gifted editor said after struggling in Boston for eight years.[2]

Such comfort as there was in the new century for journalists came by joining their principles and their account books to political factions. Alexander Hamilton and Thomas Jefferson had set up cooperative editors in the course of their rivalry in the 1790s, and the first contested Presidential election of 1800 created networks of partisan newspapers. Only fourteen publishers chose editorial independence from Federalists and Jeffersonians in that campaign. On the fringe of settlement, across the Appalachians, party and faction were less established than on the coast, so a small paper might take a more even hand with controversy. But most Americans who conducted newspapers earned a reputation as citizens who would stay persuaded (or bought). Expressions of fealty and requests for more of the patron's attention were a large part of the correspondence of these editors. Dependence, so often a virtue in eighteenth-century politics, continued to be a matter of pride. William Coleman, editor of the New York *Evening Post*, cherished Alexander Hamilton's visits just before press time to dictate pieces for the paper. "When he stops, my article is completed," Coleman said. "I have no pride of authorship," the editor told Hamilton, with the wish that nothing in an article should inadvertently offend the patron: "...alter or suppress it as with your views," Coleman said. That is the sort of consultation political leaders expected to have with journalists. In the age of Andrew Jackson, an even more aggressive loyalty was sought and, often, won. The party newspaper was "our natural field marshall," Daniel Webster observed. A Democratic journalist noted that many papers were edited as if a citizen outside the party "has no right to live."[3]

Of course it was true that newspapers sometimes circulated political information for an open mind and sober debate. The draft Constitution itself and the supporting *Federalist* essays reached the public in this way. There were feuds and arguments, as warm as when Harbottle Dorr had been watching, that turned up new information and crystallized political attitudes. Claims to "impartiality" grew even more insistent. But what America had until the third decade of the nineteenth century was a press that was political rather than a press that welcomed political reporting. Editors, moreover, had few ideas about how to win readers beyond the partisan community they served.

Eighteenth-century exposés had set about to dramatize the distance between republican virtue and the governors. Social deviance as well as unpopular public policies had been swept together in this analysis, giving life and excitement to reports of even mundane events. Independence required the press to adjust this inquiry. With the colonial authorities gone, there was no obvious way to tie crime and sin to the political order. The way to investigate a native, elected, governing class was not clear. As might be expected in a press with thin tradition of respect for controversy, shock tactics were soon tried. Hamilton, Jefferson, even Washington, found their characters blackened. This vituperation helped bring on the Sedition Act of 1798 and the early party divisions. Here the press showed its nerve, not the ability to open up the political life of a democracy. Only after much delay did the polemical editors of the new nation find effective ways to dramatize what the government did and interrogate those in power.

The early press is best defined by the political information it did not offer and the questions it had not yet learned to ask. The leadership of this society was veiled in the presentation of news. If one wants to know what people in power actually said, even what they looked like, the press of the young republic is a very uncertain guide. The bottom of this society, the life of crime and vice, rarely colored views of politics. There is nothing in these newspapers that compares with the *Journal of Occurrences* or the attention to lawlessness in the middle of the nineteenth century. Before that time, editors attracted small followings, and their failure to capitalize on political news was one of the important things that held them back. Circulation and political reporting were linked, and both grew in the second quarter of the nineteenth century.

In the first quarter of the nineteenth century, circulation of individual papers was one of the few things American not susceptible to proud boasts and wild tales. The top circulation figures were about the same during Andrew Jackson's first term as they had been when George Washington left office: something over 4000 readers. But then, in the next two decades, circulation figures exploded. The New York *Herald*, begun in 1835, had 20,000 readers by its second year, and on the eve of the Civil War it had the largest daily circulation in the world: 77,000. *Harper's Weekly* and similar magazines with pictures of current events achieved several times this number of readers and provided a visual record with political power that even presidents acknowledged.

This creation of a truly popular form of news remains puzzling. It is sensible to look, as many have, at the expansion of the market economy as well as new technology and means of transportation that made a mass media possible. However, these important factors do little to explain the political content of this journalism. Why was the popular press so political? Why didn't it dodge all of the public questions it could, just the way forms of entertainment and popular art have so often done?

The first editors to achieve mass circulation, after all, were evangelicals who had little interest in political matters. In the 1820s the American Bible Society and the American Tract Society made plans to produce a timely and steady flow of their literature into *every* American home. Their skill with the media of their time is as impressive as what evangelicals have done with television. Every month in hundreds of cities this literature reached a public that had never before had such easy access to print. The evangelicals reorganized printing while the commercial press watched from the sidelines. In the 1830s the American Tract Society alone had presses that produced five pages of religious information each year for every adult and child in America. It is surprising that the winners in the circulation contest turned out to be editors who ignored the proven religious themes. Political reporting acquired an appeal that was apparent to very few Americans in the first years of the republic.[4]

The change, throughout the nineteenth century, came in bursts and also in a slow working out of popular formulas for the telling of political stories. The speech of American politics came tumbling into print, mobilizing faction and party as never before. New ways of visualizing the city, aided by illustrated journalism, provided a compelling way to make sense of local government. At the same time new habits of detection, drawn from the reporting of crime and vice, were showing the way to make political stories more interesting. Truly national reporting of corruption, marshaling the full assets of commercial journalism, was at last achieved at the very end of the new century. The next chapters are paths between eighteenth-century reporting practices and the mass circulation of political information that was a major achievement of this democracy.

II

WORDS AND PICTURES IN A DEMOCRACY

3

"Unfeeling Accuracy"

In 1828 a milkman in Cincinnati was amazed to hear a distinguished English visitor suggest that the time Americans took to read newspapers might be better spent on something else. Mrs. Frances Trollope mentioned the repair of roads and fences. The milkman would hear none of this: "what does a broken zigzag signify, comparable to knowing that the men what we have been pleased to send up, to Congress, speaks handsome and straight, as we chooses they should?"[1]

This was commonplace sentiment in Jacksonian America. Correspondents were stationed on Capitol Hill and newspapers in distant cities competed to provide accounts of what lawmakers said. The pace of American life did indeed seem slowed down as citizens studied these columns. The same year that the milkman spoke up, an American critic called attention to "those wide, folio pages of a desolating debate, unbroken, unvaried as a wild heath or interminable prairie. . . . " Nevertheless, journalist and politician labored together sending speeches out to the people, convinced that this political reporting could win over a democracy. Few things done in America were a more startling departure from the political wisdom of the eighteenth century.[2]

In colonial America printers had no assured standing to report what people in government said. The press courted trouble when it attempted to make this record. Prior restraint through licensing—a natural function of government for seventeenth-century

Englishmen on both continents— did not vanish in the home of political debate, the representative assemblies. Printers found that reporting on legislative sessions was dangerous work. Certainly British practice did nothing to embolden Americans. In 1728 the House of Commons imprisoned and fined both the publisher and correspondent who had dared to report their proceedings. Until the end of the eighteenth century Parliament emphatically declared itself closed to journalists, and it was held to be a breach of privilege for a member to report his own words to the press. Colonial assemblies normally carried on all discussions in secret. From the mid-1740s until the Revolution, each session of the New York Assembly (and one Royal governor) asserted the right to prohibit publication of the proceedings. Two printers were called before the house and humiliated because their reporting displeased the members. In 1773 the upper house in South Carolina jailed a printer who had issued a newspaper with an accurate report of the proceedings sent to the newspaper by a member of the house.[3]

After 1776 there was no revolution in the custom of guarding the debate among men who governed. Only two state constitutions adopted during the Revolution opened the door of the legislature to the public. In peace as well as in war, the Continental and Confederate Congresses barred the press. The Constitutional Convention in Philadelphia was closed. Under the Articles of Confederation, "reporting" meant communication between delegates and the states; the assemblies did not wish to publish their work for the general public. The ubiquitous secretary of all these congresses, Charles Thomson, had won tribal honors on the Pennsylvania frontier for his care in taking down the speeches of Indians in disputes with settlers. But when the language was English and the speakers contentious white men, Thomson held back from preserving the arguments that set the course of the new nation. In the *Journals of Congress* Thomson gave no hint of the reception of the Constitution by the last Confederation Congress. Newspapers also missed that debate, and during the rest of 1787 printers brought out only a small part of what was said during the ratification of the Constitution in state conventions. In Pennsylvania, for example, defenders of the document harassed Anti-Federalist reporting and ended their own publication of the proceedings after one volume that contained nothing but speeches boosting the Federalist side. Through the 1780s, when Americans found a speech in their newspapers it was more likely to have been made in the Parliament of the kingdom they had rejected than in the assemblies of the new nation they had joined.[4]

This suspicion of reporting remained strong in the first years of the federal government. Article I, Section 5 of the Constitution required Congress simply to keep a "journal of proceedings" and to publish this "from time to time." There was, then, no requirement that speeches be recorded by the government and published for citizens to see. Indeed, there was no encouragement in the 1790s for anyone curious to know what had been said in Congress. For the first six years the Senate regularly was closed to the public and press. Well into the administration of John Adams the Senate obstructed the recording of its discussion. The House did have open doors, but its records were the merest outline of debate. Until 1800 the lower house considered the banishment and practiced the harassment of reporters.[5]

The hour glass through which eighteenth-century political debate drained into print was meant to be stopped by many hands. America was first governed by men who did not know one another and who migrated as the fragile government found shelter. The Continental Congress changed cities ten times; the new federal government three times. Even when settled, lawmakers soon felt out of touch with constituencies that lived at the end of washboard roads and cold sea lanes. Starved for news of the communities that had sent them to the Continental Congress, delegates showed no sign of wishing to publish their precise representations of citizens' interests. In this oral world an elite achieved full internal discussion without interference of distant countrymen. Under the Constitution congressmen were of course better able to keep roots in their districts than representatives during the chaotic 1780s, but these lawmakers changed too frequently to know their colleagues well. The goings and comings in the Senate made it resemble a reception hall between 1789–1801. On the average more than three men held each place in the upper house. No representative in the Seventh Congress had served continuously since the First. The discouragement of reporting gave leaders time to gauge the effect of their words both on new colleagues and constituents.[6]

The fear of casting too much political discussion into print ran deeper in this society than the worries of the upstart governors. There was a pervasive belief that debate was more likely to be effective and authority more respected if an exact record of what had been said was *not* available. The spoken word, kept free of reporting in print, was a mainstay of the hybrid colony created by the Dutch and English in New York. The strictly English precedents, especially the rationale for not reporting Parliament, touched every colony. Men trained in the law were predisposed to find this reasonable. American lawyers, like those of Great Britain, proudly clung to an oral tradition and published only a small fraction of trial and law reports. The Revolution had indeed forced political advocates to rely on publication of the widest variety of appeals and documents, but the tradition persisted that public business was not properly transacted in print. In the first decade of the Supreme Court justices made no effort to publish their decisions. The second rule of the Senate prohibited members on the floor from reading "any printed paper" (not all reading) while their colleagues were talking. In America's oldest political culture, around the Chesapeake, there is good reason to doubt that printed materials ever were as important as the ceremonies that displayed power and the oral performances of those who governed. A lightning conversion to full reporting of political life was hardly to be expected. In 1800 a Maryland candidate who followed the advanced practices of addressing voters and debating his opponent confessed that *publishing* his opinions made him feel "much embarrassed."[7]

In the young republic it was often the case that the more

incomplete the record the more the man or institution was respected. For several decades the reputation of some great orators of the Revolution grew by word of mouth, not by the printed page. James Otis's "Taxation without representation is tyranny" and Patrick Henry's "Give me liberty, or give me death" only found their way into print in the nineteenth century. In 1815 Henry's first biographer learned that the patriot was venerated at a time when there was no written record of what he had said during the entire Revolutionary era. The making of the Constitution was kept in the same patriotic haze. The nine delegates who are known to have made notes of the convention in 1787 withheld them from print during the first three decades of the federal government. James Madison's magnificent record of what was said at the convention remained secret for a half-century. Not even the crises of his own presidency led Madison to stun enemies with quotations of what the founding fathers had said in Philadelphia. It is difficult to assess all of Madison's motives for suppressing the reports, but he certainly wished to protect the reputation of old friends and to deepen reverence for the Constitution. And in realizing that printed reports of political discourse were likely to be embarrassing and even disruptive, Madison was guided by the wisdom of eighteenth-century politics.[8]

The reporting of political speech required a change in literary technique as well as political will. Americans had always been eager to copy the format of popular English journalism. Georgian Britain's Grub Street was alive with schemes to gain profit and influence by reporting political speech, but the models here were difficult for Americans to follow. The first clandestine reports of Parliament were secured by bribes and spun from the reporter's imagination. These essays were so thick with pseudonyms, anagrams, and allegories (to protect sources) that keys were distributed with the magazines. By the middle of the eighteenth century this had become a proud craft, and the real debate was known by so few that an editor's poetic license was likely to go unchallenged. (It was not until the end of his life that Samuel

Johnson told his friends that he had "reported" one of Chatham's great speeches by simply making it up.) When journalists gained entry to the House of Commons in the 1770s they were barred from taking notes and so were doubly cursed: more people knew what had been said but almost no one could remember it all. The London *Morning Chronicle* unleashed William "Memory" Woodfall, a reporter who could sit through an evening of debate and return to the print shop to dictate column after column of the proceedings. At the end of the century the press gained the privilege of taking notes, but even then full reporting required freakish skill. Though shorthand systems dated from Elizabethan times, no method was dependable or easy to learn. Doctor Johnson declared that keeping a verbatim record was beyond the reach of any mortal.[9]

Benjamin Franklin spoke of his losing struggle with a shorthand system in his *Autobiography*, and he was famous in Pennsylvania politics for taking positions that were difficult to pin down. It was ironic, therefore, that Franklin was cast as patron saint by the men who launched the American experiment in political reporting.

Mathew Carey, a young Irishman, became the first reporter to regularly haunt an American assembly in August 1785. Carey had fled British rule and been sheltered in Franklin's small printing establishment outside of Paris before finding haven in Philadelphia. Thomas Lloyd soon followed Carey into the Pennsylvania assembly for a rival newspaper. Lloyd was no artisan, for his family were landowners in England and he had been sent to school on the Continent. But Franklin inspired his career as well. A volume of Lloyd's early reporting was dedicated to Franklin's Society for Political Enquiries. Benjamin Franklin Bache, the great man's grandson, risked political reporting soon after the national government moved to Philadelphia in 1790. Bache, only 21 that year, was, like Carey, a child of the revolutionary age. He had been packed off to the safety of the Continent with his grandfather during the war for independence. In the late 1780s they returned together and Bache found himself putting that energy into filiopiety that other men put into a career. He launched his newspaper six months after Franklin died, using several different titles before settling on the *Aurora* in 1794.

Since there was no clear model from the old world on how to report the discourse of a republic, these men had to develop their own approach. The craft remained personal and eclectic, even after Lloyd's shorthand system was published. Until the middle of the nineteenth century reporters were self-taught, borrowing parts of other people's system and relying on their special knack of remembering what had been said. The reporters shared a dream that they would prosper as their craft made government virtuous. One printer claimed that Lloyd was a pillar of self-government, for his shorthand "would, no doubt, result [in] respect and obedience to the Laws of the Union, and grateful veneration for those who frame them. . . ."[10]

By the end of the first decade of the new government, journalists had found strong allies to condemn the incomplete and delayed reporting that so many legislators felt was proper. Bache's condemnation of this "skeleton of debate" was echoed by the democratic-republican societies of the 1790s who denounced secret legislative sessions. Sectional distrust also aided reporters. Southern congressmen, fearful of what the strong central government might do, insisted that journalists hear and publish as much as possible so the South could be on guard. This important episode in the making of a free press was not often an exchange on purely theoretical points. Men fought about where a reporter might perch: high in the public galleries where they could not hear every word, or in a window niche on the floor where they could meet the legislator face to face and even watch (as the *Aurora* carefully noted) one member spit upon another.[11]

A succession of small victories of this type in the 1790s opened up the new government. Dreams of profit, however, were dashed. Mathew Carey, the oldest hand, found other publishing projects more attractive and left the field. Lloyd abandoned his pioneering *Congressional Register* after one year in the House (in

the 1790s another stenographer gave up on the Senate as quickly).
Bache found, before his death in 1798, that it was one thing for
republicans to toast an open congress, but quite another for them
to subscribe to his struggling paper for the reports of what was
said. Not even scandal helped very much. James Thomson Callender planted insults and sexual innuendoes about Federalists
among luxuriant accounts of speeches and debates. The format
did not produce either the political or the financial rewards Callender expected. The journalist then betrayed his old friend
Thomas Jefferson and published the stories about liaisons with
the house slave Sally Hemmings. Callender had learned to pare
away the oratory and get right to the point.[12]

Reporting of the strictly public life of the new government
was a source of endless complaints. In the 1st Congress Senator
William Maclay of Pennsylvania saw his fears about centralized
power confirmed as his speeches were "suppressed" in the minutes and functionaries barred him from reading Senate records.
In 1794 a Boston paper warned readers against "the Jacobin
Debate Sketchers of Philadelphia" and attempted to supply
speeches that were not "mutilated." Many congressmen took
the floor in the 1790s to complain that the public had no reliable
account of the chamber. For all of the ink and breath expended
in deploring a misreported government, the institutional response was hesitant. Congress itself took no official actions to
preserve its debates before the 1820s. No newspaper outside of
Washington regularly sent a correspondent to the capital during
this period.[13]

The citizen's only dependable source of news about their government was the *National Intelligencer*, founded as a tri-weekly
in 1800 and then published daily after 1813. This Jeffersonian
newspaper had America's most competent stenographers and a
reputation of muting its republican bias in reporting debates.
Through a regular system of exchanges and reprintings, the
Intelligencer became the nation's ear in Washington. Three men
did all the listening. Samuel Harrison Smith, a would-be gentleman farmer, was the editor. He had won the final victory to

gain access to the floor of Congress in 1802 and found himself trapped there because no one else could match his stenography. The paper was also aided by Joseph Gales, Sr., an artisan radical who fled England in the 1790s and succeeded in the new world through his skill in shorthand and printing. Smith dropped his reporting duties after Jefferson left the White House. A wide search for a replacement turned up no one more promising than Gales's son. This third man essential to the reporting of Congress was twenty-four years old and lately expelled from his university after charges by classmates that he could not be trusted. In an age in which the English Parliament attracted Samuel Taylor Coleridge, William Hazlitt, and Charles Dickens to reporting, America's off-hand concern for recording speech was reflected in the limited talents of the press corps in the capital. American democracy first took shape with a precarious connection through newspapers between governors and the governed. Smith was usually the only stenographer from the paper on Capitol Hill, and he could not hope to cover everything of importance. He frequently repaired to the country to regain his health, and when this happened, news of the government stopped.

Some congressmen favored their constituents with small editions of their speeches. In the South and West, but rarely in the mid-Atlantic states or New England, lawmakers produced circular letters giving their own brief account of the past session. It has been extraordinarily difficult for historians to piece together this early reporting. It was not widely circulated or collected. Until the 1820s in fact no one sought to build a public record of congressional business. To contemporaries, much reporting was mysterious as well as ephemeral. Outside the *National Intelligencer*, reporting was likely to be erratic and suspect. A senator from Maryland rose on the floor in 1803 to rage at this mysterious process: "the account that is given in the newspaper called *The Washington Federalist* of my speech of a few days since, *is a lie*. I hope that account was not written by a senator. Sir, if I knew who wrote it, I would, indeed I would, call him to account."[14]

Congress did not make reporting easy for anyone. It appears that lawmakers seldom wrote out their remarks before delivery; certainly they tried to avoid the impression that they spoke from texts. As late as 1832 a senator's charge that a colleague had read a speech in the chamber was taken as an insult requiring an elaborate defense. In the early republic political debate in each house was staged as a oral performance, not an exchange of texts.

Listening was never easy. The acoustics of the House were notorious. Whispers moved in eddies across the floor but around many desks the loudest voice was trapped. In the winter senators gathered at fireplaces at the front of the hall and their talk drifted back across the chamber. A din of business in Congress added to architectural problems. Lawmakers walked back and forth to the snuff box on the speaker's rostrum and circulated among the stations for liquid refreshment. The desk was a lawmaker's office and den, and when sessions began, secretaries, visitors, even beloved dogs might remain to pursue their special interests. Pages were summoned by a clap. The background noise during debate made it possible for a member to whittle a pine board at his seat (as Senator Sam Houston did) without disturbing neighbors. All this happened in intervals of good behavior. Often representative government was not this calm. A presiding officer in the House of the 26th Congress called attention to the "unbridled license that has prevailed here for some time past," and a reporter of that session saw the lawmakers as unruly school boys: "They throw off all restraint, get to exchanging jocose remarks in a loud voice, and throw paper pellets all over the hall." Quite simply, the Congress of the early republic was often a poor place to be heard, to listen, or to find out what had been said. Before this state of affairs is connected to one flaw or another in the national character, it is important to note that this behavior helped the institution to do exactly what was wanted: to put debate beyond exact description.[15]

Journalists were crucial in this design. Reporters were expected to improve what they heard or at least to make sure the

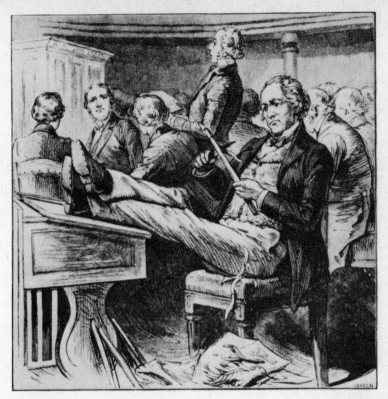

Sam Houston Whittling in the Senate. (*Perley's Reminiscences of Sixty Years in the National Metropolis*, 1886)

politician had time to improve it himself. In the 1790s Thomas Lloyd had quickly earned the censure of a competing reporter because Lloyd was a "miserable hand" in putting the speeches of congressmen in "English dress," that is, improving them. The *National Intelligencer*'s success was in part due to willingness to allow lawmakers to edit their own remarks. "Unfeeling accuracy," a cynical journalist noted, provoked congressmen.[16]

When newspapers in the late 1820s at last broke the *National Intelligencer*'s monopoly on congressional reporting, the new Washington correspondents were shocked to find that after a debate legislators were accustomed to seeing "five or six columns of fine type in a newspaper, one half of which they never imagined, and the other half they never so expressed as it appears. . . ." Congressmen then clipped their "words" and sent them home to the voters. What was actually said on the floor might be far less compelling. "No one can imagine what dreadful hard work it is to keep awake and listen to what's said," David Crockett complained when the frontiersman began his career in the House, "splitting gum logs in August is nothing beside it." Crockett learned that reporters could relieve the tedium and separate what was said from what was printed about American politics. One of the things he liked best about the East was the ghostwriters, which he used for many of his coonskin performances. He celebrated an editor of the *National Intelligencer* for boldly reworking a speech he made in Congress, "he has made me a much better speech than I made in the house or ever could make," a colleague heard Crockett say, "& I will get . . . 1000 or 1500 and send them home to my people. . . ." Crockett's happy experience with political reporting was not unusual. An early reporter of Congress, Samuel L. Knapp, noted that politicians used printed texts as veils. In *Lectures on American Literature* (1829)—the first scholarly claim that there was such a thing— Knapp dismissed the nineteenth-century record of political discourse as spurious, "for there is not one speech out of twenty given to the publick as they are delivered. The reporter, according to custom, is bound to make the orator talk good English, at least, and say nothing absurd. . . ."[17]

Such cooperation between politician and reporter had important functions in the early republic. As Crockett found, it made the tailoring of a public image easy. This was a considerable achievement at a time when parties and campaign techniques had only a sketchy form. "Buncombe" (later "bunk") were unkind Americanisms for the pretense that the politician and the

reporter created. The terms did not suggest merely a lie or pre-
posterous statement. In the congressional debates over the Missouri Compromise of 1820, a representative from North Carolina
had told his colleagues that they need not listen to an address
for he was "speaking for Buncombe." He meant only to have
the speech sent home to this county in his district. "Buncombe-
orators" might take the floor to growl at colleagues, but everyone
understood they did not wish to bite.[18]

The Missouri controversy of 1819–20 was an important step
toward the full publication of congressional debate. It is also an
illustration of the limits of early reporting. The issues touched
every corner of the nation: the admission of Maine as well as
Missouri to the Union and the place of slavery in the vast territory gained in the Louisiana Purchase. Historians have been
impressed by the amount of coverage in local papers and the
work of the new antislavery organizations to further popularize
the arguments. Citizens in every state had an opportunity to
share the mood of crisis in Washington. The South watched this
high water of reporting with horror, particularly after learning
that Denmark Vesey had used reports of congressional debate
to organize a slave revolt in South Carolina.

Viewed from the perspective of the 1840s and 1850s, however,
the reporting of the 1820s was hesitant and restrained. The printed
page told only a fraction of the debate witnessed by the white
and black citizens who filled the congressional galleries. Many
of the most important speeches made by the North and the South
went unreported. Sometimes journalists were not available to
listen, other times lawmakers simply embargoed remarks.

Henry Clay, the young Speaker of the House, showed one
way to dampen public interest. He made an argument for the
extension of slavery that was to move to the center of controversy
in the 1840s: the spread of slavery would benefit blacks by giving
the South a 'safety valve.' No version of this speech was published. Since Clay was capable of reporting his own speeches,
indeed of sending them to editors with directions as to how they
should be displayed, it is a fair assumption that the Speaker did

not want his argument to go beyond his immediate audience. The "speech" by Rufus King that ended up in Denmark Vesey's hands was not the senator's actual remarks to his colleagues, but a thorough revision King published nine months after he spoke. The antislavery address, at that, had appeared in an edition of only 1000 copies. The first comprehensive version of the debates appeared fourteen years after the issue of Missouri was settled.

The South brooded on the publication of the Missouri debates for more than a decade, and Southern contempt was an understandable response to a significant change in the circulation of political information. But journalists and lawmakers had made only modest efforts to produce this shock. Those groups in the vanguard of interloping on lawmakers reported what they were told to report. Congressional discussion was still screened from distant readers. The most telling illustration of the limit on communication was the type of reporting that reached Thomas Jefferson in the spring of 1820. Jefferson made his famous observation that the Missouri question was "like a fire bell in the night" in a note thanking a congressman for sending him a circular letter which informed constituents of the antislavery agitation. However, of the thirteen congressmen whose circular letters have been found after the slavery question came up in the House, only four mentioned this issue. Most citizens who relied on the reporting of their congressman would have had no idea what Jefferson was talking about. The closest study of public opinion during the crisis has been unable to find signs that the printed reports connected with the interests of citizens. Rather, the crisis passed with a "vast amount of public indifference." Under the political mores of the early republic, this was what reporting often allowed to happen.[19]

Early in the nineteenth century political leaders had what they would never again enjoy: separate worlds for what they said and what they published. In the oral world they could be just as accountable and flexible as they chose to be. In his autobiography Martin Van Buren called his unreported speeches of 1827 "the most successful of my senatorial efforts." The man contemporaries called "the Little Magician" had collected all the reporters' notes in the Senate, lost them, and kept his own version of the speeches a secret. When Andrew Jackson was a senator, he avoided a conflict with the simple declaration, "I never pretend to recollect after they are made remarks offered by me in public debate. . . ." At a banquet before some 100 members of Congress, Jackson challenged the South with his toast, then changed it so that newspaper readers would not be stung as hard. Before the end of Jackson's presidency no reporter was in a position to challenge this tactic in political argument.[20]

Of course the uncertainty about what leaders said was not always convenient or welcomed. The technical limitations of the reporters harmed some congressional careers. A reporter who observed Congress for more than sixty years called Sergeant Smith Prentiss of Mississippi the most eloquent speaker he heard, but reporters were baffled by his flights of eloquence, and Prentiss himself was usually unable to come up with a text that captured the performance. Citizens who did not hear Prentiss could have no idea of his appeal. John Randolph of Virginia was haunted by the fact that his outpourings of wit and learning in the House left reporters adrift. The difficulties here were both personal and political. Randolph was an assassin of syntax, able to make several different speeches in the territory between subject and verb in a single sentence. Reporting him, it was said, was "to follow the thread of the spider in its already-formed web." He spoke slowly, but at a pitch (compared by one reporter to the castrati) that shattered words. Randolph insisted a malevolent press had reported all his requests for "water" as calls for "porter" and his references to "slaves" as "Irish." In fact Randolph wished to make trouble for the *National Intelligencer* to help a more sympathetic Southern publisher, Duff Green, get established in the capital. The *Intelligencer* said that Randolph refused to clarify his remarks and even stole their reporter's drafts so he would have bad reporting to complain about. Duff Green and the *Intelligencer*'s man settled the matter in a wrestling match that broke out in a Senate committee room. The dignity of the press was not advanced by the *Intelligencer*'s report that Green went for the eyes—or by Green's defense that he had only wrenched the ears of his colleague.[21]

Not withstanding such difficult days on the job, many journalists gained a sense of dignity from their role as the public's witness to political debate. The reporters painted themselves too large on the canvas, but they were right to think they had moved to the center of much political advocacy. Antebellum reporting was not simply suppression or invention but rather a complex process of composition in which the leader and the reporter might share responsibility for the citizen's record of political discourse. Political journalism acquired stature as it filled this role. As one experienced player in nineteenth-century politics judged, it was to the lasting credit of reporters that they "inspired, if not actually prepared," the noteworthy addresses of the era.[22]

Daniel Webster, the commanding orator of the Whig party, made a deep bow to reporters. Only these journalists, Webster thought, could help him find what he meant to say. Both before and after an address, the senator used reporters as mirrors before which he primped and changed his appearance. Often he would drop in on a stenographer—or summon him to the Senate—when planning a speech. (Webster called off a Senate address on Mexican annexation when a favorite New York reporter was unable to reach Washington.) The senator attributed part of his own eloquence to the reporter and was known to sit mesmerized when a journalist told him what he had said:

> As I read over to him the successive points, to every one which seemed peculiarly clear, he would exclaim, "Good," "That's true," etc., apparently forgetting that the argument was his own, and applauding the performance of some other person.

Sessions like this between speaker and reporter produced the oratory that defines Jacksonian America. The President himself called in Amos Kendall when he wished to make an address. This experienced newspaper editor took down what Jackson said and usually recast it before reading it back. Only after a lengthy exchange did Jackson know what he wished to say.

The politician, of course, took a strong hand in the reporting process. Early in his career Webster adopted the practice of withholding addresses from the printer until the memory of listeners had grown dim and he could change them freely. Reporters honored this embargo, as they allowed other popular lecturers to avoid immediate publication. This meant that only those present to hear a leader could know exactly what was said. Those famous speeches that school children were to memorize through the rest of the nineteenth century were studied departures from the words Webster spoke. His famous reply to Senator Robert Y. Hayne (January 26–27, 1830) was kept out of the newspapers for nearly a month. The senator made extensive changes while his public waited, driven by the conviction that eloquence in print and eloquence in speech were quite different things.

Few in press or politics objected to this for the distaste for "unfeeling accuracy" was widely shared. Jacksonian America preserved a reporting process not designed to record what a leader said on his feet. The nation had no immediate record of Webster's reply to Senator John M. Clayton three years after the debate with Hayne because Webster absentmindedly gave the *National Intelligencer* the wrong speech and the reporters routinely printed what they were handed, not what they had heard. A decade later Whig editors caught themselves setting type for a Webster speech which threatened to embarrass a prominent member of the party. The editors' course was clear; they held up publication while the Whig party saw to it that Webster changed the address. The "words" of a politician were often what a party and a reporter, as well as the leader, chose to make them.

This consultative reporting process is likely to survive to some extent in any democracy, and it did not simply vanish at any point in the nineteenth century. The new practice of "interviewing" at mid-century preserved the idea of obtaining "worthy" statements. The first reporter to interview a president, Joseph B. McCullagh, saw to it that chief executive did not utter the "right idea in the wrong words." Indeed, citizens who long for reporting of this type will find it in the *Congressional Record* today. What happened in the second quarter of the nineteenth century is that politicians and reporters grew more efficient in spreading political speech, and this record of debate slipped out of the hands of trusted reporters and party leaders.[23]

There was a new dependence on print in the political life of Jacksonian America. Some of the advantages of oral discourse remained thanks to the meager resources to record what was said, and certainly the practices of delay, obfuscation, and deniability were not ended by more energetic reporting. But no person in public life could, like the Revolutionary generation, build a career on merely remembered words. The creation of a printed record of remarks was essential.

The shock of this is recorded in the diary of ex-President John Quincy Adams. When Adams left the White House and came to the House of Representatives in 1831, he learned that he had to surrender his dignity to get his speeches into the newspapers. Adams's diary of his eight terms is the record of a Brahmin slipping into the life of a clerk. "I must very rarely make speeches in the House," he noted during his first session, "it is a double waste of time—first to speak, and then to report." But he found himself spending his evenings revising reporters' notes. Adams put aside old quarrels with the editors of the *National Intelligencer* and trailed after them in the capital to protect and perfect his copy. When Adams was seventy-two, he fell on the House floor and dislocated his shoulder; the next day he was at the *Intelligencer*'s office, ready to edit a speech.[24]

Unreported speeches in Congress were impossible by the end of the 1830s, and embargoes on public addresses were fast becoming more difficult to arrange. Positions on sensitive issues were easier to pin down, while less that was said in public could be simply taken back. In the second quarter of the nineteenth century the task of documenting debate on Capitol Hill began with the *Register of Debates in Congress* (14 vols., 1825–37). The attempt to recover what had been said since 1789 yielded 42 handsome leather-bound volumes, the *Annals of Congress* (1834–56). (Appropriately, these are the books statesmen usually posed with in the photographs taken in Mathew Brady's Washington studio.) Other publishing ventures, most notably the weekly *Congressional Globe* (1833–73), also crowded the new market for reporting. (The government's own *Congressional Record* succeeded the *Globe*.) Though much of the pre-Civil War reporting was shaped by narrow considerations of patronage, political advantage, and profit, this was not all that lay behind this rush of words into print.[25]

Consider the sixteen thick volumes issued as the *Abridgment of the Debates in Congress, From 1789–1856* in the four years before the Civil War. This was a work of passion with a conscious political goal. The selection and editing were done by a defeated and dying man, former Senator Thomas Hart Benton of Missouri. Benton had entered politics editing a newspaper and spent thirty years in Congress casting a sharp eye on how he was reported. This old Jacksonian was swept out of the Senate by the divisions in his state over the extension of slavery into the territories. In his last years Benton joined his skills as an editor with the all-consuming desire to lead the nation. During the 1856 presidential campaign Benton cut back his public life and resolved to stay at his writing desk until the congressional debates of the nation were "accessible (and I hope attractive) to the whole reading community." Much of this editing was done with the senator in great pain. He forced himself to his table while tortured with a back injury. He was struck down by cancer of the bowel and became an emaciated figure, hoarsely whispering that cart loads of the *Congressional Globe* be delivered to his bed. Benton worked through the debates of 1850, the last great compromise of his generation, and died the day after this volume was ready for the printer.

Benton had more in mind than "resuscitating the patriotic

dead," though this he certainly tried to do. The project was designed to save that "brotherly Union" by presenting examples of the "fraternal spirit" of political discourse. "Controversy will be quieted or terminated," a Democratic magazine said in its review of the *Abridgment*, "... and a feeling of security and permanence diffused throughout the nation." Joshua Giddings, the dean of anti-slavery congressmen, complained that Benton's led all standard works in injustice to the cause by "garbling" the abolitionist speeches in the House. Benton's work is much fairer than Giddings charged, but there is no question that Benton took a strong hand when the record diverged from his theme of harmony.

The spirit of the reporter is well shown in the way he edited a famous exchange in the Senate. On April 17, 1850, Benton had taken the floor and made brief reference to "agitation" recently seen in the South. The *Congressional Globe* then reported that Senator Henry S. Foote of Mississippi spoke to deplore that notion that Southern leaders could be called "agitators." Senator Foote added that "their calumniators, no matter who they may be, will be objects of general loathing and contempt." Benton rushed from his seat toward Senator Foote, and the Southerner met him with a cocked pistol. "Let him fire; Stand out of the way, and let the assassin fire," the Missourian thundered. In the *Abridgment* Benton silently deleted Foote's critique and their confrontation. He did preserve a remark he had made before Foote spoke earlier in the debate that week: "Agitating, exciting, and distracting as is the subject, yet we are acting upon it like a calm and deliberate Senate, and I am willing to go home and sleep upon it, and come back tomorrow, and finish it up harmoniously and understandingly to all." Benton's was the last great effort at reporting to still the martial spirit. His final volume was published the year the armies marched.[26]

Benton's *Abridgment* sold well (as the earlier compilations had not) and was a reminder that political speech had a ready public if well edited. Newspapers had known this for a generation and had even begun to make a folklore of the energy and imagination the reporter must show in getting a speech for readers. The journalist's characteristic memoir was now the sketches of great men heard and reported, heavy with the conversations between leader and reporter demonstrating mutual respect and fellowship. Gentlemen of the press must endure the midnight sessions of Congress or last through all of the banquet toasts and then dash to the waiting ship or stage to bring their readers the words of American politics.

This generation of political reporters, the first to supply a comprehensive record of political speech, looked back on their accomplishment with misgivings. In some ways they regretted the changes in Congress that made their job easier: the practice of reading speeches. To speak from a text before mid-century was to court laughter: extemporaneous delivery or a prodigious memory was the only way to be taken seriously. Congressmen, the journalists complained, now addressed their constituents, not their colleagues or the intimate political community drawn to the gallery. There was, for many observers, a Gresham's law in congressional debate in which printed texts drove out the oral exchange of views.[27]

One of the sharpest critics of this new formality among lawmakers was the Washington correspondent for a Boston paper, Benjamin Perley Poore. He covered the capital for more than three decades with wider interests and greater self-assurance than any reporter of his time. He had grown up in Washington and always thought he understood it (his "reminiscences" of government began when he was five years old). Poore ran away from school to become an apprentice printer and then relied on family connections to gain consular posts in Europe. Before he was thirty Poore had traveled extensively on the Continent and in the Mid-East. This sharpened his appetite for all things American. The runaway became an antiquarian and lovingly restored his ancestral home. He was a connoisseur of political talk on Capitol Hill. He became the first president of the Gridiron Club, a meeting place for politician and reporter to act the part of hale fellows. Poore was among the first to take an historical view of

Washington reporters. He took the still novel position that this was a responsible group with an honest calling. (When Poore began work in the 1850s, the only book on journalists called them a "gang.") Poore was an old hand at the admiring biography, and in his memoirs he celebrated clubbiness between journalist and politician. There was insight and edge to Poore for all the sycophancy. He described how discretion and the habit of compromise had broken down with the coming of war. He was shocked by the aggressiveness of young reporters in the 1860s and looked back fondly to a time when interviewing was equated with eavesdropping. Most of all he hated the prepared speech that had become the mechanism for discussing the fate of the Union. Reporters, he believed, lost an important role in the republic when political leaders could simply issue addresses to their constituents. Political debate was a sham, and so compromise was impossible when congressmen refused to address one another.[28]

Poore's criticism can be read as a disguised attack on an old friend: Charles Sumner. This Republican was the most self-conscious and studied orator in the Senate, one of the few members for whom the toga in the memorial bust was exactly the right dress. Only on rare occasions did the senator from Massachusetts speak spontaneously to his colleagues on the grave issues of the day. From the beginning of his career in 1852 Sumner spent his nights composing thundering addresses on slavery and committing them to memory. Often the printed version of his speech—as long as 100 pages—was in his hands before he walked into the Senate. More than any senator before him, Sumner turned discussion on vital issues into a performance that closed off exchanges of views.

The power of speech in print set the framework for what the North called Sumner's martyrdom and the South, his just reward. On May 19, 1856, Representative Preston Brooks of South Carolina sat in the gallery and heard the first day of Sumner's laceration of the South over the question of slavery in Kansas. The next day, when Sumner finished the oration, his colleagues were struck by the violence and the calculation of his address. "Written with cool deliberate malignity," Senator Stephen Douglas observed, the criticism seemed fundamentally different from insults thrown out in heated debate. Representative Brooks did nothing until he could read the speech on the 22nd of May. Then he found Sumner at his desk on the Senate floor, so intent on franking copies of the speech he hardly noticed visitors. Both men recalled that Brooks's first words were that he had carefully read the speech that Sumner now hunched over. The Southerner then raised his cane and brought it down on the senator's head. Sumner was blinded by the blood and pinned in his chair. He endured blow after blow until the cane broke.

The story here was larger than the personalities, more even than the passions over slavery and sectional interest. Sumner was a victim of the new rigidity of debate and the inability of this political culture to disguise what was said and gain time for compromise. Sumner convalesced for three years and then returned to Capitol Hill. David Donald, his modern biographer, has noted that Sumner abandoned the pretense of persuasion when he again dared to take the Senate floor. Sumner declared that "no senator is reached by any argument."[29]

Others in Congress had said almost as much before, but then with important qualifications: at least colleagues could be reached at some sessions, perhaps around the fireplace while another senator held the floor. On vital issues even cynics had believed that congressional debate changed votes. From the approval of Jay's treaty during the Washington administration through the great compromises over slavery in new territories, this seemed to be true. In the memoirs of congressmen who served before the 1850s it is very hard to find men who did not believe that great orators such as Clay, Calhoun, and Webster spoke directly to them, as well as to the voters beyond the capital. In the 1850s this changed. As Sumner read from his galley proofs, his followers, not his colleagues were his public. Fellow senators might squirm, walk around the chamber, or sit stunned in their seats, tearing papers to bits during the address, but Sumner took no

notice of this. When he was insulted, the senator made no answer, simply printing the remark verbatim at the end of the text
to whip up his readers.

At times Sumner appeared indifferent to publication in Republican newspapers. It was his *own* reporting and circulation
of speeches that engaged him deeply. Through the franking
privilege and anti-slavery societies he built a network of readers
outside party journalism. In 1860, when Sumner excoriated that
moderate position on the South with which Lincoln hoped to
win election, Sumner attacked at the expense of his party. The
man who most clearly saw the uses of this new power of text
was the fiercely Democratic James Gordon Bennett, Sr., a
Northern man with Southern sympathies. He put Sumner's
speech on the front page of the New York *Herald*.[30]

Political influence was not tied closely to reporting everywhere
in the nation before the Civil War. Face-to-face politics had always been more important in the South, where lower rates of
literacy and lower density of white population discouraged journalists. In 1850 the per-capita circulation of periodicals and newspapers among Southern whites was less than a third of the figure
in the North. The scarcity of printed reports on sensitive issues
became important to the South with the rise of sectional tension.
One reason a Southern elite put so much energy in condemning
the "incendiary documents" of anti-slavery was that abolitionists
threatened to reach both white and black citizens in a new, direct
way.

The oral habits of political discussion were helpful for the "fire-
eaters" who counseled secession. William Lowndes Yancey, for
example, stated his vision of the South beyond the reach of
reporters. Yancey had edited and owned newspapers, but he
avoided journalism as he became more radical in the 1850s. This
lawyer-planter spread his secessionist dreams at great barbecues
and the gossip that followed these local festivals. He published
very little at this time and did nothing to improve the very
sketchy coverage he received in Southern newspapers. But for

many years he kept 40,000 to 50,000 citizens spellbound with his addresses. Yancey left scant record of this effective agitation, and this was a wise strategy for the making of a dangerous argument. Secession talk picked up little interference from outsiders; print inevitably opened the argument to wider comment.[31]

No single episode in nineteenth-century politics did more to illustrate the power of reporting than the Lincoln-Douglas debates. The Democrat, of course, won that senatorial campaign in 1858, sending Lincoln back to his admirers in the courthouses and taverns of central Illinois. Outside the state, reports of the debates were not widely available until after the election. But the closer one looks at the performances of these ambitious politicians and the press that struggled to report what they said, the more the debates show the future of nineteenth-century political discourse.

Led by the Republican *Tribune* and the Democratic *Times* in Chicago, verbatim accounts of the great debates circulated though Illinois that summer and fall. Never before had voters in any state such a complete and timely record of what opponents said. In 1848, newspapers had muffled the exchange between Senator Douglas and Representative Lincoln. Partisan papers ran their man's speeches and said they would report the other side only if the rival paper did this first. No editor took the dare. During the presidential race of 1856 the Republican press had allowed dozens of Lincoln's speeches to go unreported. At the momentous convention of the new Republican party in Bloomington, the state's best reporters claimed to go into a trance when Lincoln spoke and could supply no account of an address that electrified the delegates. In the campaign of 1858 candidates and reporters increasingly worked together to ensure that each man was tied to a printed record of what he had said. In these seven debates alone interested readers could find a reliable, book-length dialogue.

The *Tribune*'s reporters were the linchpins of this drive to move speeches to the public. The paper assigned Robert R. Hitt, a

twenty-four-year-old court reporter, to take down Lincoln's
words. At Freeport, with 15,000 waiting, a voice in the crowd
spoke plainly of the new imperatives for campaigners:

> "Hold on, Lincoln, you can't speak yet. Hitt isn't here and there
> is no use of your speaking unless the *Tribune* has a report."
> "Ain't Hitt here?" asked Lincoln, Where is he?"

The young man was taken up and passed over heads to the
platform so that politics could go on. The *Tribune*'s regular correspondent, Horace White, proved his worth in other ways. In
a campaign stop between the debates with Douglas, Lincoln
spoke without a text and, so White said, was unable to remember
his words. White re-created an address for the *Tribune*, part of
it so moving it soon became a chapter in the Lincoln legend.
"Well, those are my views," White quoted Lincoln many years
later, "and if I said anything on the subject I must have said
substantially that, but not nearly so well as that is said. . . ."
One way or another, "lost" speeches were growing rarer in
American politics.[32]

The clearest thing, whether reporters always knew it, was that
Lincoln's use of print was carefully calculated. He stood by the
printer at the composing bench and selected the italics for the
House Divided speech (apparently roping White into the last-
minute editing as well). The "lost" speech of 1856 was almost
certainly not reconstructed by Lincoln for reporters because he
had gone further on the slavery issue before the party faithful
in Bloomington than he wished the entire state to know. (No
Democratic reporters were there to break the convenient trance
of Republican journalists.) Lincoln asked reporters of the Douglas debates to "suppress" his inadvertent slight of a fellow Republican, and the following year he got Hitt to spike an entire
speech he delivered lest it offend that powerful Republican editor in New York, Horace Greeley.[33]

Lincoln referred, not to his printed speeches, but to "anything
that I have ever put in print," choosing just the active role for

himself that politicians had held since the birth of the republic. What was new was that in the course of the debates with Douglas, Lincoln came to see that it was far more important to be reported than to have the chance to improve what one said. Lincoln used the reporters' record in his defense as he took on the job of publicizing his own words. In the course of the debates Lincoln pasted newspaper accounts of his speeches on slavery into a notebook and showed this off to prove his consistency. In the final three debates, Douglas spent hours on the platform trying to show that Lincoln spoke like an abolitionist or a slave-holder, as it suited different audiences in the state. Lincoln invoked his clippings to show that Douglas was *"garbling,"* and he argued that the sure passage of speech to print made Douglas's charges impossible to believe: "he assumes that I do not understand that my speeches will be put in print and read North and South." After Lincoln's defeat in the Senate race the publication of what he had said across Illinois became his chief political activity.[34]

This strategy can be followed in Lincoln's correspondence and his own editorial work on a second book of clippings. In the first weeks after the votes were counted in November 1858, he made several requests for the speeches as printed in the *Tribune* and the *Times*. He was not satisfied with either paper's report of one speech so he added an old clipping from a third newspaper. The archive ran some 2400 column inches. He bought a black leather scrapbook, hired a book binder to paste in the columns, and by Christmas he was showing this off and discussing publication.

Lincoln turned editor while corresponding with publishers. He gave the book a title and took a pencil to the text, crossing out the reporters' parenthetical remarks, notes of the cheers, and questions shouted from the crowd. He restored words in his own speeches that he believed Hitt had misheard or the printer had mangled. There is no way of knowing whether, as one Lincoln scholar judged, he spent more time with this book than with any other he had owned or read. It is certain that when the scrapbook was ready for the printer, it had become a precious object. "I would not let it go out of my control," he advised a publisher. The printing would have to be done in Springfield, where Lincoln could watch his clippings. This proved unworkable, and Lincoln had only one copy of the Douglas debates when he resumed work for the Republican party in the fall of 1859. He carried his treasured book into Ohio and seems to have used it to boost the spirits of Republican officials, for when he returned to Illinois, the party declared publication "essential" to the approaching presidential campaign. Lincoln sent the scrapbook back to Ohio with a trusted courier and a reminder that his editorial work was inviolable. This edition of the debates sold briskly during the campaign summer of 1860. Stephen Douglas, now Lincoln's opponent for the presidency, watched in pain while this reporting seemed to propel the Republican toward the White House.[35]

The Civil War was not made inevitable by good (or bad) reporting. But it is hard to imagine an ideological conflict so broadly based and sacrifices made for so long without the awareness of political positions that the spread of reporting helped to bring about. After all, sectional manifestoes threatening the Constitution had been seen before 1861, issued by the New England states during the War of 1812 and by South Carolina in 1832, for example. Mere glorification of one section at the expense of another had come and gone before without bloodshed. The political system had outlasted the most eloquent and skilled propagandists, the anti-slavery work of the 1830s and 1840s. By 1850, the most delicate questions of statehood in Missouri, Texas, and California had been resolved. New territories, sectional ideology, and racial feeling had a central role in the crisis of the 1850s, but for all their force they do not explain why the dam broke. It was political institutions that gave way. The reporting system that was completed in the 1850s helped to create those fresh channels for political action that swept away patch-work groups like the Whigs and even the most adept straddlers like Stephen Douglas.

George W. Julian, a congressman from Indiana, pointed directly to the new power of reporting at mid-century. In the course of his long and principled anti-slavery campaign, Julian was a divining rod present at every source of the modern Republican party. From the 1840s to the 1870s he was a "Conscience" Whig, a member of the Free Soil party, a Republican, and a Radical Republican before finally closing his career in the Liberal Republican movement. Through five terms in Congress Julian was also a close critic of the factions he did not join. He celebrated the reporting of both friend and foe, for he saw this exposure as the surest way to end the political system built on moral compromise. In 1857 he spoke warmly of the new practice of publicizing party platforms (the major parties first issued statements of their beliefs in 1844). Planks should be a "bludgeon," Julian said, and "words taken from their own mouths" were to be used against anyone in politics who compromised party principles. Wide knowledge of party platforms made them "very convenient weapons in the exciting strifes of our times." Congressional debate in the 1850s, Julian recalled, were "caught up by the press" in a way that complemented *Uncle Tom's Cabin*. It was not simply that the anti-slavery case was heard. "Treated" to the words of the South, the North at last understood the slave power.[36]

Reporting surely did not have *one* simple role in making compromise impossible. The publication of dissent was a way of putting disputes on the table where they could be talked out. As Tocqueville and other conservatives observed, the American press often acted as a safety valve for extreme views. Moreover, orderly party life before the Civil War required the heat that reporting raised. The Whigs and the Democrats were coalitions of sectional and ethnic interests and members of one party had few principles in common. Enemies made the groups in each party pull together, and the delivery of statements that could be hated was a powerful aid to party loyalty. Partisan news-papers were admirably suited for this purpose. In Congress, parties had to win public attention before they could hope to discipline themselves and to govern. The growing concern for reporting can be seen as one of those "attention getting behav-iors" that made the legislative party system possible in the Jack-son era. The significance of this consolidation of political life has been underscored by quantitative studies that show that party, rather than sectional interests, were paramount in congressional votes until the early 1850s.[37]

It was not, then, reporting itself or the simple increase of reporting that disrupted American democracy. It was reporting that achieved national circulation outside the control of canny party operatives that made the political system less stable. Cap-itol Hill's own publications, increased franking by congressmen, the press of the new reform organizations, and the broader cov-erage of newspapers formed a new reporting system by the 1850s. The nation followed Illinois in this decade and gained a printed record of what leaders stood for. The circulation of timely and full reports of political speech was a prerequisite for the organization of politics around more systematic and more shared principles.

This flow of information was disruptive because it broke down the federal (one might almost say feudal) pattern of organized political life. As one historian has observed, before mid-century, "many voters, probably the vast majority, learned of national and even state issues only what their local politicians and news-papers told them." What antebellum politics could not long en-dure was a reporting process out of the control of these gatekeepers that furnished party members with what their *allies* said. Then the game had to change. The Whigs were destroyed by recognition of their internal differences. The new Republican party, no matter how moderate its spokesmen, could not build alliances in the South. It was a creditable bogey that broke the South's long habit of ignoring what was said up north in order to exercise power with Northern help. The Democrats were near the abyss in 1860, when Douglas was skewered by his party in the South for concessions he had made in the Lincoln debates.[38]

Reporting weighed heavily on the men who argued about the Union in Congress. The *Congressional Globe* became the official report of speeches in 1852, and lawmakers provided that it be sent free to constituents. This did not meet the demand. Contemporaries marveled and worried as they saw congressmen bend under the task of reporting. Senator Sumner was only a few steps ahead of his colleagues in his feverish pace. Senator William Henry Seward sent out 50,000 copies of an address in three weeks in 1850, a figure his political allies matched. Webster's last great act of leadership, the 7th of March speech for the Compromise of 1850, was circulated in 120,000 copies before the end of that month. During the first five months of 1858, senators from the free and slave states franked more than 800,000 speeches on the question of Kansas. Later that year Senator Douglas franked 345,000 speeches and pamphlets to Illinois voters in beating Lincoln. No wonder that in 1859 an ex-senator stood over the grave of a colleague and bitterly cited "the heartbreaking drudgery of franking cart loads of speeches and public documents to the four winds."[39]

Nothing on this scale had been seen before. The incomplete records we have for the early congresses suggest that lawmakers did not provide for the distribution of more than a few hundred copies of reports and speeches. The most eagerly sought reports of Congress had single editions of only a few thousand before the 1820s. Abraham Lincoln, known as an energetic party worker, sent out but 7000 copies of his speeches during his term in the House in 1847–48. Quite suddenly, the circulation of political speech exploded, changing the political culture of Congress.[40]

It is of course true that a political system, even a political party, can live on with warring factions that are well reported. The party may hold together if leaders can make members attend to other things. Witness the Democratic party on race questions during the middle of the twentieth century. This is rarely possible when new forms of communication make the issue prominent at the same time they allow insurgents to address the nation. In this case the party hierarchy cannot anticipate or control these appeals. National magazines and network television ensured that the Democrats would have to face Civil Rights. Similarly, the new channels for political reporting in the 1850s produced treacherous currents, beyond the skills of political conciliators who wanted to steer clear of new issues.

In a citizen's lifetime America had changed from a nation of itinerant assemblies playing to a distracted public. By mid-century no citizen with a taste for news or a vote to be won could escape detailed accounts of drama on Capitol Hill and the printed speeches. The growth of reporting, as it provided an orderly record of proceedings, was one aspect of the increased accountability of Congress to the public. The institution was becoming more open, keyed to the external rewards offered by constituents rather than by the internal rewards of colleagues. Such open phases of Congress—as in recent American history—make government more difficult and failed presidencies more likely. The critique of open systems is familiar: lawmakers will not play by the internal rules; they draw attention to themselves and play to single-issue groups. The political press becomes fascinated with such performances, ignoring many substantive issues and the process of government itself.

If this is a flaw today, it is not new in the life of Congress and political reporting. The suitability of political speech for mass distribution was an important concern in the 1850s, a matter treated as seriously as what had been said. On April 6, 1860, the day after Owen Lovejoy's address, "The Barbarism of Slavery," had created a melee on the House floor, the congressman's chief worry was that he would not be able to revise his remarks for the *Congressional Globe* so they would seem as exciting as the immediate reports of the speech that had been telegraphed to newspapers around the country. The New York *Tribune*'s first reports on April 7th and 9th barely touched on what the abolitionist had said. Readers learned little more from the Washington correspondent than "this was an excellent speech to circulate." The reporter suggested that two million copies of the address be sent out.[41]

Legislators of an earlier generation, such as Webster, thought the new opportunities for reporting and publicity might forge the compromises that would preserve the Union. This proved to be one of the many false hopes of mid-century. As Webster reached out to the South by supporting the Compromise of 1850, with its new police power to return fugitive slaves, he shattered his own constituency. He tried to protect himself by adding more illustrations of Northern grievances to the text of the 7th of March address in the Senate, but even at that the speech inspired old enemies such as Longfellow and Emerson to fresh verse on his moral blindness. Abolitionists put excerpts of the speech on the handbills that called protest rallies. Voters in remote villages were soon able to parse the Webster text and interrogate him on the exact nature of his concessions to the slave power. Publicity helped to make victories in Congress, defeats at home. In Boston, Charles Sumner rummaged through his files and put together a long record of statements Webster had published that were inconsistent with the Compromise. "Such a string of testimony would be enough to hang even a greater traitor than Daniel Webster," Sumner wrote as he sent the list off to a party newspaper.[42]

Reporting made lawmakers face pressure groups who now knew a great deal about what they stood for. The methods of reconciling differences (or of sweeping them under the rug) that had grown up with the institution no longer worked

These peace-keeping devices had been slowly put together as Congress had matured as an institution during the first half of the century. It was a large step when members of the Congress came to know one another and to accept specialized roles in handling legislation. Like-minded congressmen boarded together and learned what to expect of colleagues. By the middle of the century it was no longer necessary for a man to bow out of the House after one term (as Lincoln did) to allow another party man to have a turn. Quantitative studies of the Senate cease to use words like "morass" to describe the comings and goings of members and find at last "career senators." Committee assignments fixed by party allowed representatives to master an area of government and to shape it. In the Senate, seniority was becoming important in the 1850s. Party loyalty seemed for a time tenacious enough to bind men together through any crisis.[43]

Facing the high point of the anti-slavery movement and the most tempting apples of discord in new territories and states, the compromises and evasions continued to hold Congress together. Only in the mid-1850s did the institution break down. Reporting to constituencies beyond Capitol Hill became more compelling than the persuasion of colleagues for important factions. A public had gained the resources and the habit of mind to detect deviance from published positions of leader and party. For those interested in principled solutions to the grave moral questions that divided the nation, this was a welcome transformation. From the point of view of old national parties with their workhorse congressmen and editors, accuracy and accountability had done their worst.[44]

4

Visual Thinking: The Tammany Tiger Loose

In the spring of 1871 William M. Tweed and his associates in the Tammany Hall political club were men of some honor and considerable power in New York City. By the end of that summer these Democrats had been ruined by *Harper's Weekly* and the New York *Times*. Thomas Nast's pear-shaped Boss inhabits our mental picture of American politics, and the reporting by the *Times* of Tweed's raid on the city treasury is part of urban folklore. For all the celebration (and some recent debunking) of this exposé, fundamental questions have not been answered. Why was Nast's pen so powerful? How did the *Times* make New Yorkers pay attention to stories that were basically columns of figures copied from ledger books? These questions remain open because the major accomplishment of the press—the creation of ways to *picture* a corrupt city—has not been made clear. What was at stake in Boss Tweed's New York was visual thinking about political power. Reporting with words and pictures created images of the city that had few precedents in the American press. This political criticism was a challenge to the appearances maintained by a skillful political leadership. Pictures were the heart of the matter in Boss Tweed's New York, and when journalists learned to master them, their political reach grew.

Thomas Nast's public had only to look at the pages of *Harper's Weekly*; we have the much harder job of learning to see his drawings with the eyes of these Americans. Perhaps the most difficult thing to grasp is the attraction of abundant illustration in a culture starved for pictures. Everyone who has taken the slightest interest in political life before the Civil War thinks of a gallery of metal engravings, lithographs, and early photographs such as daguerreotypes. It is easy to take these pictures for granted. But pictures were not common and enduring things in America before Nast's day. Citizens could not expect a timely illustration of a political crisis, and they often waited years for a good likeness of politicians themselves. The handsome illustrations in modern textbooks were often not common knowledge in the early republic.

Pictures, like most products of craft and advanced technology, were more numerous in the Old World than in the New. Before the Revolution no American magazine had attempted to match the illustrations in European publications. The *Pennsylvania Magazine*, begun in 1775, showed the best that Americans could do with pictures: twenty engravings in its nineteen issues, most of these of machinery. The magazine's editors, including Tom Paine, were not able to be revolutionaries about illustrations. No American editor of the eighteenth century was. England produced more cartoons about the revolution in America than did the colonists themselves. American shops lagged behind Europe in exploiting the innovations at the turn of the century that made possible the mass circulation of high-quality pictures: cross-grain engraving on wood and lithography, the printing of drawings from stone. The circulation of illustrated magazines was small by European standards. The *Pennsylvania Magazine* had 1500 subscribers at a time when English publishers boasted of more than 20,000. London's weekly *Penny Magazine*, with a circulation of 200,000 and abundant illustrations, was beyond the dream of any American publisher in the 1830s. It would be twenty years before New York could match this.[1]

American editors also were less likely to commission illustrations; even more than the English, they lived by the ready-made. Print shops saved engravings and recycled them as events allowed. Such archives, plus specimen books of pictures, constituted the main resource for small publications until the end of the nineteenth century. Pictures waited for events to happen. The dangling man lived in the printer's case until summoned for execution stories. Publishers with large circulations could commission original pictures, but this led to a recycling of visual information. If the publisher did not save the picture to use again on a different story, it was usually sold to an editor less scrupulous.

Political pictures often tested the public's will to believe. At the end of the War of 1812 a Vermont printer issued a woodcut, "COLUMBIA, finally victorious over all her enemies—reclining in Peace, and surrounded with plenty." Columbia here has Asian features and dress, holds a parasol, and stands before a palm tree and a pagoda. Evidently an illustration of Eastern travels was the only thing at hand in the print shop. "Un-authenticity," the delicate term of one scholar, is not hard to find in portraits of the best-known Americans. During the Revolution the same woodcut was used to make pictures of John Dickinson the "Farmer" and the late British hero, General James Wolfe. Two years before his death, David Crockett wrote this on a lithographer's portrait: "I am happy to acknowledge this to be the only correct likeness that has been taken of me." Abraham Lincoln joked that campaign pictures of 1860 were "attempts on his life" and sometimes showed a man he could not recognize. Worse was to come, for when Lincoln grew a beard after winning the election, lithographers added it to their printing stones sight unseen. Some of these Lincoln "portraits" (especially one with mutton-chop sidewhiskers) would, in fact, have been difficult for the president to recognize.[2]

The camera did not, all at once, open a view on public life. Daguerreotypes, the first popular form of photography, were a common wonder in antebellum America, and the cheap *cartes-de-visite* portraits circulated widely. Stereoscopic viewers were a fixture in cultured homes. There was no shortage of picture-takers. Estimates of the number of daguerreotypists in 1850 range up to 10,000. By the end of the Civil War the Union armies were

pursued by 1000 free-lance photographers. It is an error to suppose that because we can see these pictures and ordinary citizens
at mid-century saw photographs of some type, the camera made
public life familiar. Photographs could not be mechanically reproduced, they had to be engraved by hand. This expensive,
slow work changed the quality of the image as the artisan translated the photograph into cuts in wood or metal. The illusion
that a printed page contains a photograph was achieved only at
the end of the century when the half-tone process converted
pictures to a field of dots. Before about 1900 the qualities a
modern public values in photography—the apparently unme-
diated image, timely and cheap—was not something journalism
could supply.

The incompatibility of the photograph and the printing press
was one reason that even those citizens with the best connections
were unsure of what important people looked like. In 1864, after
Ulysses S. Grant's great victories in the West and an act of
Congress made him the highest ranking general officer in the
army, the Washington press corps did not know his face. The
identification of the hero at Union Station was made on the basis
of one man's memory of a faded photograph that had shown a
corner of the general's face. In the presidential campaign of 1872,
Nast, with the resources of his magazine, could find no picture
of the Democratic candidate for vice-president, Governor B. Gratz
Brown of Missouri. He began his cartoons on this campaign
using a name card, not a man, in the drawings.[3]

All of American political illustration before *Harper's Weekly*
might be divided into two categories: the scarce and the perish-
able. Scrapbooks kept in the early republic may bulge with cards
and ribbons accumulated in political life, but they seldom have
many pictures. The archives have remarkable empty spaces.
Cartoons of George Washington are extremely rare, and it is
equally difficult to find a cartoon of Thomas Jefferson turned
out by one of his defenders. The best available records show
that between the Constitutional Convention of 1787 and the
election of Andrew Jackson in 1828, the print shops of America

issued only seventy-nine political caricatures as separate publications. Lithographs on political themes did circulate widely after 1830, but this was not a deluge. During the exciting political struggles of the Jackson presidency, separately published caricatures averaged fewer than two a month. Only a small part of the comprehensive Currier & Ives catalogue had anything to do with political questions. News to these successful picture merchants meant fires, shipwrecks, and fast horses. These were the scenes issued in color; the political pictures usually came out in black and white. Many controversies passed without illustration of any type in general circulation. One scholar has found only ten cartoons touching upon Catholics from the mid–1830s to the mid–1850s, a period when anti-Catholic feeling was a major force in American politics. No illustration of a strike seems to have been published in America before the Civil War.[4] It is not surprising that Abraham Lincoln was unable to lay his hand on a photograph of himself to send to supporters just two months before the Republican convention of 1860: the republic had never managed to meet the demand for pictures of government. There was no clear sign that illustrations would now play a larger role in journalism. James Gordon Bennett began commissioning woodcuts about current events for his New York *Herald* in the 1830s but then drifted away from the practice. Through the 1850s and into the Civil War the major dailies steadily diminished the number of pictures they printed.[5]

The technical backwardness of this developing nation does not fully explain the limited circulation of pictures. This was, after all, a society of marvelous tinkerers with eyes for the main chance. America excelled in the production of bank notes, printing the currencies of many lands by mid-century. This republic *chose* to take up many public questions free of a visual record. American democrats, like European connoisseurs, were often snobs about cheap and abundant illustration. When Daniel Webster planned the publication of his first collection of speeches he stipulated that his portrait appear in an engraving of a painting, not the new form of drawing for mass production: "I am agt. all *lithographic* things," Webster wrote. On newspapers the prejudice against pictures was strong enough to still, for a time, the profit motive. Through the 1840s, pictures (even when paid for in ads) were thought of as clutter on the page and a waste of space. Most newspapers battled against pictures and won through the 1880s. "Pictorial reporting" or "illustrated journalism" were phrases newly coined at mid-century, but few journalists used the terms naturally and without embarrassment. Some reporters went further, crying out that pictures "betrayed us into making our eyes do the work of our brains."[6]

This is why the illustrations of how New York was governed in *Harper's Weekly* were particularly significant. The dense pictorial record, more than 100 Tammany cartoons by Nast alone, focused unprecedented attention on the government of a city. Nast showed what political figures looked like and gave the public a quick way of grasping the value of their work. The editors were setting a course that was not fully accepted by fellow journalists for more than a generation.

Harper's Weekly drew power from common knowledge of illustrations as well as the public's hunger to see more of them. Both photography and the chromolithograph gave Americans frames of reference which an illustrator could use to advantage.

In Nast's generation, the chromolithograph spread knowledge of high art. This refinement of printing with stone was also a triumph of merchandising. For the first time, the middle class could see what hung in the large museums and also know the imagery of contemporary painting. In practice this meant that the prize winners at the French Salons were destined for the American parlor. Many of the cartoons that today are simply taken on their merits were issued and understood as a play on the work of the Ecole des Beaux-Arts. Only when one can feel the (now unfashionable) appeal of the stern moralizing in academic painting can one see what most of Nast's public knew he was driving at.[7]

Photography introduced a language to visual reporting that is more familiar in our day. Illustrators of the mid-nineteenth century sketched the world with the immediacy that the twentieth-century expects from a camera. They were like the artists news organizations send to court today when photography is not permitted.[8] But Nast could offer the sense of movement that the camera could not catch in the nineteenth century. In his kaleidoscope compositions he provided frames of action in which time shifts and cause and effect are clarified.

Nast also made political points that photographs missed. America's leaders benefited from the camera's slow shutter speed and the bulky equipment needed in the wet-plate process. The subject could not be surprised or caught in candid moments. The public face of an important American was almost always a dignified pose, as in Mathew Brady's portrait of Tweed from *Harper's Weekly*. The Boss seemed almost suitable for currency. Photographs, a cynic noted, turned prominent citizens into a new genus, *Homo uprights*.[9] Nast, working from photographs and careful observations of his subjects, was free to make the face mirror what he supposed to be the soul. In a series of posed photographs the leader ages before the viewer, and sadness, distraction, or sickness usually cannot be hidden (as in the photos of Lincoln and Lee in wartime). Nast denied his enemies the sympathy to be gained from being mortal. In the decade he focused on New York politics, his enemies grew no older and the only strain they showed was the hard work of crime.

The conventions of pictorial reporting, not just camera angles, favored the city as it was and tended to undermine attacks with words. Nast broke away from a whole gallery of benign urban scenes. In America and Great Britain, illustrated magazines at mid-century had only a topographer's vision of the growing cities. This was a journalism of proud panoramas. Streets were uncluttered, buildings and people were isolated; the bustling activities in an industry or a neighborhood were not allowed to get in the way of what the reader was supposed to see. One looked down on people and up at imposing buildings. Only the important people met the reader at eye level. The poor and the "dangerous classes" were swept from the city. The earliest da-

The Honorable William M. Tweed
From a photograph by Brady.
(*Harper's Weekly*, January 21, 1871)

guerreotypists broke some of these rules, but urban photography quickly found an angle of vision to make streets fit the
dreams of the town booster. Similarly, the accepted syntax for
social groups of any importance was a flattering stage setting.
An illustrated magazine from the Victorian era can be opened
almost at random to see this careful window. The artist imposed

a perspective that brought everything the reader needed to see into view. The attentive subjects of these illustrations seemed to be performing for the public's pleasure— and winning their approval.[10]

Pictures like these—even in *Harper's Weekly*— flattered Democrats. The new county courthouse, a beehive of Tammany activities, had a respectful unveiling in the magazine on September 9, 1871. On a full page readers saw a classic façade with no signs of excess. In the illustration, commerce passed on a broad avenue and a fountain splashed as if in a water company's brochure. The city appeared to work. The January 21, 1871, issue of *Harper's Weekly* covered a grand ball for the successful Democrats, with two full pages given over to the spectacle. The text made clear that at this ball there were sights to tempt a critic: a floral display rising thirty-eight feet above the dance floor, jets of water that shot twenty feet, a fountain of cologne, and 1000 canaries hung in gilded cages. This was cast in the most favorable light possible in the artist's drawing. The gentlemen of the Ring glide across a sumptuous dance floor with their ladies. Even Tweed's girth is hidden. The conventions of picturing society had been honored.[11]

In New York, as in London, "comic" illustrations were the significant exceptions to the sterile conventions in picturing urban life. Often the Victorian public got its first illustrations of the chaos and deceptions of the city through cartoons. To be sure, these were reminiscent of William Hogarth's paintings and suggested much that was in the novels of Charles Dickens's generation. But cartoons were published in such abundance during the last half of the century and punctured so many pretty pictures, they earned unprecedented attention.

This completed Nast's arsenal—comic illustration that was aimed at a field brought into view by photography and chromolithography. Thus armed, the respectful conventions for cities and their leaders could be shattered. What was Tammany's defense? It was an impressive fortress, fully as sensitive to appearances.

The New County Court-House, New York.
(*Harper's Weekly*, September 9, 1871)

New York of the mid-nineteenth century was a city fractured along lines of class, religion, and ethnic background. The leaders of Tammany made the gestures and deals that allowed a million citizens to live on Manhattan Island. Democrats handed out more than 12,000 jobs and could grant favors from the treasury or court system to influence 50,000 more citizens. But the payoff by itself was not the basis of Tammany's rule. If that had been sufficient, the organization would not have lost its ability to govern. By the beginning of the 1870s Tammany Democrats had changed the face of New York. These were accomplishments that dazzled citizens and made it very difficult for critics to gain attention. The Democrats built parks and sewers and thorough-fares. The "Ring" (as critics called it) pushed the grid of New York streets up towards the Harlem River. It made Central Park an oasis in the metropolis. It broke the stranglehold of poor sewers and docks and avenues. Tammany loved civic monuments. The New York Public Library and the Metropolitan Museum of Art were established with the support of these politicos.

One reason Tammany was formidable was that it was a highly visible meritocracy. If leaders were made in back rooms, they proved themselves in the organization's magnificent volunteer fire companies and election rallies before the test in office. Then they had to run the city, addressing the conflicting demands of the groups that might take away their power. Tammany Hall was not led by men who were easy to hate. Backslapping seems to have been as important as back stabbing (it was vital to be good at both). The lore of the organization—a Grand Sachem and his braves housed in a wigwam—did not seem threatening. The snarling tiger that became a menacing symbol of Tammany was originally the handsome emblem on the fire engine that Tweed and his friends operated in his ward.

The men of Tammany, especially Tweed and his associates, loved emblems, badges, and costumes, and for good reason: the regalia proclaimed power and loyalty. Democrats took the ritual seriously, even enduring "the Tammanical Grip of Brotherhood, which is formed by two brothers taking each other by the left hand, with forefinger of each hooked into the other and doubled into the palm of the hand...."[12] Fraternal display of this sort was a sign of character for nineteenth-century New Yorkers, and it marked the patterns of association and interest that were the bedrock of city politics. Political ritual is usually both a way to erase differences within a group and to define, however vaguely, shared beliefs. Tammany ritual brought people together but did almost nothing to clarify goals or sketch a philosophy of government. For this reason the ritual was particularly important and vulnerable. Citizens could go along with the Democrats in power because they wanted their favors or feared their punishments. Pragmatically, one could support a government that got things done. But Tammany had a very thin foundation of principled belief. Like the national Democratic party, and unlike most groups of Republicans, there were few symbols or remnants of ideology to draw constituents together. There was, indeed, little to believe in without a pleasing picture of the organization. Ridicule, as it discounted their power, was a particularly serious threat to these Democrats.

Tweed and his associates understood this. They were imaginative self-publicists. They did not rely alone on the crude and time-tested practice of subsidies to local newspapers. Tammany employed writers to send reports of its triumphs and virtues to out-of-town papers. When these were reprinted in New York newspapers, it appeared that distant, independent observers were praising the machine. The Ring paid special attention to pictures. Tweed wrote many checks over the engraving of a snarling tiger. There was a large lithograph of the Boss, suitable for display in the office of men who did business with the city. Tweed was a friend of New York's most famous portrait photographer, Mathew Brady, protecting the artist from business reverses. During 1870, the year before the exposé, four members of the Ring, including Tweed, secretly put up the money to begin *Punchinello*, an illustrated satiric review. This promised to preempt the field and guarantee that the satire of municipal government would be gentle. We cannot be sure if Tweed actually uttered that famous cry against Nast: "I don't care a straw for your newspaper articles; my constituents don't know how to read, but they can't help seeing those damned pictures." What is significant is that this is one of the earliest and most widely believed pieces of folklore of the political crisis. The assumption of this culture was that power and guardianship over visual images were closely connected.[13]

In the exposés that broke upon them, these leaders were good at little except plunder. That may have been the chief talent of New York's comptroller, Richard B. Connolly, but most of the Ring were more impressive. Mayor A. Oakey Hall "the elegant Oakey" was a fashion plate and a successful journalist, lawyer, and Broadway playwright. Hall's charm and administrative skill earned the praise of many Republicans. Peter B. Sweeny, parks commissioner and chamberlain, was also a man of cosmopolitan tastes. He was at home in France, and through his wife knew Victor Hugo, Baron Haussmann, and Jean Corot. John T. Hoffman, the governor during the years of scandal, never lost the reputation of a gentleman. Only the downfall of his friends stopped the talk of Hoffman for the presidency.[14]

William M. Tweed, finally, was a man of some private and public virtues. He was a family man who rarely took a drink, and his success was self-made. Readers of *Harper's Weekly* were told that Tweed crushed the city, but they might well know his name because his artisan family made chairs they sat on. Tweed's generosity was legend (he gave $50,000 to the poor during the winter of 1870–71), and even some of his enemies saw an element of grandeur. George Templeton Strong, an aristocratic Republican, confided in his diary that "were he not a supreme scoundrel, he would be a great man." To Strong, who had once been mayor, Tweed towered above journalists "—statuesque as a demigod in Greek tragedy. Although 'interviewed' and badgered at least nine times a day by 'one of our reporters' (as the vultures interviewed Prometheus), he is always calm and great, if not perfectly grammatical—and that defect may be chargeable to the reporters."[15]

In 1871 there were many reasons why the press had not produced a harsh picture of Tammany government. Journalism was a business with a common-sense rule: boosting paid, knocking did not. Economic power, both direct and indirect, was the most important reason why not one of the twenty-six newspapers in New York seriously challenged Tammany government in the 1860s. *Harper's Weekly* and the New York *Times* were Republican partisans, and so criticism was to be expected. But there was no good reason to press an attack onto new territory. Journalists had not yet found a way to dramatize the systematic misgovernment of a city.

There had been precursors to the Tweed story, as in the illustrated probe of deadly "swill milk" tolerated by city government in *Frank Leslie's Illustrated Newspaper* of 1858. Charles and

Henry Adams had touched the Tweed ring in an exquisite dissection of the Erie Railroad in state politics. But these were not frontal assaults to overturn the image of a whole administration. The Adams essays were filled with subtle ironies to amuse upper-class readers. Less sophisticated, partisan journalism employed abuse and sensational charges, but did not offer evidence of villainy that was easy to grasp. In the few cases when an urban exposé did give a compelling picture of corruption, the revelation came suddenly and the public was not intrigued by an attractive puzzle being put together. The political story lacked the dramatic devices to give it the clarity and pull of melodrama.

Harper's Weekly needed an angle of vision that would make the works of Tammany seem insignificant and the adept operators of the Ring loathsome and vulnerable. But more important, the magazine had to interest people in the way New York City was governed. The editors believed that indifference was the most likely response to news of corruption. The test of the exposé was to guard against the yawn or the shrug.[16] Nast's cartoons and stories in the magazine worked together to draw readers into city politics. They exploited what the public already knew, especially its prejudices, and they kindled interest in new information. The story took on the compelling form of a melodrama in which evil seemed all-powerful yet a just outcome was certain. As in the enormously popular stage vehicles of the time, the public began knowing who to blame but was led into the detection of their black deeds. The power of evil set before the public aimed to restore their sense of control. The tension and puzzle of the melodrama made the political story in *Harper's Weekly* compelling.

The most remarkable feature of the press campaign against Tammany was its ability to make the most of its lack of proof. In the 1860s the Democrats of Tammany excelled at keeping mouths (and records) closed. In the fall of 1870, before an election, the machine allowed respectable businessmen to look at the city's books. These investigators said that everything was in order. No one in the press proved otherwise until the following summer. Nast and the editors of *Harper's Weekly* threw off the burden of presenting evidence and led readers to assume what could not be shown. The refrain in *Harper's Weekly* was that the corruption was a "universal conviction" in the city and that the operations of the Ring were "familiar to every citizen" but that a much smaller number of citizens knew the whole ghastly story. These claims kept the exposé alive. The magazine built social pressure to shut up the scoffers and to make citizens wish to be in the know. Dodging the question of proof, *Harper's Weekly* was able to build excitement for the moment it would appear. Thus the assumption of guilt, "the exposure of a rascality which was universally understood," was, for all that, a good mystery.[17] When the New York *Times* finally delivered the evidence in July 1871, the magazine exploited the element of surprise, the exciting confirmation of what readers had been told they had to believe all along.

Nast found the way to have a minimum of information make the maximum impact on readers. In the thirty cartoons he published before he had evidence, he made the corruption in city government tangible and repellent. He spent three months picking through the variety of images in the cartoonist's arsenal to see which ones worked. He began the fight with the figure of the STEAL RING. In his first drawings a viper grips his own tail above the politicians and a savage Tammany chief wears a ring above his necklace of skulls. Then Nast dropped the device. He also passed through a phase of dressing the Democrats up as savages. Four of the early cartoons stuffed politicians into deerskins and war bonnets, but then these costumes disappeared. These were indeed clumsy weapons. Nast could not picture, because he did not know, what the Ring was stealing. He could not rely on the Indian lore because Tammany had for too long defused this imagery. One might as well have attacked that new fraternal organization of the 1870s, the Shriners, by making them appear to be menacing Knights Templars.

Nast needed to reach beyond the Tammany ritual and create

a threatening picture. Stereotypes of the Irish were the solution. More than half of the early cartoons portrayed a thug-like Irishman. He was an ape in a dirty suit and usually had a battered hat over his prehistoric skull. He kept a death-grip on a whiskey bottle. Some Democrats looked a bit like this, but Nast was not drawing what he saw.

In the first place, most of the leaders Nast wished to topple were not Irish. Mayor Hall was a Yankee. John T. Hoffman was Grand Sachem of Tammany and mayor of New York when Nast's cartoons began in February 1867. His family had come to America from Finland in 1657. Tweed was a Protestant of Scottish ancestry. The simian Irishman was a discovery made by British and American cartoonists in the 1860s. The long tradition of anti-Irish caricature had never before produced this sustained, bestial imagery. Nast knew the masters of this new form in London, but he did not simply copy them. He improvised and added original touches to the stereotype. It was crucial to his purpose that the Irish were types, not individuals. Real Irish misbehavior, carefully observed, would have diluted the nativist sentiment he tapped.[18]

When Nast's thugs are compared to the real New York criminals that Jacob Riis photographed in the 1890s, the point of Nast's art is clear. Riis's "Bandits' Roost" and "The Verdict of the Rogues Gallery," for example, show men and women who are puzzles—they meet our eye and make us wish to understand their world. (Photographs of Jesse James in the 1870s had the same quality.) In sensitive hands the camera showed the middle class they would have to work hard to understand their enemy across class lines. Nast's make-believe Irishmen taught only contempt.[19]

Harper's Weekly relied so heavily on generalized portraits of villains because in the first year of the crusade the magazine was in the awkward position of not knowing who, specifically, to blame. John T. Hoffman was elected governor in 1868, and twice that year Nast made him the only member of the Ring to stand with Irish beasts. Then Hoffman was dismissed as only a front man. A. Oakey Hall was the Democratic mayor during the height of the frauds, but he was scarcely noticed. Peter B. Sweeny, a parks commissioner and chamberlain was the magazine's main target from 1867 until the fall of 1870 for "everybody knows that Peter B. Sweeny is Governor of New York. Mr. Sweeny is the Dictator of Tammany Hall," the magazine said. In the twelve Nast cartoons that appeared before the summer of 1870, it was "Peter the Great, Chief of the Tammany Tribe," who whipped the Irish slaves, and wore the bones of his victims around his neck. Tweed was "the lieutenant of Mr. Sweeny" in the early cartoons.[20]

Finally in the third year of the attacks, Tweed moved to the center of the drawings. In October, 1870 Nast showed Governor Hoffman on the Tammany throne, guarded by an Irish ape and the broad axe of Sweeny. But Tweed lounges confidently behind the throne; his sword is inscribed, "POWER." *Harper's Weekly* decided that "Mr. Tweed is Tammany Hall" and made him the central villain. No new job or deed elevated Tweed. No one then, or now, has found evidence to make Tweed's power so absolute. (Indeed, few urban historians think anymore that Tweed could boss the city and one researcher is convinced that this politician was framed.) [21] His rise in the magazine seems to have been the result of his attractiveness as a symbol. Physiology and reputation cast Tweed in the role of supreme Boss. Nearly six feet tall, 280 pounds, he was the easiest man in government to portray as a menace. He was certainly Tammany's most conspicuous consumer. His waistline, his mansions, and his parties were the best-known examples of high living by city fathers. "Boss Tweed" was not Nast's label until the 22nd anti-Tammany cartoon. The epithet expressed what the magazine most feared in American politics: the bargains between interest groups and the edicts to be expected when power had thus been corrupted.

There was no place for brokers or for dictators in the America of *Harper's Weekly*. This is the moral of cartoons on national issues in the 1860s. "Compromise" was always an epithet. As Nast saw it, the Civil War brought an end to that disastrous period of American history when national policy had been made by trades among interest groups and sections. The Republican party was not totally free of this sin. Andrew Johnson, Lincoln's successor, had failed to carry out a radical reorganization of the South. But Democrats always worked for the devil's bargains. They had equivocated on the moral issues of the Union and slavery, been eager for a compromise peace, and now, during Reconstruction, they would strike a bargain to leave ex-Confederates alone. Nast did not want peace on these terms because he thought that political brokers striking deals aimed at seizing all power. *Harper's Weekly* noted several conspiracies. Friends of the South (such as President Johnson) behaved like royalty; friends of the Irish plotted to replace freedom of conscience in America with Catholic dogma. When enough bargains had been made, the country would be ruled by edicts.

Nast put Tweed in twenty-one cartoons before he knew what, specifically, to blame him for. Tweed was stretched to take the shape of both a dictator and spineless accommodator. He was a busy tyrant. Tweed appeared as a monk, a bishop, and then took secular forms—prince, monarch, emperor—before coming back to rule the city. In May 1871, for example, Nast had Tweed come into the classroom and rip books published by the Harper's firm out of the hands of children. In June, Tweed put his fist down and held Manhattan Island under the thumb. But Tweed was a colossus who bent low. In the summer of 1871, Nast had him sitting down on one stool set up by Northern Democrats as well as the stool of the ex-Confederates. He groveled in the street before the Irish.

Even as readers saw Tweed command, Nast showed them that he could be brought down. This is the cartoonist's most difficult task: to select information to make power seem illegitimate without including any of the information to make it look permanent. It was not obvious that a leader pictured as a cleric, monarch, or giant can be removed by ordinary citizens. And already in the 1870s political machines had a fine record of survival in New York City. Logically, the cartoons offered a choice:

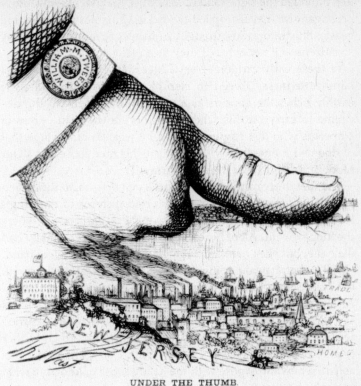

UNDER THE THUMB.

Tho Boss. "Well, what are you going to do about it?"

The Boss, with Manhattan under his thumb. Thomas Nast's drawing from the June 10, 1871 issue of *Harper's Weekly*.

fight or flee Tammany. In fact the reader was made ready for battle against the Ring because Nast's art forced his public to discount fears. To see one's fears exaggerated beyond what one dared to imagine works against fright. Nast's Tammany monsters provided the same kind of assurance that twentieth-century propagandists have supplied by making enemies into towering beasts. Illustrators must dredge up images of a monstrous enemy so citizens will not act as if they face real giants.

In these early cartoons Nast added details to guard against faintheartedness. Tweed in clerical garb was surrounded by earthly riches; he appears as a spoiled priest, without the discipline to carry out his schemes. He is shown in the dress of emperors who lost empires. When he wears a crown it is that of doomed monarchs. When he turns his men loose it is "Our Modern Falstaff Reviewing His Army."

The first thirty cartoons from Nast's pen marshaled these metaphors, not facts. He gave only blurred pictures of the Ring's leaders and did not focus on the source of graft or tell where the money went. All of his cartoons had captions and many had dialogue, but Nast handled Tammany's words with a free hand. "Well, what are you going to do about it?" the Boss sneered, but Nast seems to have simply put these words in his mouth. As far as is known, no one ever claimed to have heard Tweed say this.[22] By the summer of 1871 *Harper's Weekly* had carried readers as far as fantasy, alone, could take them. To go further required the facts held by the New York *Times*. Then Nast was able to renew the exposé with the heady sense of knowing what and who he was talking about.

The New York *Times* building on Park Row jutted high in the skyline of lower Manhattan in 1870, and from all of the five floors journalists might see the men of Tammany at work. Across the street stood City Hall, and just behind it the white marble of the new courthouse. During the halcyon years of the Ring, the politicians, clerks, and contractors with stories to tell were neighbors.

The *Times* was slow to understand and to speak about what was happening across Park Row. The paper endorsed the Republican party as warmly as *Harper's Weekly*, but Tammany rule was often agreeable to the *Times*. In the spring of 1870, editorials approved the appointment of department heads, commended the "good faith" of the Democratic leaders and said that "Senator Tweed is in a fair way to distinguish himself as a reformer. . . . "[23]

Prudence and inexperience prevented the *Times* from asking more questions about Tammany. Henry J. Raymond, the founder of the paper, died in 1869 just as *Harper's Weekly* was calling for allies against the Ring. It took George Jones, the new publisher, more than a year to consolidate financial control and to protect himself against retaliation by the Democrats. A director of the paper, who was at the same time a business partner of William M. Tweed, conveniently died in September 1870. As it turned out, *Harper's Weekly* and the *Times* had good reason to be cautious. The mayor encouraged libel suits against both publications. The school board banned Harper Brothers' books from classrooms, and city inspectors questioned the title to the land under the *Times* building.

In 1870 the paper's staff was new to the games played in City Hall Park. Jones had been the *Times*'s business manager before Raymond's death; investigation and advocacy were skills he was trying to learn. The journalists who covered Tammany were new to the city. Louis J. Jennings, the man who turned the editorial page into a pillory for Tweed and his friends, was an Englishman who had been the editor of the *Times of India* before settling in New York in the late 1860s. John Foord, the principal investigative reporter, was just off the boat from Scotland in 1870 and took on City Hall as his first opportunity to learn American civics. Jennings was thirty-four, Foord, twenty-six, when they found themselves with freedom and information to denounce the most powerful men in New York.

In the fall of 1870 these men of the *Times* began the exposé. For the next nine months, every issue of the paper contained a hostile question or an insult for Tammany. "Swindler" and "thieves" became common parlance, and in July 1871 readers were given extraordinary news pages that looked like balance sheets: New York County ledger books, documenting fraud. More than half a million copies of the "Secret Accounts" were grabbed up at newsstands. Tweed's career was ruined. The ingenuity of the *Times* was, however, even more remarkable than its persistence and courage in taking on powerful enemies.

The paper did not let the facts it knew speak for themselves, and it declined to follow where the facts led. From the start, the *Times* promised much:

BOLD DEEDS OF THE RING EXPOSED
INDISPUTABLE FACTS AND FIGURES WORTHY OF STUDY
CRIMES OF THE RING
THE RING DOOMED[24]

But the *Times*, it seemed, was whistling in the dark. Everyone who has studied the first nine months of the attack on Tammany has concluded that it was a failure, "a grand crusade conducted without fear and without facts. . . . " The paper had no concrete examples and it could not find a single city employee to confess or to cry foul. "Why so general . . . why are not names given?" The paper could not answer its own question.[25] The *Times* cast Tweed, Sweeny, Hall, and Connolly as public enemies, but enemies the journalists were unable to investigate. If reporters knocked on the doors of these leaders, interviewed their business friends, talked with the citizens who gave them votes, this information did not get into the newspaper.

New York's leaders emerged as creatures in a Nast cartoon. The *Times* cast politicians into this simple world of line drawings. Tweed's "rapacity, like the trunk of an elephant, with equal skill twists a fortune out of the Broadway widening and picks up dishonest pennies in the Bowery." Taxpayers "have folded their hands, opened wide their eyes" but done nothing, while the Ring, "thrusting their hands into their pockets, filled with money filched from the people, they have defiantly asked 'Well! what are you going to do about it?' "[26] At the end of nine months the paper could do little more than emulate Nast's sketches and repeat the hearsay that had inspired the cartoons.

The editor of the *Times*, Louis Jennings, once explained how he was suddenly able to make the corruption of New York vivid and compelling. At the beginning of July, 1871, Jennings re-called, the ex-sheriff of New York County came to his desk with an envelope. James O'Brien had been roughly handled in the Tammany wigwam (in the background of one Nast cartoon, he had been run through by a sword). O'Brien's agents had infil-trated the comptroller's office, and this angry Democrat was willing to use the Republican paper to get revenge. "You and Tom Nast have had a tough fight," O'Brien told the editor as he handed Jennings an envelope. "I said, '*had*'. Here's the proof to back up all The Times has charged. They're copied right out of the city ledgers." The legend, found in the official history of the *Times*, is that "here at last was deadly ammunition."[27]

No, the *Times* had been armed for a long time. George Jones had the evidence in hand when he *began* the abuse of Tammany. In the fall of 1870 the paper collected leads from a grand jury and transcripts of padded bills from the comptroller's office. From January to May, 1871, a *Times* source, Matthew J. O'Rourke, was a bookkeeper for the Ring. O'Brien himself remembered giving his evidence to the paper months earlier; in any case his envelope simply added to a pile. The famous "Secret Accounts" of July had been the *Times*'s secret for a long time. Beneath the headlines of July there was the quiet admission, "we were al-lowed to see the figures already printed, and some others held in reserve, fully nine months ago."[28]

This casts the *Times* coverage over those nine months in a new light. The paper said it was not free to publish the Secret Ac-counts before July, but this of course does not explain why the material was not used to guide reporters much earlier through the Tammany world of graft. The Secret Accounts mentioned nearly a dozen contractors and hundreds of suspicious trans-actions. The ledgers detailed work on more than a dozen build-ings and rent or repairs on some buildings that did not exist. The contractors routinely handed over huge sums to a Mr. J. H. Ingersoll. The *Times* need not have stood in the dark for so many months. It had scores of leads, and it might have developed many stories on its own. The triumphant publication of the facts in July loses some of its luster. It is as if Deep Throat's hints and clues to Robert Woodward had not been used by the Washington *Post* until Watergate figures had begun to confess.

The editors of the *Times* have not left a record of their motives, but their decision to play the cards so close to the chest certainly seems to have improved their game against the Ring. Withholding evidence during the first nine months gave Tammany nothing to refute and no single issue that could clear its name. The Democrats were unable to prepare a defense. Indeed, the Ring was so unaccustomed to defending itself against concrete charges, it met the revelations of July with a puzzled silence. The *Times* had led the Ring to lower its guard.

Most important, abuse and innuendo made specific facts, when they finally appeared, more impressive. By giving readers so little information to weigh and by abusing the accused every day, the paper turned readers into a hanging jury. Handling news this way amounted to a plea to the reader *not* to think:

> There is nothing inscrutable about the career of these [Tammany] gentlemen. No deepness of insight, or power of analysis, or broadness of comprehension is needed to fathom their motives. Nobody who comes to the consideration of them need prepare himself for his work by study or observation.

This *Times* editorial concluded by comparing these public officials to pigs in a potato field and dogs near a slaughter house. New York politics became the same world of simple shapes and lessons that Nast had drawn.[29]

"The day of retribution is advancing," the *Times* declared on July 8th as it began to open the Secret Accounts. "We cannot yield space to comply with the demand that is made upon us from every quarter for the reproduction of the *exposé* in full," the paper said, but in the next week editorials twice comforted readers with the pledge that the days of the Ring were "numbered." On July 20th and 21st the books were opened again— "We have, however, not yet begun to tell the story." More "Proofs of Undoubted Fraud" followed on July 22nd and 26th, "but our quotations have barely scratched the surface." Remembering these days, reporter Foord savored the power his paper held over New Yorkers: "People stood aghast at the facts which were revealed, but felt, probably, still greater alarm at the vague possibilities of what was still to be learned."[30] The *Times* could have told the whole story at once. Instead the journalists drew out the suspense, and, if the dull reader missed the point, he was hit over the head.

Popular entertainment at this time used a heavy hand to guide the imagination of the audience. Stage melodramas of the mid-nineteenth century helped create a public that welcomed manipulation in story telling. Viewed against the frozen plots of these melodramas, newspaper exposés offered mysteries that left unusual freedom for the reader to speculate on the outcome. The exposé revived a theme that had vanished from the popular stage: politics. The conventional wisdom of playwrights was that their work should be "spiced with some pungent glances at the present state of affairs without going deep enough to offend any party." Apparently only one stage production in New York touched on the Tweed Ring, a short-lived burlesque. The theater was simply not a window on politics. Mark Twain, who challenged this tradition when he brought *The Gilded Age* to the theater in 1874, would not show his audience a political villain. There was no part for that pious scoundrel of the novel, Senator Dilworthy. Journalists, in appropriating bits of the melodrama to build their stories of politics, were creating a form that was easy to understand and yet also fresh.[31]

The *Times* enticed readers by letting them count money and by having them imagine what it bought. Ledger entries were made exciting, almost sensual. The first digests of the city finances ("which we hope all our readers have carefully preserved") were pushed aside by the actual ledger sheets, spread across the front page. The paper said, "scrutinize them, analyse them, test them thoroughly."[32] Few nineteenth-century novels give as exciting an account of money-making, and the Secret Accounts remain good reading, for New York carried on its books sums that are impressive even after a century of inflation. The city paid $133,187 for two days of plastering to "the prince of plasterers"; $360,752 went for a month's work to "the luckiest carpenter that ever lived"; and a happy furniture dealer earned nearly five million dollars for a single building. The city paid four times the market rent for its armories, and the rent was more than $90,000 for armories that did not, in fact, exist.

The ledgers were filled with mysteries about an "El Dorado of Plumbers, Plasterers and Chair-Makers." The contractors rarely rested. They billed for construction during the winter and frequently reported Sunday jobs. There was always work to be done! The county courthouse stood unfinished after ten years of labor. In recent years the contractors had applied themselves to major repairs of the building they could not complete. Money moved as swiftly as time for these workmen. One contractor said he had not seen a cent of it, and the ledgers showed that all of the workmen had no sooner gotten their checks than they signed them over to one firm, J.H. Ingersoll & Co.

In the courthouse, the *Times* reckoned, the city had paid for carpets that would stretch from New York well up the Connecticut shore. The chairs in the armories would make a straight row seventeen miles long. The plastering bill was for 102 acres of walls and ceilings. Money enough for 1,884 awnings was lavished on 36 windows. The *Times* then took citizens into these buildings to see what the tax money had purchased. Hardened veterans of battle fled the dank armories, and fresh recruits could not be found to drill in the cramped space leased by the Ring. Visitors to the courthouse walked on oil-cloth because the fortune spent on carpeting was not enough to properly cover the floors.[33]

Something, however, was missing in these reports. The *Times* knew what government put on the floor and what it forced citizens to smell, but not much more about this organization. The paper did not investigate thieves so much as their workmanship. For many months the journalists had the names of these contractors, but learned little about them. An "inquisitive truth-hunter of the TIMES" confined his boasts about the investigation to the day before the publication of the Secret Accounts. The reporters were not impressive detectives. "Fillippo Donnarumma" was dismissed as a fictional artisan used by the Ring to pocket a real $66,000. A check of the city directory would have shown the *Times* that the man, a fresco painter, existed. On the other hand, it took a letter to the paper from John R. Hennessy to show the *Times* that "R. J. Hennessy" of the exposé was fictitious. And then there is the great mystery of J. H. Ingersoll. For months the *Times* had known that his company received all of the exorbitant payments—yet it knew nothing about him. To a reporter today this might well seem the most shocking part of the exposé. No political leader was mentioned in the Secret Accounts, and the *Times* constantly speculated that Ingersoll was the vital link to Tammany Hall. But the paper left "who J. H. Ingersoll really is" a matter of speculation and innuendo. This deliberately tantalizing group of facts is what the *Times* left for Thomas Nast in the summer of 1871.[34]

Nast took up the Secret Accounts at once (see illustration, Two Great Questions). In the three months before the November election he produced as many Tammany cartoons as in the previous three years. With each new issue of *Harper's Weekly* newsdealers in the city found crowds around their stands, eager to see the cartoons. The magazine's circulation tripled (to 300,000) in the course of the crusade, and in the two weeks of Nast's most feverish activity, 125,000 readers were added.[35]

The new public did not see an old show. Nast's earlier work had carried a double message about the Ring. The first message had been, here is a tyrant, a monster in the city. While the Ring seemed secure, Nast drew attention by costume or literary allusion to the weakness and servility of these men. The second message, in the same cartoons, was, here is a tottering despot. With more facts and more confidence, Nast put the Ring in starker light and more often separated the messages.

As Tammany grew weaker, Nast produced his most powerful

In the bottom panel, Tweed is joined (on his left) by Sweeny, Connolly, and Mayor Hall. The contractors listed in the Secret Accounts complete the circle. (*Harper's Weekly*, August 19, 1871)

pictures of the wealth and arrogance of Tweed Democrats. In
the three months before the November election there are revels
for New York's "masters"— they drink toasts to themselves,
while their impoverished constituents weep. Tweed, Sweeny,
Hall, and Connolly stride out of the city treasury with their
pockets bulging. They count the ballots on election day as citizens vote into a wastebasket. They grab school children to feed
to the Catholic clergy (bishops slither like crocodiles after the
young flesh). Tweed is supremely confident. He holds the whip
over both Democrats and Republicans, hangs like a gargoyle on
the ballot box, and a path to the White House opens before him.
A month before the election in New York, Tweed stands in his
best-known pose, hands in his pockets, a diamond radiating
from his shirt front, and he has become a bag of money from
the neck up. Finally, for the election issue, Nast showed "The
Tammany Tiger Loose." In this homage to the then famous
canvas of Jean-Léon Gérôme, a beast has come into the Roman
Colosseum to smash ballots and tear apart the fallen figures of
law and the republic. The Tammany politicians and their lucky
contractors gaze down on the carnage from the imperial box.

These scenes tell only half the story. During the same three
months, Nast showed the decline and fall of the Ring. In these
cartoons readers saw these politicians peek out fearfully from
hiding places. One by one they are kicked and discarded by
honest citizens. The animals in these cartoons are dying work-
horses of the Ring, not tigers. The Tammany Democrats are
vultures who stop feeding on New York when the storm of
reform crushes their perch. The men of Tammany cower and
then, losing all dignity, they run. They do not escape. Twice
Nast leads them to the gallows. Twice Nast put Tweed in the
ruins of Tammany: once with his clothes torn away and again,
more cruelly perhaps, in the embrace of the Irish (see illustration,
"Something That Did Blow Over").

Social scientists have provided a plausible model of how Nast's
contradictory images were understood. In their classic study of
rumor, Gordon W. Allport and Leo Postman used pictures

THE "BRAINS"

THAT ACHIEVED THE TAMMANY VICTORY AT THE ROCHESTER DEMOCRATIC CONVENTION.

(*Harper's Weekly*, October 21, 1871)

crammed with visual detail. The drawings were not humorous
or political, but they had the look of panels from a comic strip.
The study documented the extraordinary efforts of both viewer
and the people in the rumor chain to have cartoons "make sense."
In a subway scene the open razor jumped from the hand of the

white man to the black; on the battlefield the ammunition loaded into a Red Cross ambulance became medical supplies. The public radically simplified the drawings according to prejudice or a sense of what was appropriate. Nast's cartoons had the contradictory elements of these test illustrations, and the Allport-Postman study helps explain why a public is rarely confused by social commentary in illustrations: the complexity is swept aside as the reader rushes to find the moral. This is why Nast risked nothing in his later work by picturing the Ring as triumphant. His public was well prepared to screen out all implication that this was really so.[36]

Nast's purpose was served just as well if his public did hold contradictory ideas. It could not be true both that Tammany was unassailable and that Tammany was beaten. But anyone fighting the machine will have use for such a conception, for it produces an animating sense of outrage, while at the same time this vision builds confidence that the giants are helpless. Contradictory ideas give power to the people who make them believable. Followers enter the propagandist's world and lose touch with actual political life.

It has long been standard practice to discount the reforms that come from this type of political journalism. It is important to know the limits of this type of visual thinking, but to dismiss the exposé for its lack of substance misses the point about nineteenth-century politics.

With the November election reformers gained control of the city's treasury, but they proved unable to punish the men who had looted it or, in the long run, to keep spoils away from the political machine. The governor, the mayor, and Tweed himself continued in office, and the legal system was slow to touch the Democrats. *Harper's Weekly* said that the caricatures "never can be lived down," but this was wishful thinking.[37] Tweed was the only leader to go to jail and to die disgraced. Connolly became a wealthy exile. Sweeny lived comfortably in Paris and struck a deal with the prosecutors that allowed him to bring most of his money back to the country. He often returned to Manhattan and

The Tammany Tiger Loose. "What are you going to do about it?" (*Harper's Weekly*, November 11, 1871)

Something That Did Blow Over. (*Harper's Weekly*, November 25, 1871)

retired in upstate New York. Hall chose London and lived long enough to gain respectability on both sides of the Atlantic (before he returned to New York, Hall was appointed to the General Council of the London Metropolitan Ratepayers' Association). The small fish also avoided the net. Ingersoll was the only contractor to see the inside of a cell and he was out in a few months. No civil suits were carried through to recover the city's money, and the prosecutor's deals to bring in some cash did not far exceed the costs of the legal actions. The Democratic machine, of course, did not die; it was renewed with new leadership. Tammany was a phoenix, not the tiger that Nast imagined.

There is no mystery about why this was so. Tammany's constituents would have reinvented the machine had the blueprint been destroyed in 1871, for the political structure served them well. The taste for exposure faded because its partisan uses were played out with the November election. Both insurgent Democrats and Republicans realized now that an investigation would incriminate many public officials and businessmen. A quiet ending of the prosecutions served everyone's interest. Journalists had not brought enough mental capital to this political story to make further investments. The *Times* and *Harper's Weekly* were far better at getting citizens moving than in telling them where they were going. Neither publication was really curious about how Tammany worked, nor did either encourage readers to think very hard about the city they lived in. *Harper's Weekly* mused that "there are probably a great many people who think that TWEED'S Ring had more really valuable political knowledge and practicality than any other body of citizens." But the magazine was proud that it never entertained this idea. Settling for a visual squelch of Tammany left journalists with few new things to say as the contest to govern New York went on.[38]

Criticism of the press must be tempered by the realities of American politics in the Gilded Age. To a great extent the extravagances of Tammany *were* the substance of city government, and making these men absurd or monstrous struck at the heart of their administration. It was not incidental that Tweed had a

wigwam he loved, a diamond on his shirt-front, and a snarling
cat imprinted on his checks. Like the contortionist grip of Tammany brothers or the elegant suits of the mayor, these were
tools of governing in an age that provided few others. How was
a metropolis to be ruled if not by the loyalties and gestures of
a fraternal organization and by arrogant display? New York was
governed without telephones, typewriters, or card files. "Bureaucracy" and "civil service" were awkward new words in
American English. Public works and public welfare were not
widely understood as legitimate aims of city government. Display and payoffs made New York governable. Ridicule, especially in the new form of pictures, was the most effective criticism
available in this political culture.

This remained true for the rest of the century. The lively and
informed essays of the *North American Review* and the *Nation*,
for example, glanced off political leaders, while the illustrations
in *Harper's Weekly*, *Puck*, and *Judge* drew blood. The founding of
the nation's first illustrated newspaper in 1873, the New York
Daily Graphic, was a sign of the times. When Joseph Pulitzer
came to conquer New York a decade later he quickly discovered
that his newspaper must have cartoons, especially to make political points.[39] William Randolph Hearst challenged Pulitzer in
a newspaper war of the 1890s that was often a battle of pictures.
On many days readers opened Hearst's New York *Journal* and
saw bulbous plutocrats from the masthead to the bottom of the
page. (Americans who attended Hearst political rallies saw en-
largements of these cartoons, not icons of Hearst himself as the
film *Citizen Kane* had it.) The final measure of the importance of
illustration in political reporting is that when a reform movement
at last gained support in the established press, these critics too
were compelled to find new pictures. Progressivism at the turn
of the century could not rely on the word alone, and the movement tried to change the way the public pictured men in power.
The simple visual way politics was presented in the Tweed exposé was now a part of all plausible definitions of the aim and
power of government.

TOWARDS THE
TWENTIETH CENTURY

By the last quarter of the nineteenth century the American press had settled ways of presenting the words and pictures to take account of this democracy. Newspapers were edited so that citizens could see what people in power said. Politicians and reporters worked together to ensure that a record of debate was in circulation among the voters. A new abundance of pictures aimed to reveal both the vices and the virtues of national leaders. Republicans and Democrats established an orderly two party competition in the 1870s on the basis of this political reporting, taking for granted that these were the ways citizens would follow politics in the press. Judged by circulation figures, the public wanted this reporting. At least this is the political information that the editors of large metropolitan newspapers and successful magazines thought citizens should have.

Nineteenth-century journalists were quick to insist on their reliability, but they were slow to develop a philosophy about objectivity. Exactitude in reporting political speech and fantasy in political illustrations were the appropriate, joint achievements of the media, for accuracy was not yet at war with bias in this profession. Fact and prejudice both had a revered place in the presentation of news. "The new editor of the GAZETTE desires to make a clean, honest local paper," William Allen White told Emporia, Kansas, on June 3, 1895, "He is a Republican and will support Republican nominees first, last, and all the time. There

will be no bolting, no sulking, no 'holier than thou' business
about his politics. . . . '' This confidence in one's ability to get the
facts and to keep a prejudice is the most striking difference
between journalists before and after the turn of the century.[1]

White's *Autobiography*, like the memoirs of many journalists
of his generation, made fun of the naïve way they swept questions aside as they gathered the news in their youth. Perhaps
they underestimated what the cocksure dailies achieved. Nineteenth-century voters got a patient, full record of what was said
in politics, and they also got a sharp kick from the editor. On
the national level this political reporting made for vigorous competition between Republicans and Democrats and a massive turnout of voters. The press made democracy (as the two parties
understood it) work.

One reason that journalists seldom wrung their hands over
objectivity in the nineteenth century was because other problems
in gathering news were more troubling. Political reporting lacked
perspectives that are taken for granted today. An important
limitation was set by the photograph and the state of the printing
process. The camera was a poor tool for investigation and comment. The expense and trouble of getting a photograph ready
for publication yielded a picture that was almost always simply
the face an official wished to show the public. The press did not
know what to make of all it saw. American newspapers and
magazines hesitated to draw political lessons from the underclass. Criminal behavior, especially, was rarely connected to
public life. The press could not make the whole nation see itself
in local corruption. The partisan networks of papers, superb in
circulating the news of a national party, could not easily pass
information *up* from a local political crisis or from an underclass
of criminals. It was not until the beginning of the new century
that editors learned how to extend the reach of political reporting
in these directions.

"Muckraking" in the Progressive Era attracted new readers
and added new issues to political debate. Local scandals and a
country-wide pattern of crime came into the idiom of national

political reporting. Editors learned how to put the camera to sharply partisan uses. The powerful new vantage points of muckraking were anticipated by the newspapers of Joseph Pulitzer and William Randolph Hearst. It was muckraking in the magazines, however, that finally broke free of the most serious limitations on political reporting in the nineteenth century.

III

PATHS TO MUCKRAKING

5

Reporting from the Bottom

Mark Twain told his Victorian readers that when he visited a Paris cabaret he placed his hands over his eyes—but watched through his fingers. This is what editors did with crime stories until well into the nineteenth century. News gathering had no older tradition than the interest in crime, but telling the story normally required that one not look too closely or say too much. The Revolution did indeed make rogues in the street the subject of detailed examination and political comment, but this illustrated what was possible, not what the press wished to do. Free of a crisis, the hand went up to the eyes in embarrassment. Crime as a vantage point on politics had to be rediscovered in the nineteenth century. When the popular press learned to report on the bottom of society, political reporting had a new range and appeal.

In the colonies the drama of crime and punishment entered into much of life. The link between rogue and ruler was made in popular protests such as the Pope's Day celebrations in Boston with grotesque effigies and scurrilous verse. Every theater company offered a look at underworld characters with political motives in *The Beggar's Opera* by John Gay. When a printer got in trouble he was likely to be stigmatized in a ritual acted out by the authorities. The first action the government of New York took against John Peter Zenger was to order that four issues of his newspaper "be burnt by the hands of the Common Hangman," a standard practice in England. In New England, offensive publications were sometimes first whipped before being put to the fire.[1]

There was also the real thing to color political imaginations. Pillory and whipping post stood in the market square inviting both silent and loud reflection on the life of the rogue. Executions drew large crowds. Especially in New England, the good citizens and the condemned heard a sermon preached in church on the preceding Sabbath or at the execution ground on the appointed day. There was keen interest in the last words and the expression on the prisoner's face before the white cap was put over the victim's eyes and the fire or the gallows did its work.

There were costumes for the execution, trials that were swift enough to sit through, and even the opening of court could be brilliant theater. The very display of the early legal system— "status degradation ceremonies" as one scholar has viewed them—may strike the modern citizen as a good substitute for reporting. It was not. There was a great hunger to know more. For all their vivid procedures and punishments, courts frustrated the telling of clear stories. Indictments often had multiple, contradictory counts. In important cases these approached Rashomon tales as prosecutors tried to anticipate different presentations of the evidence in court. The accused was not a competent witness in most American courts before the 1860s. Sworn statements by the men and women on trial were rare. Face to face with criminals in early America, citizens seem to have been in as much need of help to understand deviance as any later generation.[2]

Printers labored to speed the news of crime and punishment. Though this colonial society produced nothing to rival the comprehensive *Newgate Calendar* books in Britain, American printers did their best with the lower level of violence and the smaller market in the New World. The astute printer of the eighteenth century could publish the execution sermon as a pamphlet. On single sheets (broadsides) the printer might issue special editions of crime news: the rogue's last words and a ballad to make the story live. Unlike newspapers, which were printed for subscribers, the cheap broadsides were peddled and hawked to the public:

> Good People all I you beseech
> To buy the Verse as well as SPEECH

These timely publications show varied attention to the criminal. Ministers sometimes asked probing questions and frequently made acute psychological as well as scriptural interpretations. But the clergy could not resist improving on confessions and seldom issued the criminal's own words to the curious public. The ballads prepared for the execution crowd were almost always silent about dying words and confessions. Later verses kept crimes alive over several generations but placed the rogue in a legend, speaking in rhyme, if indeed the rogue spoke at all.[3]

The broadside reports of last words were the most vivid account of crime and punishment in eighteenth-century America. Like the execution sermons and the ballads, this testimony was laden with the hackneyed language thought to be appropriate for "the borders of the grave" just "before launching in to the eternal and invisible world."[4] But the broadsides offered something distinctive: comprehensive reporting. And these hastily prepared sheets pioneered in the taking of testimony and showed how a journalist might address the questions raised by crime.

The broadsides, first, asked to be trusted. They often noted when and where the criminal spoke, cited witnesses to the interviews, and added the death wish that this story be believed. There were good business reasons for such guarantees—claims that went beyond what eighteenth-century newspapers issued in the normal course of printing news. The execution field was highly competitive. A great trouble to all printers, readers might well have witnessed the last moments and know something about the life of crime. Much more quickly than in weekly newspapers, facts acquired a cash value.

Fortunately for the printers many criminals used their last moments to talk about their careers. A few hours before she was hanged, Rachel Wall knew what was expected of her: "Without doubt the ever-curious public (but more especially those of a serious turn of mind) will be anxious to know of every particular circumstance of the Life and Character of a person in my unhappy situation. . . . " The condemned not only reviewed their upbringing and fateful sins in these broadsides, they set the record straight about both their known and unknown crimes. Rachel Wall gave an accounting of her thefts (more than she was hanged for but less than gossip had it) and even cleared up the mystery of how her accomplice had escaped from jail to help her pillage New England (Rachel had put tools in bread she sent to his cell). The broadsides were the first record for the public of horrors they had only imagined and losses that had gone unsolved. Here a citizen could read exactly how Samuel Frost killed his father with a handspike and his employer with a hoe. Or how a young Irishman beat up a wife-beater while the poor woman held the light. The largest part of these narratives tell of more prosaic mayhem: clothes taken from the line, cheese from the press, tools from the field. The typical broadside solved a mystery for many different families and communities by reporting how valuable spoons, tankards and buckles had been snatched, year by year, town by town.[5]

A look at any collection of broadsides is likely to reveal a woodcut of a body hanging from a rope with a crowd pressing close to the scaffold—the same body and the same crowd at different executions. Broadsides boasted of their accuracy, but they were usually the hurried work of printers who had not the time to get new woodcuts or to make thorough investigations. Nor did they have the space to tell all they knew. By the end of the eighteenth century criminal infamy inspired a variety of longer reports that explored roguery in greater depth. Thick volumes of English crime reports were reprinted in America, ranging from that *summa* of criminal lust, *The Cuckold's Chronicle* (1798), to the higher moral tone set in accounts from the famous prison in London, the *Newgate Calendar* series. Pamphlets on the lives of criminals also became more common in the early years of the nineteenth century. Some of these show an unprecedented interest in reporting on American rogues.

In *The Convict's Visitor* (1791) a Rhode Island minister went beyond the simple presentation of last words and took down the vernacular of the criminal underworld. William Smith's pamphlet, based on wide experience counselling the condemned and taking their confessions, presented the secret vocabulary, songs and oaths of criminals. Similarly, when a printer in Dedham, Massachusetts had the good fortune to have a murderer in the village jail, he hit upon a new approach in getting the man's story. The printer explained that the murderer's "singular trait" was that he never volunteered new information. Therefore the printer devised an "interrogation" that was "calculated to rouse his attention." The printer rearranged the murderer's answers but took pride in keeping his exact words. (The criminal was indeed given his due. When the printer made pious mention of the Book of Psalms, the murderer pointed out that David had sent a rival to his death, "But David was not *hung!*")[6]

These reporters of American rogues carried their questions beyond the simple moral lessons that they claimed to illustrate, and, if one has the street literature of crime in England or France in mind, it is tempting to look for an "ideology of crime" here and an expression of social tensions. This literature does underscore a transition that has been noticed in trial reports: crime in the decade after the Revolution became less a sin and more a threat to the society. Criminals were not simply "fallen" citizens who had yielded to temptation but might rise to join the community. Criminals were increasingly viewed as a breed apart who were expected to remain outcasts. In the nineteenth century Americans discovered that criminals were different, and stressed their isolation from the social order as well as their danger to it. The investigations that came from print shops were the natural response to this new perspective on deviance.[7]

There are folklore materials, especially electioneering songs, that connect outlawry with political life. But the most striking feature of the printed accounts of crime is their failure to develop political ideas. The connection of lawlessness to misrule and the use of detailed crime reports to score political points were features of journalism during the Revolution that lay dormant during the first decades of the republic. To be sure, a rhetoric drawn from the criminal world still enlivened political commentary. The newspapers of the Federalist era unmasked George Washington as a "common defaulter," John Adams as a "ruffian," and Thomas Jefferson's "crimes of the deepest dies." Now, however, the reader got little beyond the epithet. Rarely did the vitriolic editor investigate these matters or make a clear connection between the hated governor and the breakdown of law in society. A reader with Harbottle Dorr's relish for political evidence drawn from the street would have found little to collect in the first newspapers of the republic.[8]

Reporting from the bottom of society in the broadsides and pamphlets remained popular but grew more isolated from the news that was judged suitable for a newspaper or periodical. Before the 1820s, no journalist seems to have learned a thing from the investigations and reports of rogues. The American newspaper had a regimen of an inch or two of crime stories. But no editor grasped the idea of expanding the form. The Dedham murderer was interviewed in a newspaper office by the editor, but subscribers never learned what he said. Publishers would not ruin the sales of broadsides and pamphlets by putting a good crime story in a newspaper. Sensationalism in a newspaper did not make good business sense. Most papers had to be ordered in advance. Often, a single issue cost six cents, the price of a serving of beef for dinner. News in this form could not hope for an impulse purchase. The broadside that could be peddled for a penny was a far better medium.

The practice of keeping crimes out of newspapers was more than a prudent trade habit. A moral distaste for the spectacle of punishment and the fame of criminals was common. "The less that is said about it the better," was the advice to editors of that arbiter of enlightened taste, Dr. Benjamin Rush of Philadelphia. Even on the frontier, editors seemed to agree, no matter how good the story. Consider the example of two of Thomas Jefferson's nephews who moved to Kentucky and there killed a family slave in 1811. In front of witnesses they had tied the man down, hacked him apart with an axe, and fed the pieces to the hearth fire. The cremation was interrupted by the most severe earthquake in the recorded history of North America which knocked the fireplace down and exposed the grisly evidence. A grand jury indicted the men. Before a trial could be arranged, Jefferson's nephews made a suicide pact. They met in a graveyard to kill each other; one accidentally shot himself, the other fled west to an unknown fate. The story quickly spread across Kentucky by word of mouth and letters. But here and elsewhere in the republic, newspapers paid little attention to the tragedy.[9]

Even for excitable, vituperative critics, crime seemed out of place in printing the news of public affairs. William Duane, whose newspaper work was radical enough to earn him an indictment for sedition at the turn of the century, boasted in 1820, "I never admit into my paper accounts of murders, robberies, crimes and despertitions, because habits make good or bad news, and familiarity with tales of crimes will blunt the faculties and form habits of indifference to crime." As late as 1824 one of America's most experienced editors observed that the nation's criminals were not to be found in its periodicals. "Such things," he said, "are chiefly circulated through the agency of those who pass through our streets with almanacs and ballads for sale."[10]

The logic of incorporating this popular street literature into newspapers was not widely recognized until the Jackson era. Looking abroad, editors saw that British newspapers won readers with crime stories. John Wight's anecdotes about English justice, *Mornings at Bow Street* (1824), helped to set the fashion of sending reporters to court. It was the American edition of these news stories that seems to have inspired editors in several cities to find the equivalent of battling cockneys and titled drunkards. The expensive subscription papers found a place for court reports by 1830, while in the middle of that decade an explosion of "penny papers" that were hawked in the street brought notice of seductions and bloodshed to the humblest citizens. At the same time, dozens of new labor papers, tied to the new Working Man's Party, experimented with crime stories. By the end of the 1830s, crime news had escaped from the broadsides. It was back in the newspapers where editors of the "Journal of Occurrences" era had thought it belonged.[11]

Much more than the broadside tradition of crime reporting, this was an urban publishing venture. A new complexity of city life had much to do with the attention to deviance in these newspapers of the Jackson era. Journalists noted that the cross-hatch of streets was fast becoming a world too elaborate and distant to explore. Other people's business was increasingly conducted out of sight. Newspapers, as they noted this change, offered to open up "the depravity and infamy which abound within every little district of this large and populous city." This was the theme of many religious tracts before the 1830s. Hundreds of thousands of these pamphlets circulated through the hard work of evangelical societies. But clerics rarely described the city they deplored, preferring scenes of country life, often in England, for their moral instruction. Thus the commercial press had the freedom to open a landscape left dark by its first explorers in the mass media.[12]

Crime news in cheap newspapers also performed a service that a modern community could not otherwise provide: shaming punishments. By the 1820s the whipping post and the pillory were banished in the North, and executions were closed to the general public. Here, too, journalists learned they could profitably report city life that, a generation earlier, citizens could see for themselves.[13]

Until the mid–1830s newspaper editors were no more interested in putting crime stories to a political use than the peddlers of broadsides. The British newspaper articles on crime had suggested only that readers celebrate what Wight called in his preface "the prosperous and orderly portion of society." Even

American labor papers did not venture onto riskier ground before the 1830s. Many of the "penny papers" made crime a tame subject in the next decade. But in some cities, and in some radical circles, reporting about the bottom of society acquired a more serious purpose.

"We mean to begin a series of Police Reports on a new and improved plan," James Gordon Bennett announced in his New York *Herald*. This was late in the summer of 1835, and by then no New Yorker could doubt Bennett's determination. This Scotsman had offered lively columns on Washington in the 1820s for the *Courier & Enquirer* and gained further attention as that paper's reporter at a sensational murder trial in 1830. Three years later Bennett was inspired by the first successful penny paper, the New York *Sun*, and made several attempts to launch his own. He began the *Herald* in the spring of 1835 and quickly built circulation and advertising. He lost everything in a fire, but it took him less than three weeks to set the press moving again. He announced a rush of new ideas about covering vice. "The mere barren record of [prison] and crime amounts to nothing—to something less than nothing," Bennett wrote. "There is a moral—a principle—a little salt in every event of life—why not extract it and present it to the public in a new and elegant dress?"

Bennett's prospectus is notably vague on his course of political reporting. A decade earlier he thought he had found the key to covering Washington in the Library of Congress: an edition of Horace Walpole's letters! For a time Bennett had managed to turn the debate of a democracy into court gossip told with Augustan phrasing. Readers were not reminded of that experiment and he implied that they would be little troubled by political reports of any type.[14]

There were risks enough in this business without political coverage. Shortly after Bennett started the *Herald*, the Philadelphia *Public Ledger* boasted of a "police reporter" in its prospectus. Drunkenness, wife-beating, and pig-rustling filled the news columns in the first issues. After a week of this in the spring of 1836, the editors came to work to find their offices smashed.

This penny paper concluded that it was its crime reporting and its high moral purpose that was being tested and promised readers "the discharge of a duty which we deem imperative, viz: to expose vice and infamy wherever found."[15]

A few days after the *Ledger* mused over the good moral work that crime reports might do, the penny press found the story to launch a crusade. Bennett broke the news on April 11, 1836:

MOST ATROCIOUS MURDER

Our city was disgraced on Sunday, by one of the most foul and premeditated murders,that ever fell to our lot to record. The following are circumstances as ascertained on the spot.

Richard P. Robinson, the alleged perpetrator of this most horrid deed, had for some time been in the habit of keeping (as it is termed) a girl named Ellen Jewett, who has for a long period resided at No. 41 Thomas street, in the house kept by Rosina Townsend.

Having, as he suspected, some cause for jealousy, he went to the house on Saturday night as appears, with the intention of murdering her, for he carried a hatchet with him. On going up into her room, quite late at night, he mentioned his suspicions, and expressed a determination to quit her, and demanded his watch and miniature together with some letters which were in her possession. She refused to give them up, and he then drew from beneath his cloak the hatchet and inflicted upon her head three blows, either of which must have proved fatal, as the bone was cleft to the extent of three inches in each place.

The bedroom had been set afire in an attempt to hide the crime. Bennett paid at least three visits to the site and filled columns in the *Herald* for weeks with his detective work. In other cities his reports were reprinted by the cheap papers, and in New York his competitors hungered for the scraps of evidence he might miss. The *Herald* made the plausible claim that it was ahead of the police investigation. Perhaps no journalist before Bennett did more to place himself at the center of an inquiry, looking and listening for his public as well as offering theories to put the evidence together. He had a police officer uncover the corpse and reported his search for clues on the body ("as polished as the purest Parian marble"). The editor persuaded the madame, Rosina Townsend, to tell what she knew. Under his questioning she described the last evening of the couple known as "Helen" and "Frank" in the demimonde:

> I knocked at the door, and Helen said "Come in." I opened the door and went in.—I saw Frank lying on the bed.
> *Question*: What was he doing?
> *Answer*: He was lying on his left side, with his head resting on his arm in the bed, the sheet thrown over him, and something in his other hand.
> *Q*: What was that ?
> *A*: I can't say.
> *Q*: Was it a book
> *A*: I think it was—either a book or a paper.—I saw his face.
> *Q*: What did he say?
> *A*: Nothing. Helen said to me, "Rosina, as you have not been well today, will you take a glass of champagne with us?" I replied, "No, I am much obliged to you, I had rather not."—I then left the room, as some of the other girls called me from below.—I neither heard nor saw anything more from that time.[16]

Bennett pushed the madame to account for everything she had seen that night and then conducted a cross-examination. The *Herald* cited witnesses to the answers and set them down verbatim in the paper.

The talk about Ellen Jewett's bedroom has fascinated a great many people. The crime reports created a run on editions of the *Herald* and made New Yorkers bid a shilling for the paper on the streets. The popular press, both in New York and in other cities, followed Bennett and threw open their papers to this killing of a prostitute. Scholars around the world have paid close attention to Rosina Townsend's testimony. One Swedish researcher, drawing on German studies, has underscored a point that Americans long did not see clearly: the madame was one of the first people to be interviewed by the press. The face-to-face meeting to obtain statements intended for publication coincided with the development of crime stories for newspapers.

The first large public to find a source quizzed in the newspapers consisted of the readers who clamored to know who killed Ellen Jewett.[17]

Bennett's inquiry yielded broken pieces of information, stunted memories, and a jumble of clues from the brothel. It is a reasonable assumption that these facts alone did not sell papers. The *Herald* made the facts add up to an intrigue, a mystery for the journalist and the public together to unravel. Bennett played with the details as fondly as Edgar Allan Poe was soon to do in his detective stories. The reporter parsed the books and the love letters he found at the scene. He studied the hatchet and the charred bed. Ratiocination shaped news coverage. Bennett's omniscient narrative of the crime in the first story was thrown out in the course of reporting. On his second day on the case he became suspicious of the neat solution provided by male revenge. "There is some mysterious juggle going on. Look to it— look to it." (Jurors eventually felt the same way and did not convict Robinson.) Female aggression was Bennett's pet theory, spun out in a series of articles. Bennett, fully as bold as Poe's C. Auguste Dupin, threw out the circumstantial evidence pointing to Robinson and pinned the crime on a woman, basing his inspired guess on a painting he noticed in the brothel. The sifting of evidence was more remarkable than the misogyny. More than any earlier reporter Bennett had assembled the raw materials for a detective story and prompted citizens to think like criminal investigators. Poe in fact paid a sort of homage to Bennett in his second detective story, "The Mystery of Marie Roget" (1842). This was a reworking of the news coverage of the murder of Mary Rogers in the *Herald* and the other New York papers that Bennett had led into sensational crime reporting.[18]

Through this first half-century of crime coverage in newspapers the stories were something more than an aid to circulation. The invention of the crime beat boosted political arguments. This happened in two phases. On the heels of Bennett in the 1840s the exposure of deviance became a common way of making political points. The detective work was applied to political stories. Looking ahead to the 1890s, police reporting heralded the arrival of a new generation of political reporters, the muckrakers.

James Gordon Bennett did not see this future clearly as he filled his columns with even more speculations about the Robinson case, but he did find political sting and political hope in this material. "The death of Ellen Jewett," the *Herald* declared, "is the natural result of a state of society and morals which ought to be reformed. . . . it as naturally springs from our general guilt and corruption as the pestilence does from the waters of death stagnating under an August sun." Bennett was just as sure that powerful men were corrupt as he was that fallen women were violent. The *Herald* singled out "a large race of merchants, dealers, clerks, and their instruments." On this observation of the rapacity of the upper class and the joining of sexual and financial corruption, Bennett was willing to praise the most radical party in Jacksonian America. "The loco-focos are half right," he wrote, "the same princely virtues which debauch a legislature and rob an assembly or senate of their virgin innocence, also succeed in rifling the young. . . ."[19]

This thundering judgment that crime was emblematic of political disorder was not one of James Gordon Bennett's many eccentricities. In turning vice into big news the press of Jacksonian America insisted that an investigation of the sordid facts revealed a general pattern of corruption in society. In Philadelphia the *Ledger* had no sooner given over its columns to the Ellen Jewett sensation than the paper said "these things call for an inquiry into causes. They compel us to ask if there be not something wrong, radically wrong, in the state of society in our cities?" The *Ledger* was just as quick as the *Herald* in discovering the merchant class and sons of the wealthy at the root of the Jewett murder.[20]

In both New York and Philadelphia the penny papers noted that the meaning of crime was changing in America: it was becoming a reference point in debate on social questions. Bennett saw that news of crime was a political force. As the journalist drew readers into the investigation the newspaper became the "hinge of a course of mental action" that would result in "a total revolution in the present diseased state of society and morals." The *Ledger*, as it heard readers clamor for more reports of murder, also noted the increased "sensibility to crime" and the important role of the newspaper in bringing this about. Americans, it seemed, were no worse in the fifth decade of the republic. The editors could easily remember when drunkards, thieves, and thugs were more common. But public figures, the paper observed, were now expected to prove their distance from rogues. "Not thirty years since, drunkenness, gaming and licentiousness were no disqualifications for public trust. Now, proof, clear, positive proof of intemperance, gaming, licentiousness or fraud would defeat the election of any candidate for public favor. The search into the private life of candidates for office was never so keen as at present."[21]

In the 1830s, the political vision of the penny press was fixed at the local level. In these early years the editors were impatient with campaigns outside their community. All through the election year of 1836, the *Herald* and the *Ledger* ignored the presidential candidates. Martin Van Buren and the three Whigs who sought to take Andrew Jackson's place were rarely mentioned. Van Buren earned coverage in the *Ledger* only by walking into the office to buy a paper. The editors returned the vice president's visit during his stay in Philadelphia but reported only on Van Buren's walk through the labyrinth of Philadelphia streets, not his political course. Bennett professed affection and support for Van Buren. The editor said that "Van" had opened his eyes about politics. But Bennett put little in print about what his candidate stood for or the personal qualities he would bring to the White House, interesting though these were: Bennett told readers that his friend had helped to turn the Capitol into a brothel and was fitted to marry a whore. Other editors professed to be shocked by such talk, but no matter how high-minded, they bragged of their indifference to national politics. "We care not one straw about the result of this general election," the *Ledger* announced in the fall of 1836.[22]

While the clash of national parties seemed distant and confused, the shape of injustice in the city was made vivid in the penny press. The editors who wished to "hold our noses and look on" found they could smell local corruption. Citizens who handed out two pennies for the *Herald* (Bennett doubled the price and crowed twice as loudly about its value) were promised knowledge of "the secret springs of actions which regulate society in this corrupt and over-grown city." The space saved by ignoring the presidential campaign of 1836 was filled with stories about the "higher game" of corrupt New Yorkers. Bennett reduced the national debate about currency regulation and banks to an exposé of New York speculators. Making the nation's fate seem to hinge on the city's, the *Herald* printed the names of the financiers, gave a detective story of their crimes and compared them to the murderer of Ellen Jewett. Similarly, in Philadelphia the *Ledger* asserted a special guardianship over the city. As readers prepared to choose the President in 1836 the editors claimed they could carry the state for the Democrat, the Whig, or Beelzebub, if they cared to, "but the municipal affairs of the city are our particular provinces; and as we now exercise an overwhelming influence, and can command a majority of votes upon anything, we shall speak to our city authorities in a style to be neither misunderstood nor disregarded."[23]

The process of exposure was more significant than the product. No one—certainly not a journalist—could boss the fragile government and hardening interest groups of the antebellum city. Newspapers were only one of the loud voices asking for changes that urban governments were hopelessly unprepared to make. But the investigation and crusading of newspapers was not an idle activity. The conviction that a closer look at the underside of society would bring reform had wide appeal in the 1830s. This way of thinking produced new forms of political argument in Jacksonian America.

The editors of the penny press stood in the company of many publicists who were disgusted with the established political parties and ready to report on the bottom of society in the cause of reform. A literature of exposure grew from many roots in the 1830s. Each branch linked claims of moral enlightenment with details of hidden vice. In most reform movements, this decade was the first time that talk of sin and crime took compelling form for a large public. Here, as in the 1970s, there is evidence that the exposure of one form of corruption led to increased notice of other kinds.[24] Antebellum feminists, for example, turned the *Advocate of Moral Reform* into a weekly that rivaled the circulation of popular magazines. One reason for the success is easy to spot. In a campaign against the double standard, the editors showed how men preyed on women in New York and then turned readers across the nation into reporters of local seductions. The *Advocate* chronicled illicit sex more dutifully than the penny press. Through new publications such as William Lloyd Garrison's *Liberator*, the anti-slavery movement reported news of plantation life that had been passed over in silence by most earlier critics: "THE SOUTHERN STATES ARE ONE GREAT SODOM." More than the penny press such material deserves the term "egalitarian" because the editors reached out to rural America and shaped the stories to allow women (and children) to learn of injustices that had been hushed up. Similarly, temperance workers discovered the exposé by the beginning of the 1840s. They went beyond the medical evidence and the Biblical exegesis that had long been their ammunition and revived the war against alcohol with reports from the gutter and personal confessions from ordinary citizens.[25]

Reformers and sensationalists said different things, but they often used the same language. It has never been easy to draw a line between the committed and the crass. P.T. Barnum moved from editing the reform-minded *Herald of Freedom* to the exhibition of "curiosities," but in Barnum's mind the showmanship would bring social renewal. George Wilkes, editor of the *Police Gazette*, found one outlet for his radical republicanism in this titillating magazine. His *Lives of Helen Jewett and Richard P. Robinson* (1849) was prurient and political. The young man with the fresh pen name of Ned Buntline threw himself into the slums

of New York to produce reform tracts before he found his calling
out West as the myth-maker for "Wild Bill" Hickok and "Buffalo
Bill" Cody. The editors of the penny press kept their distance
from most reform movements and loathed some. But all successful publicists of the 1830s and 1840s were driven the same
way—toward the discovery that the bottom of society revealed
the need to change public institutions.[26]

After Bennett, most publishers who succeeded with a mass
public gave considerable attention to unraveling cases of the
Ellen Jewett and Mary Rogers type. Joseph Pulitzer, William
Randolph Hearst, and members of the Scripps family took pride
in their detective work, adding to the newspaper vocabulary of
crime all through the nineteenth century. "Sleuthing" threatened to take over editorial careers. The founder of the Chicago
Daily News worried that posterity might believe his activities as
editor "were wholly confined to thief catching."[27] Following the
tracks of criminals to local government was a hallmark of popular
regional papers—Pulitzer's achievements will be examined in
the next chapter. The distinctive feature of this interest in crime
is that it was much more likely to intoxicate the reporter and
sell papers than to lift readers' sights beyond their immediate
community. Reporting on the bottom of society did not bring
national issues into view. The dreams of the idealistic (and the
crass) did not come true. There was no nineteenth-century
equivalent to the "Journal of Occurrences." Communities were
not tied together through crime reporting and neither the law-
man nor the outlaw came into the news to score political points.
At the turn of the new century a jurist in New York deplored
sensationalistic coverage of crime, not so much for what it had
done to justice, but for the way it shrunk the field of vision of
the community: "These papers constitute beyond question the
greatest provincializing influence in metropolitan life."[28]

The muckrakers of the first years of the new century were the
legitimate heirs of the crime story and the first to make the whole
nation take notice. Often the police beat was their school in the

1890s— it gave them a vantage point on society and politics.
Crime reporting looked fundamentally different when the best
of the muckrakers were through, for they took the police story
to a radical conclusion.

On the metropolitan newspapers of the 1880s and 1890s the
crime beat was often given to the reporter who was too imaginative for conventional assignments or too green to be trusted
with them. In New York the assignment was often pleasant exile
to the "shack" across the street from the Mulberry Street police
headquarters. The poker game at number 301 brought together
some of the closest students of urban America. There is a photograph of that game, taken by the most distinguished reporter
of the bottom of society, Jacob Riis. *How the Other Half Lives*
(1890) came directly from his police stories for New York newspapers and was the first book to show with both photographs
and text what the slums produced.

We turn to Riis to be reminded of street urchins and sweat-
shops, and there is no question that poverty was his obsession.
But Riis earned his salary by covering the police, and his work
honors conventions of beat reporting. Much of his documentary
is told as an exciting chronicle of what Riis called "raiding parties." He did not exaggerate. On the early trips to take pictures
of the poor the police came along. Riis used a revolver to shoot
off the flashpowder in the first tenements he visited. Riis's camera frequently strayed from the pathos of the tenement to show
thuggery. There are murder scenes, thefts re-enacted for the
camera, gangs in their hideouts, a rogues' gallery, and one photograph of the police in pursuit of thieves.[29]

Riis's encounter with the police helped to shape his notions
of authority, just as similar experiences would for many of the
leading journalists of the Progressive Era. He never forgot his
own treatment by the police during his desperate early days in
this new country, so much of his exposé was directed at the
police lodging houses where he had suffered. What Riis learned
in life a younger generation learned through reporting. The police educated the muckrakers, as many of their memoirs make

clear. Mark Sullivan, who made a fortune editing for reform tastes, started out in journalism paying close attention to the police of sleepy Pennsylvania towns. This, he recalled, was sufficient, "in my relation with the police, in part camaraderie, in part impish truculence, there was the beginning of an attitude toward authority, government." Another man of legendary success with the reform themes of the day, Alfred Henry Lewis, told fellow reporters in 1906 that they should be "the police of politics," watching office-holders the way the constabulary kept posted on rogues in the city.[30]

It was harder to learn from the underworld than it was to learn from the police, but the most imaginative journalists of this age of reform tried. In the 1890s some of America's most talented journalists joined the poker game Riis pictured, shared his pride about the beat, and tried to make sense of the disturbing documentary he had begun.

Around 1880 Charles E. Russell heard of the detective work accomplished by the journalists in New York from the tramp printers who came through his father's newspaper office in Davenport, Iowa. Russell's notion of what a reporter should do was not what he saw done in Davenport. Nor at first was his family's long tradition of reform causes very important. What this young man heard and read made it clear (as he recalled) "that the true glory of newspaper work lay in the unraveling of murder mysteries. . . . " Russell sought to awaken Midwesterners by reporting sensational crime, and at twenty-six, he was able to break into the fabled circle of New York reporters of the underworld. As a police reporter on the East Side, Russell found "the only education I ever had that amounted to anything."[31] The courts for Russell were what they had been for Riis, a window into the poverty and despair of immigrant life. Both men called the middle class to look at this nether world and to understand that it threatened all parts of the city.

So far, such reporting fit a conventional political outlook. The Lexow Committee hearings and report of 1894 brought the New York police to the attention of the nation and established a connection between street crime and corrupt government. Many genteel reformers were bringing these facts to light with no thought of upsetting the political order. Theodore Roosevelt, in his term as president of the board of police commissioners in the 1890s, proved that crime was a good way to catch public attention, work for reform, and remain in the mainstream of political debate. What set Russell and other prominent reporters apart is that they used what they saw in police court to shake politics. Reporting from the bottom taught them that American justice was an illusion. The governing class was tied in with a web of criminal conduct. Business itself was not fundamentally different from the shady conduct that landed the poor in jail. "What are we but all little crooks together?" was Russell's conclusion. Socialism seemed to him the only answer to what he had reported.[32]

The most celebrated equating of crime with the American way of life was made by the reporter whose charm and guile has seldom been matched in journalism, Lincoln Steffens. Nothing was typical about his path to Mulberry Street except his conviction that it completed his real education. Steffens grew up rich in Sacramento in the 1870s, a pampered only child with a disarming way of drawing older people out. His father allowed the young man's schooling to stretch from Berkeley to Heidelberg to Paris to London before closing the checkbook. Steffens was out of money in New York in 1892. He found that the social capital of a golden youth was all he needed to launch a career. In a letter to his father Steffens traded notes on how different color suits affected potential employers as the young man waited for the family connections to win an opening. Steffens's social standing won him a tryout with a newspaper in New York famous for refinement, the *Evening Post*. The young man proved to be a natural reporter. He also was so lucky with money that by the time he turned twenty-eight he really did not have to be good to be comfortable. The *Evening Post* sent Steffens to Wall Street. The brief walk from there to the Lower East Side of Jacob Riis was a world away. Editors of this high-minded paper avoided the sensational stories in this quarter almost as carefully as the founders of the *Post* at the beginning of the century. To Steffens, the "beastly work" on the "horrible East Side" was a dark legend, but he burned to cross this line. "Indeed," Steffens wrote after speaking with his city editor, "it is the problem of modern journalism, this of decently and interestingly to report police news." Steffens walked into the shack on Mulberry Street in 1893 with weak cries to his family ("Will it degrade me? Will it make a man of me?") and dreams of achieving fame. Steffens discovered that crooks completed his education and that the underworld revealed the true nature of government. "What is being done in the police is the material of politics," Steffens wrote to his father in amazement in 1894. He would simply follow along this line, he wrote home, "so my occupation is defined for some time into the future."[33]

Crime helped to change Steffens's mind and, more importantly, his methods. His own reporting from Mulberry Street and the larger story told by the Lexow report made lawlessness seem to be an extension of government. The police, Steffens found, were the keepers of street criminals and set the rules for plunder. Pickpockets, for example, knew exactly where they could operate and cooperated with the authorities so that constituencies important to the police were not bothered. Drinking, sex, and gambling were protected by New York's men in uniform. The police took money from the criminals, passed it up the political organization, and received the gratitude of the prosperous and ignorant citizens who thought law prevailed. As this civic order mocked the ideals of American government it helped move Steffens, as it had Russell, to the left.

There is more to Steffens's reporting than this. What the police story demanded was a detective's heart for intrigue and detachment. This temperament made his later political reporting possible. Steffens had proved himself on Wall Street, gaining the confidence of businessmen and plungers. But these men were not far different from his merchant-father, and Steffens's own playing of the market in the 1890s also gave him common ground.

Cops on the take, codes of honor among pickpockets, the social functions of the saloon, these were topics that Steffens was ill-prepared to understand. Bluffing dangerous people below his social level was a new lesson. He learned quickly and took his readers into this alien world. In Minneapolis, for example, Steffens fell in with the criminals being investigated by a grand jury. He walked into the gang's hideout and spoke so convincingly of the underworld that they allowed him to walk away with the evidence of corruption needed for an article in *McClure's Magazine*.

Steffens sought the insights of crooks to understand how American was governed. At the beginning of his investigation of urban government, Steffens had his pocket picked on a train by a "dip" he had helped in New York. The thief was being friendly and returned the wallet with a warning to watch out. Steffens invited the crook to dinner and got intelligence on the cities he was exposing. The lesson to be learned, Steffens said with a drumbeat of articles, was that the business classes do the same work as the criminals in American society. He found his way through a labyrinth of corruption in San Francisco with the detective who marched the city fathers into court. Their confessions of guilt, the article concluded, were a "perfect sketch" of how America was governed.[34]

Often, the progressive journalist's view of politics was focused by an encounter with the culture of crime. Few readers can forget the slaughterhouse scenes from Upton Sinclair's *The Jungle* (1906), but most of the novel was a descent into the underworld of Chicago. The immigrant Jurgis slips from proletarian to crook until at last he, and the reader, can see the intricate alliance between criminals and politicians.[35]

There is a photo of the young Brand Whitlock that documents the exotic sources of political conviction on the eve of the muckraking era. Whitlock sits with his fellow Chicago reporters at a table in the Whitechapel Club—so named after the scene of Jack the Ripper's activities. Instead of a card game the press corps is diverted by the skulls of criminals that lay before them. Bloodied weapons, ropes used in hangings, and pictures of executions complete the décor. Here reporters talked about their art and assassinated the reputations of city fathers. Whitlock's bright political and literary career continually drew inspiration from criminals. He left newspapers for a brief legal career and kept a scrapbook of his defenses in criminal cases. Whitlock's scrapbooks, like Russell's, show a connoisseur's interest in murder cases. Whitlock settled in Toledo, Ohio, at the turn of the century, a community alive with radical sentiment in local politics. He found that championing the underdog, especially citizens who stood on the wrong side of laws, could be the basis for a political career. Whitlock was elected mayor. Through four terms at city hall he managed to keep night sticks away from the police and petty criminals out of jail. The mayor told critics to read Tolstoy on Christian love. Skeptics could also read Whitlock, for he was constantly on the fiction lists and in the pages of reform magazines with testimony to the virtuous example of the underworld. "There is not great moral difference to be discovered between those in prison and those outside." Whitlock announced in *Everybody's Magazine* of 1907. His autobiography reached the magazines a few years later and was consistent with this insight. He began by celebrating a jail break arranged by his grandfather and moved through Brand's many successes in letting jailed citizens go free.[36]

In Whitlock's novel of 1907, *The Turn of the Balance*, he tested his readers' willingness to listen to criminals. Convict #2656, a reviewer for the *Anamosa Prison Press*, complained that the underworld banter was so thick in the story that prisoners would read it with difficulty. Lincoln Steffens stayed up all night finishing the novel, disappointed only in the fact that some good citizens had been dragged into it. He wrote Whitlock, " . . . I found that my interest deepened in the book every time I was among the thieves. I wish you could write a story or a novel about them only, or at least about only the acknowledged grafters. They are really interesting people." " . . . Glad that you liked my thieves and grafters," Whitlock replied, "what you like about them, of course, is what I like about them, that is; their essential

honesty." The cant and hypocrisy of respectable citizens made
the mayor long for the company of thieves.[37]

Empathy with the criminal was a strong current in the magazines of the Progressive Era. It was not normally so pure, so
Tolstoyan, as Steffens and Whitlock professed, but much of the
reporting from the bottom was designed to shake the confidence
of readers. The most popular authority on petty criminals was
the journalist-tramp, Josiah Flynt Willard. Willard did not use
his family name in the dozens of articles he contributed to popular magazines, protecting the reputation of his aunt, Frances
E. Willard, the president of the Woman's Christian Temperance
Union. No reader could fail to see that Josiah Flynt had dropped
through several layers of class. He wrote with detachment and
understatement of his life as a vagabond and an associate of the
confidence men and women who rode the freight trains. He was
a compulsive refugee from Victorian society though never a consistent critic. He celebrated the lure of the road and low company; measured the "criminal in the open" against the textbooks,
and also turned policeman and informer to see if he could end
the way of life that attracted him. By the time of his death in
1907, Willard's reporting filled four volumes and had built a
Whitmanesque record of proud self-contradictions.

What connected Willard with writers on the left was the conviction that there were profound lessons to be read in crime:
"the league between the Powers That Rule and the Powers That
Prey." He wanted crime reporting in the newspapers to become
a mirror for the republic to see itself. Willard satirized reformers
but held out hope for cities transformed through the knowledge
to be won by living on the bottom of society. At this point
Willard's contact with progressivism ended in a haze of cocaine
and alcohol; he was dead at thirty-eight. His enduring contribution to muckraking was an angle of vision and a catch-word.
His "True Stories from the Underworld" began running in
McClure's in the summer of 1900 and alerted both the editors
and readers to the ways petty crimes might bring illegitimate
power into focus. The magazine made elaborate efforts to doc-

ument lawlessness. Finding a "carnival of crime" in America, the publisher frankly set out to use it to snare readers and reform institutions. Samuel S. McClure pursued Bennett's dream of an accounting from the underworld that would, at the same time, build circulation and change the political order. Willard's "In the World of Graft" appeared in *McClure's* during the spring of 1901 and changed the language of political reporting. "Graft" was a word from the underworld that had never been applied to politics. The term quickly became the center of reformers' efforts to understand how American government worked.[38]

Willard personally trained several journalists through invitations to come drinking with crooks. His best students were two young men out of Harvard, Alfred Hodder and Hutchins Hapgood. Hodder was a lapsed professor of philosophy when he found Willard, and he soon made clear that more works in metaphysics were not to be expected from his pen. He helped Willard produce the stories in *McClure's* and felt at home in the underworld. Hodder made his own contribution to the literature of reform with *A Fight for the City* (1903), the story of five weeks of campaigning to defeat Tammany and to elect a new district attorney in New York.[39] Willard's sensibility made the book distinctive. Municipal politics were reduced to the maneuvers of competing groups of criminals against a compassionate reformer. The crusading D.A. was celebrated for his understanding of the crooks; there was little animus against the criminals or against Tammany. Most reformers were slighted because they had no feeling for the underworld.

Go one step beyond Willard and Hodder and the reporter becomes a naturalist of low life, too busy watching to judge. Hutchins Hapgood went slumming with Willard and practiced this detachment. The reporter's *Autobiography of a Thief* (1903) was the story of an ex-con, Jim Caufield, whom Willard had asked Hapgood to entertain. Many drinks later Hapgood had his story. Some reviewers found a reform theme in this confession, and in his memoirs Hapgood remembered he had tackled the labor question through this reporting. To read *The Autobiog-*

raphy of a Thief this way is to miss the point. The ex-con had tried to steer the book toward prison reform, but Hapgood eliminated this as well as every other reform theme. In its resolute unwillingness to judge, this journalism slipped outside even the broadest definitions of progressivism. Half the royalties for this book went to the ex-con who used the money, Hapgood said, to buy cocaine and improve his wardrobe so that he could pick the pocket of a higher social set. One wonders if the thief found the time. Ellery Sedgwick, the editor of *Leslie's Weekly* before moving to *McClure's*, monopolized Caufield. Sedgwick, a Brahmin Yankee, dressed like a crook in order to accompany Caufield on his round of Manhattan dives.[40]

It is not possible to separate a connoisseurship of crime by journalists of this generation from the sober calls for changes in government that fill their publications. So often both impulses guided the reader and the reporter in the Progressive Era. The appreciative sketch of criminal life was a commercial success that hurt no writer with reformers. Alfred Henry Lewis became one of the most successful journalists of the era by assuming the role of ambassador for the outlaw to a wide public. Perhaps no muckraker appealed to more diverse people. Citizens who viewed each other as enemies of the republic might often find that they both read Lewis with pleasure. It is enough to say that Theodore Roosevelt and William Randolph Hearst both courted this man. TR was drawn by Lewis's tales of a lawless West and trusted him to edit his first collection of presidential papers in 1904. For Hearst, Lewis set to work on the urban underworld with its detectives and gangsters circling the political bosses.

Lewis lived a great many of the lives he wrote about. He was the prosecuting attorney in Cleveland for a year, then in sure leaps, he became a cowboy, a frontier editor, then Hearst's chief Washington correspondent, before settling on magazine work in New York. Lewis played Boswell to Tammany Hall's Richard Crocker and produced two books that made a legend of the boss. This reporter liked the company of Manhattan toughs, and his drinking companions were often a mix of lawmen and felons.

Charles E. Russell liked these people too; Russell and Lewis graced the same New York saloon.

In the Progressive Era, up until his death in 1914, few months passed without a story from Lewis either boosting some reform measure or offering a titillating account of lawlessness. Lewis's reform interests were bound up with the criminal element he followed. "The Apaches of New York," a monthly accounting of mayhem that ran for more than a year in a muckraking magazine, began with the promise of political enlightenment. In *Confessions of a Detective* (1906) a crooked police officer interrupted his exciting tale from time to time to tell readers to enact progressive reforms in the city.[41]

Crime was not a metaphor for all muckrakers, and fascination with the underworld tried the patience of some reformers. As David Graham Phillips lectured Whitlock, "I should hesitate to base an indictment of our social system upon the woes of the criminal class."[42] But crime told progressives what to think about if not always what to think. Testimony from the depths of the social system had a fascination and power for muckrakers rarely seen before by political commentators of any type.

Ray Stannard Baker's "Following the Color Line," one of the most original investigations made by progressives, shows the pull of the crime story. Baker set out to study black-white relations, a topic that had been ducked by journalism for a generation. The *American Magazine* brought out the series, a publication newly controlled in 1907 by Baker and his friends from *McClure's*. There was, then, a clear field for the progressive mind to work.

"The Riddle of the Negro" read the editorial announcement. Above this a proud black woman in profile looked out at the reader from the corner of her eye. The prospectus then posed fundamental political questions. Readers found, in the first installment, that Baker was working the crime beat and that, like Riis, he could not approach social injustice without this perspective. The portraits now, fully as handsome, were blacks of the "criminal type." Baker reported the cycle of black-white crime in Atlanta, the scene of a recent race riot. He made an investigation of every crime committed against a white woman in the months before and after the violence. Baker wrote "without excuse for the horror of the details. If we are to understand the true conditions in the South, these things *must* be told." "Following the Color Line" would finally range to the broader questions Baker had promised. But in assuming that fundamental political issues began at the bottom of society, with the crime that a newspaperman was trained to cover, Baker paid homage to one of the assumptions that had come to guide the muckrakers and their public.[43]

The attraction of crime stories of course owed much to cultural forces that lay outside of journalism and outside of politics. Many different strains of realism and naturalism in literature pointed to the bottom of society by the end of the nineteenth century. The muckrakers were inspired by better writers who had charted these depths. Jack London, Stephen Crane, and Theodore Dreiser competed for the attention of the public, often in the same periodicals with the muckrakers. Mark Twain was still alive to give a good name to the study of social dregs (in *The Adventures of Huckleberry Finn*, for example, Twain had not covered his eyes in reporting the theatrical con game played by the Duke and the King). Perhaps the only thing distinctive about investigative reporters was their first-hand knowledge of the city and the niche on the police beat that had allowed them to live thoughtfully between respectable society and the abyss.

The writers and the reporters shared, as Americans, an unexplored frontier. The American student of crime did not begin, as one would have in Europe, facing a century of popular literature working over these themes to the point they became dull. Crime had won only grudging acceptance in the popular press of this young democracy, and it had not added fresh colors to political journalism since Bennett's day. Thus the political investigations announced with such excitement in the new century gave readers a new outlook on government. Reporting about the bottom of society in the muckraking era completed an investigation that the American press had never before carried through. As in so much of political reporting, stories that began with the underworld formed a vernacular that freely mixed new and old narrative forms, creating a way of talking politics that was up-to-date.

6

The Provincial Scandal

In 1908, with the prospect of national leadership before him, Woodrow Wilson despaired of the press. Like all Democrats he was uncomfortable in a land so well supplied with Republican dailies, but partisanship was not his main complaint. Journalists, Wilson argued, rarely saw the big picture of America as they gathered news: "There is no newspaper in the United States which is not local, and narrowly local at that, both in the news which it prints and the views which it expresses."

Wilson had been hitting this theme since his first writings as a political scientist nearly a quarter century earlier, and he took the idea with him to the White House. Early in his presidency he considered forming a publicity bureau that would drive news the public needed past the provincial editors. The mobilization for World War I in 1917 brought a solution. The Committee on Public Information watched over the nation's more than 2600 dailies. America's first official daily newspaper set a model for reporters. Publicity specialists in Washington rushed copy to editors, neglecting not a page of the typical daily. A Bureau of Cartoons, for example, aimed at "centering the minds of every community on the same subject." No president tried harder to reduce the cantankerous localism of the nation's press and to encourage reporting of a clear national purpose. In this Wilson fulfilled the wish of many in the progressive movement who had helped bring him to power.[1]

A century earlier, no such bureaucracy was needed to ensure that newspapers took a national view. Editors followed the cues of national parties. This was common-sense economics for a publisher. Partisanship appeared to be the glue that kept readers. Patronage was more important than advertising dollars. The press was often unfair to political rivals, but it was seldom parochial and local in the way men of Wilson's generation complained. Party leaders set the tone and the priorities for papers stretching out across the land. An editor in a minor city with standing in his party could set the agenda for much larger papers. In the contests between Whig and Democrat, journalists in Boston, Philadelphia, and even New York found their political lines in Thurlow Weed's Albany *Evening Journal* and Thomas Ritchie's Richmond *Enquirer*. At the end of the nineteenth century one journalist looked back wistfully to the time when a few papers "made known the sentiments of the two great organizations, and the press of the interior endorsed them as pure gospel, without the crossing of a t or dotting of an i." Here was one of those numbing uniformities in the early republic that drove Tocqueville to despair. From the point of view of those who sought to govern, partisan papers were an almost providential instrument. The loyal newspapers were bridges to the island communities on the frontier. The press imposed some order and sense of purpose on an unpredictable electorate. Woodrow Wilson needed to look no further than his own family to see how this had come about.[2]

The decentralization of the American press and the partisanship that tied papers together were carried out by men very much like Wilson's grandfather. The printer James Wilson came over from Ulster to Philadelphia in 1807. His first job— indeed, it appears his first bed— was in the print shop at Benjamin Franklin's last residence. There Benjamin Franklin Bache's old *Aurora* continued the fight for Jeffersonians. In five years, at the age of twenty-five, James Wilson ran the paper. Had American printers aped their English or French cousins, Wilson would have stayed in Philadelphia or gone to New York, dreaming of vast circulations and national importance. But in a nation with an open frontier and waves of immigrants, most ambition was spread wide. Many printers and editors chose to leave competitors behind. No more capital was required to start a paper in a small community than in the time of James Franklin. The flatbed press was not much changed and 500 subscribers were still enough to tempt a newspaper publisher. James Wilson went to Ohio, establishing a combative paper in Steubenville that was fiercely critical of the new Democratic party of Andrew Jackson. Wilson was busy in state politics but found time to start another paper in Pittsburgh and to edit a campaign sheet for the Whigs in 1840. Wilson's political judgments are the sort that Tocqueville collected in the Jacksonian period to amaze Europeans with the sulfurous tone of the American press. "The Goths & Vandals, now seated in high places, must be pulled down, and when down *kept down*," Wilson wrote of Democrats in office. He had a chance to go back to Philadelphia and purchase the *Aurora*, but the national stage was finally too long a step. James Wilson taught his ten children to set type, and some of them founded new papers farther west. The scholarly James Ruggles Wilson made the cleanest break from political service on small newspapers through a career in the Presbyterian church. His son, Woodrow Wilson, longed for something beyond party loyalty to lift journalists' eyes above their own community.[3]

There are no simple ways to explain how a city comes to see its problems writ large across the country or how readers see themselves as they learn of other people's corruption. Nor are there pat answers as to why critics demand recognition at the centers of power instead of prizing success in more sheltered positions. It is clear that political reporting had a major role in expanding the citizen's concern beyond the community to take in the nation at large.

The passage from local to national journalism cannot be made into the story of a key institution, the wire services. These were the great nineteenth-century achievements in cooperative news gathering. At least in theory they made one city's news available to distant newsrooms and gave political leaders access to front pages across the land. In fact the wire services were poor at focusing the attention of the nation. They did little to bring local events to the center of national politics until this change in mental habits was well under way. The nineteenth-century wire services were regional, patchwork affairs, of little weight in determining what an editor would print. Much of their energy went into business conspiracies and court actions to settle disputes about turf. This changed quickly in the twentieth century. The formation of the Associated Press in 1900, the United Press Associations in 1907, and the International News Service in 1909 did much to tie the nation's newspapers together, but they came after magazine editors had beaten newspapers to the discovery of how to exploit provincial scandals. One has to go to a region and see what the magazine editors found to understand their success. The city of St. Louis offers the clearest picture of the powerful centralizing forces that gave local reporting national importance.

The railroads and the rivers of commerce built St. Louis in the nineteenth century, but the city's most remarkable export was its journalism. Here Joseph Pulitzer began the *Post-Dispatch* in 1878 and worked out the techniques of investigation and self-promotion that enabled him to dominate American journalism from New York in his later years. Lincoln Steffens came to St. Louis at the turn of the century and produced the first urban "muckraking" article of the Progressive Era. Many journalists fed on scandals during America's Gilded Age but nowhere was the interest in corruption so sustained. The New York *Times* dropped the story of municipal boodle after Tweed went to jail. No publisher before Pulitzer marshaled both news columns and editorials year after year to attack corruption.

In the 1870s St. Louis spread along the limestone bluff on the western side of the Mississippi and looked over a levee that was crowded, in good weather, with the products of the Midwest. Measuring itself against the upstart city of Chicago, St. Louis preserved the old world in the exclusive residential "places" and the formal plantings in the generous public parks. Eads Bridge, three arches of steel lace work, brought the railroad from the East into the city. Smoke that appalled travelers and delighted civic boosters stretched from the steamboats to the city's major industries in tobacco, sugar, and beer. The pleasures, no less than the work of St. Louis, were palpable. Beer gardens were the Sunday haunt of ordinary citizens. The fine hotels gave America the highball, Planters Punch and Southern Comfort. The self-intoxication of St. Louis increased after the census of 1870, which supported the boasts that here was the nation's fourth largest city—some 310,000 by this count, surpassing the arch-rival Chicago for dominance of the Midwest. This did not stop the boasting. *Saint Louis: The Future Great City of the World*— a book the city ordered printed in six editions—explained how ten million Americans would come to St. Louis and control the earth's wealth.[4]

St. Louis lived on an illusion. Its trade on the Mississippi was fading in the 1870s as markets moved away from the North-South course of the river to the East-West network of railroads. Chicago, not St. Louis, was the master of this commerce, and Missouri entrepreneurs were not bold enough to compete beyond their beautiful bridge. The Old-World look of St. Louis included the crooked line of tenement blocks, a sign that America's poor might sink as low as the European proletariat. The census of 1870 was false comfort. That count had been rigged to make the city seem more prosperous than Chicago. The census of 1880 told the truth and marked the fall of St. Louis from dominance of the Midwest.[5]

The man who led St. Louis to measure the distance between appearance and reality came to Missouri ignorant of this society. Joseph Pulitzer had emigrated from Hungary and fought in the Civil War. He came west after Appomattox with no money and little English. His entrance into the city as a friendless teenager, his rise through menial jobs and long hours in the public library,

these were stories that Pulitzer liked to tell and that friendly
biographers have embellished. The young Benjamin Franklin's
arrival in Philadelphia comes to mind. Pulitzer, it must be remembered, was not a gentle stranger content to let virtuous
industry alone open the door of opportunity. The first form of
communication he mastered in his new home was the harangue.
Pulitzer succeeded as a reporter for a German-language newspaper because of his skill in intimidating sources and political
enemies. (When a politician he had attacked in print questioned
the young journalist's integrity, Pulitzer shot him in the groin.)
Before he was thirty, Pulitzer found political patrons among St.
Louis Germans who helped him practice law and win a Republican seat in the state legislature. Pulitzer used an inheritance to
speculate profitably in a bankrupt newspaper, and at thirty-one
he brought together two struggling afternoon dailies, the *Post*
and *Dispatch*, and bent them to his will.

The six-foot-two-inch Pulitzer was a restless giant in the newsroom. Colleagues felt they were always within his reach: "his
sanctum was a corner cut off by a dusty curtain from the room
in which his city editor and reporters sat. And about every twenty
minutes a long arm would sweep the curtain aside, the proprietor's head and long neck would be thrust out, and his shrill
voice would shower suggestions mixed up with violent condemnation or praise, uttered in a high, harsh voice. Nothing escaped
his keen, gray-blue eyes."[6]

Pulitzer chose young men with a taste for melodrama. John
J. Jennings, twenty-five, was news editor and star reporter in
1879, the first year of the paper. At twenty-nine, Henry W.
Moore directed the news staff. Both men wrote extensively about
the theater, and the time they spent with show people seems
to have helped them understand their boss and his news judgments. John Cockerill, thirty-four, became managing editor at
the end of the first year. He shared the publisher's taste for vivid
writing about crime and vice, and Cockerill thundered in unison
with Pulitzer against the urban underworld on the editorial page.[7]

The first hundred days of the *Post and Dispatch* (the hyphen was not yet in place) brought a storm of exposés. "Decks" of boldface type ran down the columns:

SOME GLIMPSES AT THE ST. LOUIS GAMBLER'S RING
HE ALLEGES HE MADE THE GOVERNOR DRUNK AND PUT HIM TO BED

THE SOCIAL EVIL
SOME OF THOSE WHO RENT THEIR PROPERTY FOR IMMORAL PURPOSES

TAX-DODGING
HOW THE RICH MEN OF ST. LOUIS PAY TAXES

THE VEIL IS RENT
AND THE DOORS OF THE STAR CHAMBER FALL FROM THEIR FASTENINGS

THE GREAT SCOOP
A REVELATION THAT FELL LIKE A BOMB UPON THE CITY[8]

When stories grew complicated, the journalists urged readers on— "there is a good chance that they will now have unraveled to them many perplexing mysteries." The catharsis for St. Louis was to come as readers measured the boosters' dream of the city against this reporting: "the contrast between the braggart pretense and the beggarly performance." Pulitzer addressed citizens whose faith in their city had been shaken and who found in the *Post and Dispatch* a way to acknowledge guilt: "Their deepest wish," he wrote, "is to throw off the disgrace which oppresses them, to purge themselves of the guilt of acquiescence in corruption: all they need is an organ, a voice to speak what their heads think, what their hearts feel. Well! Six days in the week at least the truth will be spoken for them without fear of favor; the work of purgation is begun as soon as the secret evil is dragged into the light of day."[9]

As in the Tweed exposé, the reader was awash in names,

addresses, and sums. In a single month, Pulitzer published the locations and owners of dozens of brothels and the detailed tax returns of several hundred property holders. (No doubt one selling point of the *Post and Dispatch* was the guide it provided to prostitutes and the cash value of other people's household goods and jewelry.) The references to "ring tribes" were shadowy, and there was none of the ethnic politics of the Tweed exposé. Indeed, Pulitzer encouraged prurient interest about both honest citizens and rogues:

A MOST UNSAVORY SCANDAL, IN WHICH GOOD AND BAD NAMES ARE MIXED PROMISCUOUSLY

The *Post and Dispatch* disclaimed partisanship and was exuberantly even-handed.[10]

This was an important departure for an American newspaper and worth examining closely. Pulitzer marks the course taken by many newspapers in his generation away from dependable partisan service. "Independent journalism," a slogan that first gained currency in England, was a rallying cry for American editors in the 1870s. They meant that political commitments should be earned, not automatic, and that support for a political party did not require one-sided reporting. The ideal had of course been professed often before in American journalism. Now, however, the practice took hold in covering a major city. This was a most surprising development in this region.

In Missouri the newspapers had often been only one step removed from armed struggle. During the Civil War the Democratic state government had been faced down by armed Unionists, while many Democratic voters were disfranchised by the Republican government of Reconstruction. Democrats were no better than rebels to some Republican editors. The opposition press was defiant (in the town of Linn, the paper was the *Unterrified Democrat*). Partisanship went deeper than this two-way battle, for Republicans also fought one another. Radical Republicans of the late 1860s drove moderate Unionists into opposition and their own newspapers. It was the organization and press

of the Liberal Republicans that put iron in the young Joseph
Pulitzer.

Liberal Republicanism in Missouri was the cause of the German community and the *Westliche Post*. Pulitzer learned to cover
news on this paper and to fight a party battle in the 1872 campaign. He also learned the importance of political dexterity with
these German-Americans and joined a revived Democratic party
after the defeat of Liberal Republicanism. On national issues the
Post-Dispatch was belligerently Democratic. Readers learned that
"Grabber Garfield" was the Republican candidate for the presidency in 1880. During this campaign the paper ran a series on
scandals within the Grant administration—"The Secrets of the
Whiskey Ring Exposed"—lest there be any doubt about what
could be expected from Republicans in power.[11]

This makes the non-partisanship of local coverage striking.
Here Pulitzer's disclaimers of party bias seemed to mean something as he suggested pervasive corruption in the state and city
government controlled by Democrats. This "independent journalism" was the product of economic, aesthetic, and political
opportunities.

Pulitzer was one of the earliest editors to realize that in local
reporting, narrow partisanship no longer paid. One reason
newspapers ignored stories that embarrassed their party was
that they did not expect circulation to grow beyond its loyal
defenders. The penny press had made the breakthrough in circulation by ignoring, but not biting, the hand of the party. In
antebellum America, there was no incentive to make this attack.
The partisan community was familiar and known to be powerful.
The idea that cities were markets of much greater scope and
potential profit was slow to take hold. Advertisers aimed at a
class or a neighborhood, not the whole city. In an age without
cheap public transportation, a city was in fact a mosaic of small
local markets. It was in the 1870s that the economic drawbacks
of the party press became clear. The streetcar and the department
store created a more centralized market (and commuters who
wanted something to read). Advertising revenue, keyed to the

new commercial opportunity, grew more important to the newspaper. Printing costs dropped sharply in the industrialized nation. The older partisan dailies were often too distracted, too accustomed to insulting readers outside the party, to make the most of this new setting. The prosaic work of managing elections and making political lieutenants look good made it harder to gather exciting news.[12]

There was an imperative for writers here too. Reporters looked at the city and found vice, poverty, and hypocrisy on a scale that begged for impassioned description but which did not nicely fit party interests. Though journalists continued to find villains who, like Tweed, happily confirmed party prejudice, many of the best stories of the 1870s had to be told at the expense of both parties. The newspapers were not the first to see this. Magazines edited for the elite such as the *North American Review* and the *Nation* often gave each party a cold look. Mark Twain and Charles Dudley Warner gave the name to the era in their novel about Western boosters, *The Gilded Age* (1873). What the authors had in common was a realist's eye for how things got done in America and indignation over this use of power. Newspapers discovered that readers wanted scandals that were closer to literature and farther from partisan jibes.

Consider what the *Post-Dispatch* printed about gambling. Pulitzer hinted in his first year that men in power made St. Louis a "Gambler's Paradise," but the newspaper offered a travelogue, holding back on the political side of the story. An expeditionary force of seventeen reporters was sent out New Year's day, 1881, and "not a single hell was left unvisited" the paper claimed. There were seven columns of news about location, décor, and clientele. The reporters noted the narcotic effects of the games: "the scribe bent to the game and was for five minutes just as oblivious to all the ills of life as though drunk with hasheesh." The gamblers proved to be intriguing characters, some "ecclesiastical" in their dignity, others with the "hard look" of street gangs. The prize catch was Robert Pate, the owner of a large casino. A reporter "buttoned his overcoat up to his chin and set out to track the festive tiger in his lair." One is struck by how frequently the dime-novel language yields to discoveries that fit no stereotype. The journalist who tracked Pate found that his games were the most honest in the city and that Pate followed the socially responsible policy of excluding workingmen and minors.[13]

An urban landscape was opened, a frontier that American fiction was just beginning to explore. The partisan press had long ignored or simplified the spectacle of illicit pleasure and dirty work. Pulitzer's reporters took readers inside "opium hells" and "dago dens," aware that newspapers, novels, even gossip had not captured this low life: "Curious tales had been told . . . but not one-half of what can be seen has been described." This was not a journalism of characters credited with homilies or wisecracks (the abiding vice of reporting on the poor). The reporters took down the broken and flat conversations of everyday life. Readers learned, for example, how a black roustabout ordered a beefsteak in his cheap boarding house.

Pulitzer also filled his paper with information about the respectable classes that had not before been considered "news." The extraordinary intrusion into the tax records was followed by other lists: the salaries of elected officials, judges, businessmen, and the Protestant clergy. Pulitzer, with a genius for making piety serve the needs of the prurient, also published a guide to where the social belles of St. Louis could be seen in church.[14]

"Independent journalism," finally, was also a form of political revenge for Pulitzer, directed against the party that shunned him. He had courted the local Democratic organization when he began the paper. Pulitzer wanted the nomination to Congress that the "Dark Lantern" machine could deliver. Accordingly, the *Post-Dispatch* dismissed reports that nominations were for sale in St. Louis at the same time Pulitzer paid for his. The evidence suggests that he was double-crossed when the machine was pressured by wealthy Democrats who feared the crusading editor. Ed Butler, a blacksmith who was the broker for such deals, switched enough votes to defeat the publisher in the primary. Pulitzer wrote the epitaph for his career as a politician on the editorial page: "All is vanity—vanity of vanities, said the editor as he contemplates politics."[15]

Pulitzer got even as well as mad. Soon after the rigged primary election he backed a reform group within the Democratic party and gave his exposés a new cutting edge. The renegade Democrats were soon beaten by Butler's organization and faded from St. Louis politics. The exposés in the *Post-Dispatch* endured. The stories, as before, were graphic reports of city life, but now villains came more clearly into focus. Pulitzer, first, offered "a little inside history" of how garbage was picked up. The *Post-Dispatch* saw the soiled hands of the "Butler clique" and a system of corruption reaching up to the mayor. That man, Henry Overstolz, was a popular figure, long praised in the *Post-Dispatch*, and the candidate of both parties in the last election. Ed Butler had enticed him to cut his ties with the Republicans and used him to block reform in the Democratic party. Through the winter and spring of 1881 Pulitzer attacked the respectable interests who, like Overstolz, had made accommodations with the Dark Lantern organization. The gas and streetcar monopolies that the paper had often sniped at in the past now were connected with the Democrats in power. St. Louis, it appeared, cradled strong men gathered around "the public teat."[16]

In the early 1880s the *Post-Dispatch* did a great deal to back up these charges and to encourage political support for change. The paper reported the high profits and poor service of the gas and streetcar monopolies, published questionable real estate deals, described fraud at the polls, and paid regular visits to the protected gambling halls and brothels. Pulitzer goaded the police, the mayor, and grand juries to do their duty. When powerful men escaped punishment, the paper used the confessions of boodlers with bad consciences. Politicians talked about "de customary han'some consideration" for putting friends on the city payroll and for handing out franchises to corporations. The *Post-Dispatch* reported the price list of the elected Municipal Assembly: the cost of buying a seat from the Democratic machine and the great profit to be made for voting right. Representative government in St. Louis, readers learned, had elaborate customs. "Bunkum bills" threatening monopolies were introduced so that "reformers" could extort bribes from the corporations (then the legislation was killed). Insurgency within the Municipal Assembly was the sign that a representative was on the take. "If I don't buck, I don't get anything," a lawmaker explained. Democrats understood one another but did not place too much faith in words. One delegate told how he insisted that bribes be put in a safe place before he voted.[17]

Pulitzer's exposés had some success. In three years circulation went from 4000 to 23,000. The crusades helped to put some men in jail and improved a few public services. After the defeat of Mayor Overstolz, politicians realized that his newspaper had power at the polls. But, as the *Post-Dispatch* admitted, corruption continued to be part of the usual public business of St. Louis. Ed Butler tightened his grip on the Democratic party and reached into the Republican organization as well. He was now the broker for the gas and streetcar interests. Like Tweed, Butler was probably ahead of the journalists of his time in collecting information to help government as he knew it (among his other feats, Butler set up a telegraph company whose sole business was to receive bets).[18]

The exposés may have left many readers conscious of their guilt and ready for reform, but the machine did not seem worried. Butler ran display ads in the *Post-Dispatch* for his livery business and published the names of leading citizens attesting to the quality of his work. Smaller operators showed as much nerve. "I don't mind tellin' you about it," one bribe-taker remarked to a reporter for Pulitzer, "It'll be an advertisement of my business. . . . De people dat didn't know afore dat dere was anything corroked in de House of Delegates knows it now, an' if dy wants anything done dey'll pony up a dime or two."[19]

With such taunts in the air in the spring of 1883, Joseph Pulitzer left the *Post-Dispatch* and came to conquer New York with his purchase of the *World*. This move from a prosperous regional paper to New York was rare before the Civil War, but the metropolis was a magnet now. Thurlow Weed came downstate after the war and directed a paper. William Randolph Hearst left his paper in San Francisco and bought the New York *Journal* in 1895. The next year Adolph S. Ochs left Chattanooga and bought the New York *Times*. The pull of talent and fortunes to New York was a sign of the frustrations of regional journalism. To be influential, one must work at the urban center of the nation. Pulitzer watched over his St. Louis editors and encouraged them to follow up on corruption in the 1880s and 1890s. This they did. But the *Post-Dispatch* illustrates how a stone may drop, with a small splash and no ripples.

Between the founding of the *Post-Dispatch* in 1879 and the big stories of the shame of St. Louis in 1902, only about a dozen assessments of the city appeared in national periodicals. Not one article took its cue from Pulitzer's work. The political outlook of these observers was diverse. Charles Dudley Warner wrote about St. Louis after the encounters with Missouri government that he put in *The Gilded Age*. A local minister, John Snyder, spoke to the American people without such dark adventures (his taste ran to the fake ruins and real mausoleums in the city parks). But all the authors gave a picture of how St. Louis carried out public business, and they all sounded the same theme: St. Louis government was, in the main, a fine example of American democracy.

St. Louis was a pleasing sight to most professionals concerned with urban government. A history professor reported that the city was protected against extravagance and corruption alike by the charter of 1876 and that in the decade that followed the vices of patronage and election fraud had been cleaned up. The National Municipal League heard the Municipal Assembly praised in 1897 and learned that St. Louis "has not suffered from political bossism." The expert opinion was that "the financial management of St. Louis has always been good," and even the most sober student maintained in 1901, "I do not think it can be fairly said that our city was made the victim of serious raids upon the treasury."[20]

Journalists who wrote for popular magazines also looked on the brighter side. Typically, they spoke about how well the streetcars ran in St. Louis, not the franchise scandals on the routes. This journalism backed up a booster's dream: "the carnival city of America." In these reports the government was not above criticism, but its virtues were what the writers cared most about. If the lower house of the Municipal Assembly was "unprepossessing," the upper house seemed a "credit to any legislative body in the land." If St. Louis had no more public spirit than other cities, at least here there were "no great and arrogant political 'rings' which it would require gigantic effort to throw off." In 1888 Charles Dudley Warner saw nothing from the plot of *The Gilded Age* in St. Louis. He found no sign of corruption and a town with "immunity from the ward politician." St. Louis, Warner mused, "seems to me a very good place to study the influence of speculative thought in economics and practical affairs."[21]

The journalist who changed the nation's picture of St. Louis from a carnival or model government to a spectacle of corruption came to the city by accident. In 1902 Lincoln Steffens was sent away from New York by his boss, Samuel S. McClure—"you can't learn to edit a magazine here in the office," McClure said. Steffens had no itinerary and poked around Chicago and St. Paul before he heard about a political scandal in St. Louis. Steffens had grown up listening to stories about the California legislature, covered the political and financial news of New York as a young man, and so, at thirty-six, he was not making his first discovery of how America was governed. His was an editor's view, simple but arresting: "to take confused, local, serial news of the newspapers and report it all together in one long short story for the whole country." The three articles that Steffens published in *McClure's Magazine* did at last place the provincial scandal Pulitzer had shouted about for so long before the nation.[22]

On the surface, St. Louis did not look like a civic abyss in 1902. A dignified "reform" mayor had just been elected. City fathers were turning two square miles into "unexampled beauty and sublimity" for the World's Fair of 1904. Steffens, like Pulitzer, was able to show what the boasts hid. The Municipal Assembly, he explained, had long ago put the city up for sale. Street and railway franchises were sold at a fraction of their true value to the men with ready cash for votes. The streets that had been taken away from the people were cleaned, lighted, and repaired at enormous profit to political favorites. "Debate" in the Municipal Assembly was an intricate screen for back-room deals. Steffens described how a safe deposit box was stuffed with money by businessmen so that representatives would trust the capitalists long enough to vote as they were paid to vote. The city fathers longed for bigger deals. They discussed selling the city hall, and some visionaries had fixed a price on the city's water works. "It will be done some day," a boodler predicted.[23]

Steffens blended local color with rumination about the soul of the nation. Like Pulitzer's reporters, he had a good ear for the talk of Missouri politicos. "You have the moon yet—ain't it?" a mayor said in defense of arrangements for lighting the streets of St. Louis. But not even the cracks of Col. Ed Butler (the title had come with prosperity) led Steffens to see the scandal as a local story of a few bad men in the raw West. He reported that "a fellowship had grown up among boodling aldermen of the leading cities in the United States," and that across the nation respectable citizens cooperated with this underworld. Classes of Americans—businessmen, lawyers, jurists— found corruption to be safe and profitable. Steffens made a term fashionable that took corruption out of its local setting: "the system." The catch-phrase aimed to bring the whole country into the scandal and to make even the most upstanding readers share the guilt: *BUSINESS AS TREASON—CORRUPTION AS REVOLUTION*. Perhaps unsure that all his readers would stick with the grand political theory to the end, Steffens concluded with a less abstract matter, Missouri baking powder. The manufacturers, he found, bought and sold the men who governed the state and pushed powder that might not be safe into America's kitchens.[24]

The editing of this story of corruption was much more difficult than getting the facts. Steffens heard the whole story from the circuit attorney, Joseph W. Folk, in the lobby of the Planters Hotel on the day he arrived in St. Louis. The former city editor of the *Post-Dispatch*, Claude Wetmore, wrote the draft of the first story, and Steffens produced the final two articles from the public record of Folk's prosecutions. The editors at *McClure's* wanted to publish this material, but they struggled to find the right voice and the right timing for the revelations. Steffens tore apart the story sent in by Wetmore and made it fit a national drama of corruption. The New York editors also roughed up the friends and sources Wetmore had protected. McClure shot back the second article that Steffens did with a lecture on the technique of the exposé:

> You know the ideal method of writing is that pursued by Alexander Dumas in his great D'Artagnan romances, once in every so often the narrative came to a powerful climax. This article must be arranged in the same way; for example, working up the climax of this man Butler, and of the convicted bookmakers still being members of the Assembly and passing laws; the climax of the tremendous robbery of $50,000 followed by another climax in the scheme for robbing the city $50,000 more, making it the greatest carnival of loot in recent times.

"A trick, a political trick!" was Steffens' verdict on some of his own editing. The editors labored hard to make the news of St. Louis shocking. McClure, who sometimes addressed journalists as if they were members of a ring, wanted to "keep to ourselves all these plans and schemes that we have in hand . . . for the sake of the effect we expect to have on public opinion. . . ."[25]

The exposé bears the mark of this theatricality. Much was

borrowed. "Tweed Days in St. Louis" opened the series of three articles; Tweed was invoked in the second, and even the jokes about St. Louis had been part of Tammany folklore. The St. Louis stories had nothing to do with overpriced municipal buildings, but *McClure's* ran photographs of the city's unfinished hospital and city hall in a sort of homage to the Tweed courthouse. Boss Butler was introduced late in the story to personify the graft; he was only an unnamed "legislative agent" while the scene was being set for his villainy. The names of the boodlers were withheld and saved for a rogues' gallery toward the end of the story. The detective work was fast and sure. Attorney Folk, the hero of the piece, got a tip from a reporter and quickly made a "single handed exposure of the corruption, high and low." Steffens pictured citizens as innocents ready to make the most of the initiation provided by *McClure's*: "St. Louis, indeed, in its disgrace, has a great advantage. It was exposed late; it has not been reformed and caught again and again, until its citizens are reconciled to corruption."[26]

Steffens knew perfectly well that corruption had been a running story before the Folk revelations—veterans of the *Post-Dispatch* crusade had helped him with the articles.[27] But Steffens was right to claim that his exposé placed the facts in a new light. Pulitzer had gone beyond the partisan exposé but could not capture national attention. *He* left town, but his stories of corruption did not. Steffens's success at making St. Louis a national story was a measure of how journalism and politics had changed.

The most that the Republican or the Democratic organizations would do was to reward newspaper crusaders who were loyal to their side. Before the turn of the century, no national reform organization spread the word of corruption at the local level. No third party at this time was able to place grievances from the states on the national agenda. The Populist agitation of the 1880s and 1890s was a powerful political movement with a genius for publicity, but it failed to win over the national magazines or to establish new ones of wide influence. Most metropolitan newspapers treated the Populists as if they were a rabble. The agrarian insurgents had slim chance in the journalism of their day to make their critique of industrial America seem coherent or attractive.

Trade practices as well as prejudice discouraged the nineteenth-century press from making local investigations fit political movements. Only the editor or owner of the paper could court fame through exposure, and this was rarely the prudent business practice. A reporter's story, in the first place, did not normally carry a byline. Though this was true at many magazines of the day as well, the difficulty of making a name locally was especially galling to newspaper reporters. Ray Stannard Baker recalled with bitterness that "when I wrote for a newspaper I never had the feeling that I had any readers."[28]

The reporter who sought fame or a new career through stirring up trouble at home was not making a rational decision. Opportunity beckoned to those who printed less than they knew. Journalists in St. Louis had a tradition of using inside information on the black market. "Red" Galvin—a reporter who helped Folk—had become a legend in the city by keeping the secrets of friends in the underworld. Theodore Dreiser competed against Galvin in the 1890s and considered him no different from the crooks, so perfectly did the reporter get on with his sources. St. Louis's most cosmopolitan journalist, William Marion Reedy, was also at home in the local world of graft. Reedy was a connoisseur of scandal (and of the best literature of his age) who moved easily between the city's dives and drawing rooms. For a time in the 1890s Reedy seems to have subsidized his literary publications by taking blackmail for not writing about prominent citizens. The "shame" of a community was worth more suppressed than printed. A career in journalism was more easily lost than found in this reporting.[29]

It was the progressive movement of the new century that made scandal less insular. New magazines and new political organizations enlarged the public for exposure and the rewards for investigators. The "muckraking" magazines such as *McClure's*

had triple the circulation of the older monthlies and sold at a
third of the price. They had not all gained their readers with
investigative stories, but editor after editor concluded, in the
first years of the Roosevelt presidency, that this was the way to
keep the circulation figures of their dreams. With bolder editing
and greater use of photographs, the new monthlies brought
vivid stories of corruption to hundreds of thousands of Americans who were used to nothing more than disjointed newspaper
accounts.

The reform magazines did a poor job of hiding their impatience
and even contempt for the timidity of the newspapers that had
bought peace at home. When muckrakers wrote about the daily
press, it was most often about the evasions and lies citizens
must contend with. The editor of the *Arena* magazine said his
career as a reformer had been spent printing those stories local
editors faced "blind, deaf, and dumb." *McClure's* reported that
even the tramps of Chicago could see the papers were afraid of
the truth about municipal government. *Collier's* commissioned
Will Irwin to make a study of the dailies, and he jabbed at the
press corps in several cities, especially the newsrooms in Pittsburgh and Cincinnati. Irwin's series ran from January to July of
1911, and a contest followed with prize money to local citizens
for letters on the revelations. The logical step had already been
taken by the reform magazines—a publication that would free
readers from their local newspapers. Erman J. Ridgway used
the profits from publishing a series on "Frenzied Finance" in
Everybody's to start a magazine published simultaneously in fourteen cities. The editors spoke to local conditions, opened each
city to distant readers, and built a network for national reform.[30]

St. Louis understood the superiority of the national forum for
exposure provided by magazines. Attorney Folk, who was a
master publicist of his own cause in the St. Louis papers,
"dropped everything" (Steffens recalled) when the editor appeared. Folk wanted St. Louis to read about itself in a national
magazine. "Our only salvation seems to be the scourges laid on
unsparingly by outside hands," a St. Louisan wrote to Steffens

after reading the stories in *McClure's*. Even the "globe-trotting boodler" the magazine had pictured in the exposé asked to confess "to the Public through your Magazine." The mail at *McClure's* was filled with evidence of guilt and narcissism. One overworked staff member was convinced that cities took "morbid pleasure" in the investigation. So many towns asked to be exposed that Steffens could not visit them all.[31] Six communities earned a place in *The Shame of the Cities* (1904), and St. Louis came first. The volume was as much a monument to the new willingness to make scandal national as it was a sign of the determination to reform America's cities.[32]

Not all of this can be credited to muckraking magazines. The "yellow press" prepared the way with its chains of dailies and enormous circulation. Pulitzer earned this epithet in New York, while other press lords such as Edward W. Scripps and William Randolph Hearst had even more energy to attract national attention to their newspaper exposés. In 1896, for example, Hearst's snarling employee, Ambrose Bierce, was brought to Washington from the San Francisco *Examiner* to attack the Southern Pacific Railroad. Bierce's acid stories about California helped defeat the subsidies the Southern Pacific sought from Congress. However, the national influence of the yellow press is more fable than fact. James Creelman, a star reporter for both Pulitzer and Hearst, gave up working for dailies in the Progressive Era with a blast that "the American newspaper has become practically a local institution." Creelman saw that regional papers had destroyed the wide influence of the old party editors and that magazines were now the only way "to get national utterance for what I may have to say."[33]

Creelman signed on with a reform magazine he called "unfettered," an apt term for the appeal of muckraking. The writer gained influence over the government of a community but shed worries about living there. Thus Mark Sullivan nourished the grass roots of Midwestern politics from the office of *Collier's* in New York in the first decade of the twentieth century. Sullivan gave the congressmen he favored an attractive name as they battled an autocratic Speaker of the House: "the insurgents." Week after week *Collier's* kept this faction before the nation. Further, the *counties* that sent these men to Congress were much praised and Sullivan used the magazine to start a letter-writing campaign from these home districts. Reform in the Mid-West was being defined from the outside. As an independent movement and as a faction in both the Republican and Democratic parties, progressives were patrons powerful enough to free journalists from local constraints and temptations. Prudence and the payoff were now much less likely to keep reporters in line with local political organizations. Claude Wetmore, the reporter who had demanded that Steffens take responsibility for publishing what he knew about his city in 1902, now spoke for himself and started a magazine of exposure in St. Louis. The alchemy of progressive journalism might transform the shadiest characters into uplifters. "Red" Galvin, for so long the corruptionist's friend, was celebrated across the nation once he sided with Folk.[34]

The new attention to the scandals in distant cities opened doors for reporters in New York and Washington. President Theodore Roosevelt was quick to see the power of such exposés. The President courted McClure and Steffens so they would understand who the hero was in his administration. TR brought the editors to the White House to give them documents and kept them there until after midnight with talk about how to write the story.[35]

Western journalists probably gained the most from the notion that a writer who could find the scandal close to home had a calling to awaken the whole nation. Reporters found that their journeymen days looking up tax records and franchise schemes in San Francisco, Kansas City, or Chicago led to jobs with national magazines and progressive leaders. Branching out did not always disturb roots. William Allen White, for example, left a big city for a small one— Emporia, Kansas. His national reputation grew through every fight of the Progressive Era. White did love Kansas, but he played the angle of being a prairie editor for all it was worth. His best reporting on national politics went to editors back East. (In 1905 *McClure's* had him sum up the Folk story in Missouri.) The 3000 readers of the Emporia *Gazette* did not learn much of the proprietor's role in progressive fights, for most of the articles he wrote for them stuck close to the community. White was quick to understand that speaking "from Emporia" won him eager welcome in popular magazines. White's bibliography as well as his travel schedule show he had limited interest in speaking simply "to Emporia." White wanted the national stage, and he understood that a homespun reputation could place him there.[36]

White's goal as a political insurgent was not far different from that of David Graham Phillips, a Hoosier and star of Cincinnati papers who had left the Midwest behind: "the corruption that is vital is not in ward politics, or state politics, but in national politics. It is at Washington. . . . " There was a migratory path for progressive journalists, almost always East. Ray Stannard Baker and Will Irwin, for example, left the West to edit *McClure's*. George Creel and Brand Whitlock went from city hall beats to jobs as municipal reformers that brought them into Eastern progressive circles. Charles E. Russell came through Davenport, Minneapolis, and Detroit before his assaults on the plutocracy with Hearst and the muckraking magazine. Their next step was to the center of power.[37]

Woodrow Wilson brought these reporters—and many more with similar backgrounds—into his administration. The key agency was the Committee on Public Information during the mobilization for World War I. This was a bureaucracy run by journalists who had specialized in the investigation of injustice at the local level. Creel, the head of the organization, began his political education covering the Tom Pendergast machine of Kansas City. Two of his three associate chairmen were, like Creel, muckrakers who had made their names in the West. Harvey J. O'Higgins had exposed Denver and Utah. Edgar Sisson was a reporter for two Chicago papers before becoming editor of a reform magazine.[38]

The Committee on Public Information adapted muckraking themes to the national emergency. Mobilization promised to fulfill many of the dreams of the pre-war literature of reform. The government would demand equal sacrifice from its citizens and trusts would bend to the common good. Patriotism would win out over clannishness and selfishness in every class. War-time measures such as votes for women and prohibition made a strong case that what reformers had asked for, they now had won. The discovery that the Kaiser was the great menace to democracy fit the muckrakers conspiratorial frame of mind. Indeed, for a popular journalism that had done much to view American criminals with understanding, even admiration, the picture of this brutal, external enemy offered psychological comfort. It was fitting that the most creditable reports of the evil Germany had brought to conquered Belgium came from Ambassador Brand Whitlock. Germany provided something more concrete to fight than a pervasive "system" run by self-deceived businessmen.

The excitement of war propaganda, like the appeal of muckraking itself, came in the opportunity to see a story unfold and build shock upon shock. There was much of that editing skill within the CPI, as with the posters that reached young Americans with news of German barbarism "so terrible that only whispered fragments may be recounted." Muckraking was a triumph of story-telling, reaching those citizens who had earlier shown little interest in hearing about these political or social problems. The selling of the war was done in the same spirit, making popular entertainment accommodate serious appeals to the public good. The old muckraking magazines warmed quickly to the theme of military preparedness, for it offered the exciting stories they had always sought. *McClure's*, for example, gave little space to political reform when World War I began, but in 1915–16 the magazine offered two serials that told how American defenses might be smashed and the land conquered by a Prussian-like invader. Most importantly, the CPI played upon the distaste for the process of two-party government that muckraking did much to build. When Charles E. Russell spoke on the war for the CPI, for example, it was to identify those traitors in the U. S. Senate who frustrated the national will. This, it will soon be clear, was language that muckraking had taught in its heyday.[39]

With the Committee on Public Information, President Wilson did create journalism with a unified sense of national purpose. A group of reporter-civil servants shadowed and corrected the press corps. America's first daily newspaper by and for the government, the *Official Bulletin*, was sent to be displayed in post offices and training camps and tens of thousands of influential Americans received their own copy. It has been estimated that every newspaper in California received six pounds of copy from the news bureaus of government every day during the War.[40]

As political reporting shifted weight towards Washington, both politicians and reporters felt the strain. Wilson used the skills and ideals of reporters that had been won on small battlefields of the Progressive Era. The effect of such publicity by the government in Washington was to make these local skirmishes seem less significant to all concerned. This was one sign of a paradox the muckrakers themselves had made: the political reporting aimed at reform themes in the new century was not able to make politics compelling for the general public.

IV

REPORTING FOR A PHANTOM PUBLIC

Collier's
THE NATIONAL WEEKLY

THE GAME BEGINS

December 9, 1905

7

The Civics and Anti-Civics
of Muckraking

The political reporting of the Progressive Era has often been viewed as a grand civics lesson. Muckraking, the investigative journalism in the successful magazines of the day, has usually been understood as a way of waking citizens up to their political responsibilities. There is much evidence to support this view. From the beginning of the century to World War I, the magazines with progressive themes sounded a call to political action in both the facts and the fiction they published. Readers were asked to raise their voices against illegitimate power. Over and over again the case was made to extend the citizen's power through the direct primary, initiative, and recall so that the simple act of marking a ballot could choose a candidate, depose an official, or make law directly. Part of the credit for woman suffrage belongs to this literature of reform. More than this, progressive journalism tapped the national genius for voluntary organization. In leagues, clubs, churches, and social settlements, reformers built a fellowship around political goals and the periodicals of the movement often helped to bring citizens together in these ways. Lincoln Steffens alone convened the citizens of several New England communities to lead them through a civics lesson.

The impact of all this on political parties was greater than any other reform movement of the twentieth century. Roosevelt's Bull Moose campaign of 1912 was the most successful third party challenge of modern times. In the decade before 1912 both Republicans and Democrats sought the banner of progressivism, and the leading figures were devoted to the magazines of reform. A number of progressive senators had familiar bylines in the muckraking magazines. Senator Robert M. La Follette of Wisconsin started his own weekly. It survived into the 1980s as the *Progressive*. Even before the Wilson administration, reform journalists frequently took government jobs. Ray Stannard Baker, George Creel, and Brand Whitlock, for example, were immersed in the details of state politics as officeholders. There were celebrated cases of muckraking in which public officials simply told what they had learned at work. Christopher Powell Connolly, for example, had been a district attorney in Montana before exposing the state for the readers of *Collier's*.[1]

There is a paradox to the civics lesson provided by progressive journalism: overall political participation declined in America as this reporting gained strength. For all the new constituencies we may credit to progressives, for all their skill in mobilizing protest, it remains true that this age of reform was an age of voter apathy.[2]

In the Progressive Era the percentage of the electorate that voted was sharply down from the extraordinary high turnouts in the decades when citizens could expect little in the way of inspired investigation of political ills on a national stage. In 1912 the population was a fifth greater than during William Jennings Bryan's futile campaigns for the presidency, but Wilson gained the White House with fewer votes than Bryan had attracted. In that year of passion, the total vote for President Taft, ex-President Roosevelt, and Wilson was lower than Taft and Bryan drew in 1908. At the national level there was a steady fall-off in voting by those eligible in the progressive years. Most of the large industrial states lost 15 to 20 per cent of their voters in presidential campaigns between the election of McKinley and Wilson. At the local level this was not always so, but many urban and state reformers won during periods of decreased voting participation. At a time of easier transportation as well as communication, this drop-off in interest at election time is a puzzle.

It is not possible to explain the slide in voting by demographic changes, the fracture of parties, or new voting rules. The immigrants of the 1870s and 1880s marched to the polls, and it is hard to find anything in the newcomers of the turn of the century that should have held them back. Besides, in sections of rural America where new immigrants were rare, the same decline occurred as in the major cities. The fall-off in national vote totals is not simply a result of the practical disfranchisement of so many blacks and poor whites in the South at the end of the nineteenth century. The graph of electoral participation makes a deep valley in the Progressive Era for the North and East as surely as in the South. Twenty-six of the thirty-four non-Southern states participating in both the 1896 and the 1916 elections showed a decline in participation. Women, of course, do not skew the figures in national elections until 1920.

Progressives did crack party loyalties, but that by itself need not have discouraged participation. In 1896, Bryan repudiated the traditional economic policy of fellow Democrats, dismissed the party establishment, and drove "gold Democrats" away. His appeal for the free coinage of silver also split the GOP. Yet for all this damage to party loyalties, the Democrats and Republicans managed to attract more voters than in the election of 1892. Insurgency by itself is no explanation for voter apathy. Nor is the existence of party machines the heart of the matter. Today, states with abundant patronage and efficient party organizations do *not* have greater participation in elections than the "reform" states.[3] When progressives attacked political machines they were not bringing down a way of conducting elections that was inherently better at turning out voters. Progressive support for the secret ballot and tighter registration laws undoubtedly discouraged some voters, but these reforms do not account for what happened. The downturn in voting preceded the secret ballot in many states. Where rural voters did not have to register, their participation dropped along with the urban voters faced with controls.

The fall-off in voting was not an isolated sign of lessened

participation. That venerable institution, the monster campaign rally, also went into decline. As the presidential candidates divided on progressive issues their organizations were not able to match the "Sound Money" parades of 1896 (in Chicago the procession took five hours to pass the reviewing stand). The new century brought no spectacles of commitment to compare with those extraordinary gatherings at the front porches of Republican candidates. In 1888 Benjamin Harrison drew nearly 200,000 well-wishers to his home in Indiana, a figure approaching 80 per cent of the Republican voters in the state. The crowds outside William McKinley's home in Canton, Ohio, during the campaign of 1896 equaled more than 10 per cent of the Republican vote nation-wide in November.[4] Judged from the candidates' front porches, as well as at the polls, something fundamental was happening within this political culture to reduce interest in elections.

Recent scholarship has demonstrated that the origins of nonvoting lie in strategies of the national party organizations in the 1880s and 1890s. For a number of reasons (not all of them pragmatic) the old rituals fell out of favor in high party committees. Distaste for the "ignorant" voter and the spectacles that moved him to the polls led both parties to try and raise the intellectual level of campaigns. Some of the most thoughtful journalists of the Gilded Age, such as Edwin L. Godkin of the *Nation*, favored this course and hoped it would leave the unqualified voter behind. Journals that deplored mass democracy to a small group of readers influenced American politics because they reached a party elite ready to listen. Metropolitan dailies with more talk of their "independence" and less space available for national party materials also signaled the end of the full mobilization of the voter that had been possible before 1900. The daily paper now had too many new interests and sources of support to be effective missionaries for their party.[5]

The new priorities for party and newspaper do not by themselves explain why voting lost its appeal. Party professionals often do not get what they want and must backtrack. There must have been a powerful cultural sanction for their efforts to dispense with the ritual that had carried so many Americans to the polls. The independent dailies were evidently not crucial to the change, for turnout also fell in small towns where dependable party newspapers remained to urge voters on.

The fashion of muckraking in popular literature of the Progressive Era does much to explain why the habit of voting declined. It must be admitted that the best-known generalizations about muckraking shed little light on this change. Reporting bad news about American institutions and branding some politicians scoundrels was not a new activity of the press. It would appear that if press attacks on the competence of government could drive voters from the polls, that would have happened early in the course of American democracy. To show that muckraking lessened trust in government is not the same thing as showing why the habit of voting weakened. There is some evidence that today the cynical and the disaffected vote at about the same rate as citizens with confidence in their government. Broad statements about the "negative" tone of the muckrakers are little help in explaining the drop in political participation.[6]

To understand the impact of the muckraking texts one must read them with the common sense of nineteenth–century politics clearly in mind. For it was the discrediting of some basic assumptions about how democracy worked that made muckraking both shocking (as the authors intended) and (as they did not wish) a message to pull back from political life.

Before the Progressive Era, Americans voted for two fundamental reasons. The issues touched their deepest concerns as members of an ethnic or religious group, while the parties drilled citizens to act on their feelings. The best local studies we have suggest that class interest and economic factors do little to explain the late nineteenth-century electorate. Religious orientation and ethnic loyalties were the basis of politics. They set the tone and defined the issues for orderly party conflict. Mobilizing these powerful loyalties was the business of politicians.

The imagery of war does not distort the democratic process

of the nineteenth century. The two parties *looked* like armies. In election campaigns they marched in review before their leaders, wearing uniforms, chanting slogans, carrying flags, stepping to brass bands. The attitude toward the small number of citizens not in the ranks—the swing voters—was that of a regular army toward mercenaries: it was necessary to buy their services, and questions of honor were beside the point. Patronage (the "spoils") was the chief objective of each party. The partisan dailies of the nineteenth century were heavy with speeches—there was an abundance of information about the issues of the day—but editors saw to it that citizens could make simple choices. Blind loyalty was more often a virtue than a vice in these publications, and at election time the drumming for loyalty grew louder as many new party newspapers were set up. National magazines did not reach a large public with a more complex view.[7]

Progressivism, and especially its journalism, undermined the ritual of political participation. The reformers lacked the enthusiasm of party regulars for indoctrination, social pressure, and, if need be, the payoff. Progressives asked the public to overturn old assumptions and to view issues in new ways. Muckraking magazines attacked the notion that a citizen's vote should be an act of loyalty set by tradition and sprung by election spectacle. Political participation was redefined as a thoughtful search for that true principle obscured by the "surface play" of the parties. Implicit here was a heresy to both Republicans and Democrats of an earlier generation: that detachment was the right course if there was no clear choice or the issues seemed too complex. In 1903 the *Independent* called on reformers to recognize that "the more conscientious and the more intelligent the voter is the more likely will he be at certain times to decide that duty and common sense admonish him to play golf or go fishing on election day."[8]

The old politics had anticipated the difficulties of the new. In 1892 Democrats and Republicans emphasized educational measures over the traditional ritual. The result was the lowest rate of voter turnout in twenty years. It appears that both parties pursued citizens with open minds so well they left some of their loyalists confused and distracted. The drill of the faithful was sloppy. Progressive journalism was a major, disruptive shift toward political education, confusing the voter's cues and teaching him to hesitate.[9]

Party loyalty itself was a virtue of the old politics that progressive journalism helped turn into a vice. This was the lament of that Tammany stalwart, George Washington Plunkitt, in his "very plain talks" on American government. When a leader "hustles around and gets all the jobs possible for his constituents," Plunkitt thought that a "solemn contract" was made and voters must return him to office "just as they're bound to uphold the Constitution of the United States." Plunkitt spoke out in the midst of progressive attacks on this self-evident moral truth. There had always been the "crime" of ingratitude in Tammany, he admitted, but reformers were worse, for they added ridicule to moral turpitude. Plunkitt cited *The Shame of the Cities* as a sign of this confusion about the proper basis of politics, and he probably had in mind cartoons of the type that *McClure's Magazine* featured: party voters with rings in their noses, pulled by the reins of party leaders. In the eye of leaders like Plunkitt, reporting by progressives turned the moral order upside down.[10]

Progressives exposed the forced system of participation. In some of the most prominent muckraking texts the manipulation of voters made electoral politics a chamber of horrors. *Cosmopolitan* ran a four-part series by Charles E. Russell, "At the Throat of the Republic," to demonstrate "that nine of every ten elections are decided solely by the methods of the vote broker and the ballot box stuffer. . . . " When Ben Lindsey and Harvey J. O'Higgins made patronage and electioneering part of *The Beast* (1910), they used a term no stronger than was common in the new reporting about city elections in that decade.[11]

It is less well known that muckrakers delivered the same shocking news about the voting of rural America. This theme was so striking to reporters and editors that it was used many times. Early in his series on the states, Lincoln Steffens noted that voters in Rhode Island's villages had sold out. Ray Stannard

Baker found that the swing votes of Springfield, Ohio—1500 Americans—were for sale in every election. David Graham Phillips began *The Plum Tree* with Hoosiers at the polls lined up like addicts, exchanging their vote for the favor of the local party official. Brand Whitlock created an anti-pastoral in rural Illinois with *The Thirteenth District* (1902). Every autumn, Whitlock wrote, campaigns drew the small-town lawyers and businessmen to a terrible harvest: "Amid all this beauty and mystery, men were fighting one another, bribing, deceiving and coercing one another, in order that the offices of the republic might be taken from one set of men and turned over to another set of men." Adams County, Ohio, where both parties ran buggies down country lanes delivering payoffs to farmers for their vote, was exposed several times. Whitlock reviewed press reports of this kind in 1912 and said the public had seen nothing yet, for "if the muckrakers were to report to their magazines what they know on this subject, I am sure they would reveal conditions that are worse than those urban States they have so minutely examined." [12]

For all this criticism, the face-to-face community of the small town attracted and bedeviled progressive journalists. Reform required coalitions of urban voters, citizens united in politics by recognition of their common interests, not from trust developed in living together. Muckraking was ambivalent about whether democracy could survive in America's cities of enlightened strangers.

Ray Stannard Baker argued both sides of the question. He put his name on major investigations of industrial America and posed issues that required close study and the mobilization of voters if solutions were to be found. Baker's faith in an informed public spanned the Progressive Era. At the same time, he published the "Adventures in Contentment" series under the name David Grayson. These were idylls in the countryside of a free-thinker. The David Grayson stories began in that bright new hope of progressive journalism, the *American Magazine*. Sometimes the stories appeared in the same issues as Baker's investigative pieces.

He did all he could to keep authorship of the Grayson stories a secret. There was no reason for the reader to think the same man was responsible for the fiction as well as the facts. One of the earliest stories contrasted politics in the city and in the country. Grayson confessed that in the city he and others dodged political responsibilities and were hopelessly confused. Grayson said this was perfectly natural. In the country there was "elbow-knowledge" of public issues gathered in the plain talk of one neighbor to another. In the city Grayson found only newspapers and books on politics offering "sham comfort" and "mock assurance." "It was good to escape that place of hurrying strangers," Grayson said, to gain neighbors who could help make sense of politics. The Grayson stories acknowledged that country folk needed to educate themselves, but there was more than a hint that citizens who did not keep a corn field or one-room school within sight could not be trusted to govern. Written by a muckraker, edited by reformers, and loved by readers drawn to progressivism—the Grayson stories imply that the literature of exposure was beside the point. In the cities there would be apathy and confusion for in the absence of community, reporting did not matter.[13]

America's cities were "a wilderness of careless strangers," William Allen White said. With his home in Emporia, Kansas, and his eye on reform across the country, White addressed an urban nation that (by his own analysis) could not respond adequately because the "instincts of humanity" decayed as citizens grew up outside a country town. White helped edit the *American Magazine* and fought for insurgents in the Republican party, finally carrying the banner for Roosevelt in the Bull Moose campaign of 1912. But all of this work to draw readers to national reform was undermined by White's writing that was designed to make urban citizens feel misplaced and damaged by the rhythms of their daily life. Like Baker, White sometimes made political participation forbidden fruit. The citizen from the big city could not taste it.[14]

The eclipse of rural communities worried a great variety of

social critics and cast a shadow over the ideal of political participation in reform literature. The "small-town fetish" (as one
scholar has called it) helped to channel progressivism to the
urban neighborhood. This reform movement placed so much
emphasis on community organizations, particularly social settlements, because nostalgia for the country towns was widely
shared and cut across many other differences. Several progressives dreamed that newspapers could aid them in re-creating an
intimate community in the city by supplementing personal contact, relaying conversation, and helping citizens to act as if members of a town meeting. The reality was that much reporting in
reform journals added to the traditional fears about democracy
in cities. Progressives stumbled, as Bryan had tripped in the
1896 campaign: appealing to urban workers through references
to the moral superiority of rural life. Voting studies show that
this cognitive dissonance hurt the Democratic party. Progressivism got into the same trouble. Anti-urban appeals had been
effective in nineteenth-century politics and remained potent in
the new century. But they were drawbacks in a reform movement attempting to mobilize America's growing cities. Muckraking opened up the perplexing variety of urban scandals to
the whole nation and gave a vivid, documented picture of how
far the metropolis departed from fond memories (and folklore)
of democracy in face-to-face communities.[15]

Progressives wished to populate both rural and urban America
with different citizens than the ones who happened to form the
electorate at the turn of the century. Reform journalism was
directed at Americans whose ethnic or religious ties left them
free to be disinterested voters. There was to be a "new citizenship" in which all ethnic or religious loyalties touching on politics
were suspect. It was wrong, muckrakers said, to use politics to
protect parochial interests, either by enforcing the moral rules
of one group on another or by using politics for tribal advantage.
Much ink has been shed arguing about whether this conception
of politics was the narrow vision of a middle-class, Anglo-Saxon,
Protestant group. It is certainly true that some progressive meas-

ures, like prohibition, were in part the revenge of some ethnic groups on others. It is not necessary to face the difficult questions about the exact tensions within this broad reform movement. Whether there was a cosmopolitan ideal or a coercive 'Americanization' plan at the heart of progressivism (and both had a role), the attitude toward ethnic or religious loyalties was usually the same: they must give way to make a good citizen.[16]

The muckrakers wrote to refute the notion that some ethnic groups were at fault for the troubles of American government and also to show that parochial appeals would do no good. Thus Lincoln Steffens set out to explode the theory of scapegoats in the cities. He examined old immigrants (St. Louis), new immigrants (Pittsburgh), and Yankees (Philadelphia) to show that political systems were not determined by ethnicity. *All* these cities were corrupt. Steffens taught that no one group in society had inbred talent for governing. Confidence in any ethnic community was misplaced. Similarly, Upton Sinclair's *The Jungle* (1906) paid close attention to Lithuanian and Polish families in Chicago to show that they had no special standing as victims in Packingtown. A socialism embracing and transcending all parochial loyalties was the lesson of Sinclair's investigation.

Muckracking was troubled by the loyalties that kept urban Americans apart and ambivalent about the city itself. But this was where this journalism brought the reader. Muckraking usually meant reporting on the work place and tenements, on urban vices and concentrations of power best revealed in cities. Washington itself became the focus for most of these concerns in the reform magazines.

In this respect the journalism of the Progressive Era followed the reform-minded presidents. The office became a "bully pulpit," in Theodore Roosevelt's phrase. Presidential press conferences and regular opportunities to interview the chief executive replaced congressional debates as the most important news from Washington. The muckrakers were only a part of this shift of attention, but their national magazines had the greatest reach.

• • •

In the first years of the twentieth century David Graham Phillips took political reporting where few journalists had dared to go. His steps were the ones reporters dreamed of; his conclusions were bolder than successful journalists had been willing to make. Phillips was a celebrity and a scoffer. The gray routine of a reporter's life was not for him, nor the pulling of punches. Phillips snarled at the political process. He brought to the surface an antagonism toward government that was at the center of muckraking.

Phillips led a double life: the man of letters standing free of the demands of the newsroom and the reporter in harness who would chase any story. Phillips is easy to spot in the photographs of the press corps of this era, the peacock amidst the dark, wrinkled suits. His first editor in Cincinnati was so appalled by his fashionable tailoring that he would not speak to the young man for several days. In New York, conversations started over his white flannels and the large chrysanthemum he chose each morning for his lapel. Editors could not find an assignment too trivial, humiliating or dirty to discourage him. He scored on the stories other reporters found hopeless. Colleagues credited Phillips with finding a missing child and then wringing the last tear from the discovery. He got a full account of a British naval disaster into the New York *World* before the Admiralty knew the details.

Phillips's advancement followed the daydreams of a generation of colleagues in the newsroom. Reporters were paid the wages of clerks and often lived as if they were paid less. Phillips commanded the unprecedented sums that Pulitzer and Hearst bid for star talent in New York. Many reporters worked themselves sick as they supplemented writing for a newspaper with stories for other publishers. Phillips could take or leave newspaper work as he chose, and for a time he happily covered a beat during the day and wrote fiction through the night. (In the photo chosen by Phillips's admirers for the memorial biography, the journalist stands at his writing table for the night, wearing an embroidered robe, pencil poised.) He published seventeen novels, seven short stories, and one play before his death at age forty-three. Phillips was assassinated in Gramercy Park in 1911 by a deranged reader of his novels. Somehow this self-sufficient, nocturnal dandy thrust himself into the middle of the great public questions of the Progressive Era. It was Phillips's series on government for a Hearst magazine in 1906 that provoked President Theodore Roosevelt to brand it "muckraking" and to warn the American people where such reporting was taking them.[18]

Any reader who even skims the nine installments of "The Treason of the Senate" soon notices two things: the pictures that tell Phillips's story and the reporter's insistence, over and over again, that the words of senators mean nothing. These may be the most important things about this reporting, for they upset the conventional way of telling political stories.

William Randolph Hearst had bought *Cosmopolitan* in 1905, and the Senate exposé was his first opportunity in a magazine to show his characteristic extravagance. Phillips was allowed to name his price. Talented researchers were hired. The series was relentlessly advertised. There was full-color art work on the first covers, and important cartoonists produced frontispieces. The most striking feature was the photographs Hearst obtained. The first installment of March 1906 began with New York's junior senator, Chauncey Depew, tilting his head back and laughing in the reader's face. This shot was followed by photos of the senator's three imposing residences and his drawing room in Washington. Depew was shown at play in his automobile and at work at the Republican convention. Three more senators were caught on the street with snap shots in the first six installments, and the story was frequently interrupted by architectural specimens. The fine modern edition of "The Treason of the Senate" reproduces only the cartoons from this run of illustration, and this is unfortunate. The photos said something about politics as startling as Phillips's words.

Cosmopolitan was the first magazine to find a place for pho-

MARCH

COSMOPOLITAN

TEN CENTS

The
Treason
of the
Senate

by

David Graham Phillips

1906

tographs in the tested format of the exposé. Juxtaposing public servants with their lavish possessions had been a staple of illustrated journalism since the rise of *Harper's Weekly* a half century earlier. Without making an argument, without attempting to prove graft, the sumptuous setting of men in power was a visual indictment. Hearst used the new half-tone process to fit photographs into this scheme, and editors made sure readers got the point. The photo of Senator Depew in his auto had been published a year earlier by *Leslie's Weekly* captioned "A Statesman-Automobilist-Senator Depew, of New York, en route to the Capitol at Washington in his Horseless Carriage." The wide view of the avenue did make it seem the senator was going to work. *Cosmopolitan* cropped the photo to take the senator off the road and chose a caption to make it seem that he was idly sitting in his plaything—"one of the Senator's Favorite Recreations." Hearst's editors added the off-guard shot to this syntax of derision. Officeholders no longer control their public face. They can be "snapped," feet in the air or frozen to the sidewalk; they usually appear to be fleeing the camera or caught at playing a children's game of statue.[19]

The governed were not used to seeing the governors in this way outside a cartoon. *Cosmopolitan* had not published an unposed photo of an American politician before "The Treason of the Senate." The magazine had gone beyond the studio portrait before Hearst took control, showing reformers bent over a desk or gripping a telephone. Also, like the Hearst newspapers, candid shots of the rich at play were common, but *Cosmopolitan* had never printed a photograph designed to fit a political exposé. *McClure's* had been just as conservative with pictures. The boodlers and bosses of Lincoln Steffens's series appeared as they chose to appear before the camera. "Snap shots" in political stories were not unprecedented in 1906, but they had not stung. Wounding photographs linked to an attack with words formed a new arsenal for the press. A few months after the Phillips's series, for example, a photograph of the political establishment

in California appeared in most of the progressive publications
in that state as well as in national muckraking magazines. The
camera had caught a Republican celebrating his nomination for
the governorship in the company of the biggest money men in
the state. The candidate's fingers gripped the shoulder of Boss
Abraham Ruef of San Francisco. The photograph acquired a
name, "The Shame of California." Veteran reformers, especially
working for Hearst, made much bolder use of photographs towards the end of the first decade of the century. Muckraking
had hit upon a new way to picture men in power, anticipating
candid shots and even the "ambush" techniques of television.[20]

"The Treason of the Senate" overturned conventional reporting because it changed what the reader was to hear as well as
see. Phillips had contempt for the debates of Congress, and he
wanted the public to stop listening. He rarely quoted a senator
and gave only the haziest account of what their positions were
on the issues. Repeatedly he dismissed public debate as "sham
battles" designed only to fool naive citizens. "Orators of the
treason" pretended to disagree in order to disguise the conspiracies arranged in the committee rooms. To listen to these
men was to be caught up in this deception, Phillips explained,
for "all the speeches of these secret traitors to country and people
... abounded in virtue, piety, and patriotism. . . . " An honest
minority felt bound by senatorial courtesy and muffled criticism
so the hypocrisy of the majority was never exposed. Phillips
spoke of "the dust of senatorial debates" and described an atmosphere so close and fetid that a healthy citizen must keep
away. He marveled that the senators who sat through the debates did not break into laughter.[21]

"The Treason of the Senate" began by pointing out the "stu-
pidity" of the electorate and frequently offered a sneer at the
gullible public. Taunts at the average citizen crept into muckraking after the first discoveries about government. The general
public was scorned in *The Jungle* by Upton Sinclair, an exposé
that was frightening Americans at the time Phillips's series appeared. After 1906 Americans were not allowed to forget how

little they knew or to escape blame for their ignorance. The deceptions worked! This was the chorus of the investigative magazines, with Phillips and Sinclair the loudest voices. Sinclair took his story through several election campaigns, showing how bread and circuses produced any outcome the capitalists wanted. Voters were handled as efficiently as cattle in Packingtown. Phillips drew attention to the occult nature of politics, "the mysteries of the Senate—all its crafty, treacherous ways of smothering, of emasculating, of perverting legislation." A reader might reasonably conclude that the upper house consisted of nothing but buncombe speeches. "Slathering treason with cant," Phillips said, was the normal business of lawmakers. Behind the "black art of politics" stood "the Interests," —a term Phillips coined to describe the American plutocracy. He predicted that the lower and middle class would be crushed by this exercise of power in Washington. The humble citizen had only himself to blame. Phillips baited his readers, asking if the Senate's contempt was not justified.[22]

Phillips had built his reputation in fiction by mocking the political process, so his reports on the Senate could not have surprised his large number of faithful readers. The Americans in these novels, like Jurgis in Sinclair's *The Jungle*, lived through an anti-civics lesson. Machines decided elections. Bosses controlled their own party and, usually, the other one as well. Higher up "the Interests" bought the outcome plutocrats favored. Politics was a matter of "puppet peoples and puppet politicians" according to *The Cost* (1904). This was a tour of the "sewers of politics." "The Plum Tree, or, the Confessions of a Politician," made the cover of *Success Magazine* a month before the nation elected a president in 1904. The novel was a great success on the book lists the following year. In sending Phillips to the Senate in 1906 Hearst was asking little more than to make fact follow popular novels of the day.[23]

Phillips's point in fiction was the same he made as a reporter. America's trouble was not merely that the plutocracy ruled, but that honest exchange of views was impossible. In *The Great God*

Success (1901) an editor who dared to give space to all sides and to crusade for the right finally sold out. His wife froze in her chair as she heard the betraying editorial read. The general reader was cast as a helpless victim of the commercial ties of the press. One Hampden Scarborough was the hero of these bleak novels in which everyone else with virtue is impotent. He was the progressive cast as savior and modeled after Phillips's college friend, Albert J. Beveridge. Beveridge, a senator from Indiana, was eloquent, but also pragmatic as he worked for reform within the GOP. It is noteworthy that Hampden Scarborough's career was free of all those activities that would seem central to governing a democracy. There was no debating of positions or adjustments as more facts became known. Compromise and reconciliation were never goals, and minds were changed only as the leader cast a spell over a confused and frustrated public.

It was politics itself that was attacked in a good deal of the literature of reform. In *Success Magazine* Charles E. Russell condemned "the fatal virus of 'practical politics,' the very name of which is always a sign of something rotten." Alfred Henry Lewis told readers of *Human Life* that "politics is the art of arousing the ignorance of mankind." There was contempt not only for the compromises a practical politician must make but also for the calculating mind that seeks partial good in the political process. Muckrakers like Phillips and Sinclair turned from the dissection of democracy as it was to an orgastic vision of what it might become. At a convention, Scarborough's first words set off "huge waves of adulation, with his name shouted in voices hoarse and voices shrill like hissing foam on the triumphant crests of billows." Pauline Dumont, the betrayed wife of a corruptionist, listened to this voice and was seized: "Pauline felt as if she were lifted from her bodily self, were tossing in a delirium of ecstasy on a sea of sheer delight."[24]

Sinclair's Jurgis found political virtue the same way. He had learned that citizenship was a license to stuff ballots and that political work was all trickery and payoffs. He sank so low that he had only the warmth of a GOP rally to save him from the streets—"he must listen—he must be interested!" But a senator's address made him snore, and Jurgis was kicked out into the cold. Finally, a Socialist rally was salvation. The image of the slumbering labor giant brought the workers to their feet "and Jurgis was with them, he was shouting to tear his throat; shouting because he could not help it, because the stress of this feeling was more than he could bear. . . . There was an unfolding of vistas before him, a breaking of the ground beneath him, an upheaving, a stirring, a trembling; he felt himself suddenly a mere man no longer—there were powers within him undreamed of, there were demon forces contending, age-long wonders struggling to be born; and he sat oppressed with pain and joy, while a tingling stole down into his finger-tips, and his breath came hard and fast." Sinclair needed several hundred more words to describe a political conversion that was at once an ecstasy of body and soul.[25]

Progressives rarely made good cynics, and neither Phillips nor Sinclair could walk away from the political institutions that each condemned. Sinclair gave advice to the President—sometimes more than once a day—on how to regulate the meat packing industry through legislation. It was not until many months later that Sinclair acted as if he believed what he had shown readers of the *The Jungle*: piecemeal reform through the parties was a delusion. (Packingtown *had* federal meat inspectors, and this troubled the bosses not at all.) The *Cosmopolitan* articles fit into Hearst's campaign for the direct election of senators, and Phillips, too, put stock in this reform. He expected great things from a few insurgents in the Senate and believed an attack on the plutocracy might yet come from this body. The GOP, he once wrote, "has become chiefly a mask for burglarious operations and nauseating exploitations of helplessness and ignorance. But the moment of awakening is at hand. . . ."[26]

What were readers supposed to make of this reporting? How could a political process worthy of such contempt be fixed so quickly? How could a government of traitors doing the bidding of the wealthy disappear? Theodore Roosevelt touched the play of defeatism and hope within reform sentiment in an address on April 14, 1906, "The Man with the Muck-Rake."

Roosevelt's remarks, made during the dedication of the House Office Building on Capitol Hill, were calculated. He had tried out the argument weeks earlier before journalists likely to be in good spirits at a bibulous Gridiron Club dinner. The public address identified not a single story or reporter and was filled with encouragements to honest criticism, embracing even the attacks of "merciless severity." More, the president closed with a deep bow to the left and gave vague endorsement of a progressive tax on large fortunes. Some social critics did feel that the nice things they heard before Roosevelt punched them were not enough. As the reporters took offense at the suggestion that they delighted in filth, TR rushed to assure them *their* work was not being questioned. The president also conducted a long correspondence with Sinclair and lured Phillips to the White House for soothing treatment.[27]

TR's private papers show that he had Phillips and Sinclair uppermost in mind and that the term "muckraker" was designed to blacken their names and discredit their point of view. Writing in confidence to William Howard Taft, the President credited these muckrakers with "building up a revolutionary feeling." This was probably not TR's deepest concern in the spring of 1906. He reminded Taft that Republicans had stopped such threats before. In private as well as in public, the president seems to have worried more about political indifference than about revolution. Roosevelt told the crowd on Capitol Hill that an indiscriminate attack on the powerful "means the searing of the public conscience." He worried about "the hard scoffing spirit" and "the vacant mind" of citizens nurtured on exposés. In private the president fumed about what literature was now doing to politics. He had stopped halfway through Phillips's *The Plum Tree* in disgust but returned to it shortly after the muckrake speech on the urging of the editor of the *Saturday Evening Post*. In a letter to the journalist that was longer than any published review of the novel, TR spoke in confidence about how little the political process matched the story. "Now, I feel that almost each individual fact brought forward by Phillips is true by itself," the president conceded about *The Plum Tree*, "and yet these facts are so grouped as to produce a totally false impression."[28]

The criticism at base was that Phillips did not know politics, the mixture of motives that seemed so obvious to Roosevelt after a quarter century of public life. What most exasperated the president was that *sincere* men stood against his policies! Men "with no earthly interest at stake" could frustrate his will! TR seems to have grown angrier as he thought about it, and eleven days later he added a note to this letter about "The Treason of the Senate." Phillips's reporting was now more dangerous, the president said, for the articles "excite a hysterical and ignorant feeling against everything existing, good or bad. . . ."[29]

This was not quite fair. The editors of muckraking magazines were obsessed by charges that they were too negative, and they responded with demonstrations that this was not so. As in Phillips's and Sinclair's work, exposés were almost always connected with a piece of legislation that would set things right. Open one of these magazines at random and read for a half hour: there is assurance (probably more than once) that an aroused public opinion will fulfill the promise of democracy. But this said, the President was a discerning critic of the literature of muckraking. The process of government was usually denigrated so effectively that participation in it—even as a voter—was made to seem futile. The imaginative literature and reporting repelled the citizen from political life.

Of all the progressive journalists, Brand Whitlock knew best what he was talking about when he developed this theme. In the 1890s he left the Chicago press corps to become an assistant to the reform governor of the state. In the early years of the century Whitlock's name was continually before the nation as the mayor and great innovator of Toledo, Ohio, and the author of stories about how America was governed. William Dean Howells, the celebrated man of letters, called Whitlock's novel of a campaign for Congress "the best political story I know." The voters of Toledo returned Whitlock to office three times, and such was his popularity that he was continually asked to baptize, marry, and eulogize his constituents.[30]

Editors, especially at *McClure's*, sensed that Whitlock had something new to say about public life. Mere cynicism and elegantly expressed disgust were not by themselves new in political literature. There had been plenty of that in the bohemian world of Chicago journalism, and many across the nation knew of Mark Twain's fulminations as well as that wicked novel written by Henry Adams and published anonymously, *Democracy* (1880). The worst that could be said about the American experiment in government had already been said. Again, the distinctive feature of the muckrakers was not that they were first to say things, but that they were the first to say these things from *within* the political culture they described. What impressed writers of Howells's generation was that Whitlock wrote as someone who breathed the air of politics on the ward level and could create believable characters at home in this world.[31]

Whitlock was vastly more knowledgeable than Phillips about how public questions are settled but the mayor's eye was just as cold. During the Progressive Era Whitlock issued an autobiography testifying to his "disgust" with the old parties and customs. His biographer has noted "the almost visceral dislike" for politics in the early stories. In much of his fiction the political process was an invitation to nausea or boredom. Washington, for this muckraker, was not peopled with the lively rascals Twain and Adams had seen. Politics was posturing and indolence. Congressman Jerome Garwood in *The Thirteenth District* lived only to dodge any coalition that could send him back to his wife and law practice in Grand Prairie. Power and position translated into stuporous loafing: "To saunter over to the House at noon, to saunter back, to lean at the corner of the little bar in the Arlington, one foot cocked over the other, his broad hat on the back of his head, and the Havana cigar between his teeth tilted at an angle parallel with the line of his hat brim, thus preserving to the eye the symmetry of the whole striking picture he knew he made—this was existence for him." Whitlock was surely one of the first moralists to suggest that corruption in America did not keep bad rulers busy.[32]

The muckrakers scoffed at politics as they labored to make politics better. They said that traditional outlets for political feeling led the wrong way. Party and ethnic loyalty were snares that the good citizen must avoid. The agenda for the nation now consisted of complex, sobering problems. Is it likely that some in the electorate were driven away from politics by this message? Were some Americans less impressed by the example of activism the muckrakers set than by the perplexing and discouraging course of politics they wrote about so well? We do not have modern survey data to profile the citizens who stopped voting (and attending rallies) at the beginning of this century, but magazine circulation figures offer important clues to the impact of muckraking.

Between 1902 and 1912 about a dozen popular journals tried many times with exposé material. The effect in the marketplace was unpredictable. The circulation of *Everybody's* went from 150,000 to 700,000 in the course of the "Frenzied Finance" series. *Ridgway's* (under the same editorial hand that guided *Everybody's*) never caught on and quickly went bankrupt. *McClure's* found in muckraking simply a way to hold onto the large readership it had won in the 1890s. For all of Hearst's money, *Cosmopolitan* attracted few new readers with muckraking. The staff from *McClure's* that took charge of the *American Magazine* achieved no breakthrough in circulation. Both *Cosmopolitan* and *American Magazine* boosted their readership only after editors gave up, reluctantly, on investigative reporting. *Collier's* doubled its readership, to over half a million as it featured reform themes. The *Saturday Evening Post*, serializer of six novels by David Graham Phillips, climbed to one million circulation by 1910. The popular appeal of social criticism in the magazines was volatile but the editors' commitment to these stories was remarkably steady. This has become a familiar state of affairs in the mass media.

The magazine business in the Progressive Era looks very much like television networks in later decades, convinced by a political mood in the nation and a few hits that the public has unlimited appetite for programs blended to a formula. The popular recipe is the one sure to be, in time, force-fed.[33]

Perhaps the most important feature of muckraking was that it became such an ubiquitous and insistent trade practice. The number of magazines truly dedicated to reform has often been set too high, but the error stems from a correct perception by researchers: the investigation of social problems and impatience with the political *status quo* seems to be everywhere one looks in the periodical literature. It is reasonable to assume a readership in 20 million American homes. In a total population of about 90 million people, the great majority of American families with anything topical to read were exposed to muckraking material. No wonder Senator Beveridge in 1910 called the exposés a "people's literature" amounting to "almost a mental and moral revolution." Not all of this, of course, carried an extreme critique of government. But writers such as Phillips, Russell, Sinclair, and Steffens had a great deal of exposure, both as contributors and as celebrities in the news. As with any heresy, we may assume that their outlook grew congenial to citizens as it was merely described, or, indeed, as it was refuted. If muckraking did nothing more than break the silence over the wisdom of political participation in America, it did a great deal.[34]

What today would be called the "demographics" and "reader profile" of muckraking was discussed in 1905 by those sure judges of public taste, Finley Peter Dunne's Irishmen in the Archey Road saloon:

> "'It looks to me,' said Mr. Hennessy, 'as though this counthry was goin' to th' divvle.'
>
> 'Put down that magazine,' said Mr. Dooley. 'Now d'ye fell betther? I thought so. But I can sympathize with ye. I've been readin' thim mesilf.' "

Mr. Dooley said that he didn't used to read magazines, or when he did open one, "I'd frequently glance through it an' find it in me lap whin I woke up. Th' magazines in thim day was very ca'ming to the' mind.' " No more, Hennessy and Dooley agreed, as they reviewed the exposés of muckrakers. "Is there an institution that ins't corrupt to its very foundations? Don't you believe it."[35]

The extraordinary reach of muckraking meant that much of its audience had nothing like the first-hand knowledge and love of politics of a Mr. Dooley. The magazine distribution system was so efficient and the price so low that historians have spoken of a "revolution" in publishing. There was little cost in money or time to have these stories. Even citizens who did not ask for this material found it without looking far. Indeed, there was a system of rewards to see that they found it. In 1906 when *Success Magazine* organized a "People's Lobby" to fight a corrupt Congress, the editors offered deep discounts to subscribers who would take magazines such as *Good Housekeeping*, *Country Gentlemen*, and *Yachting*. These "clubbing" subscription plans also allowed a reader to combine magazines with a taste for reform, but the offers were advertised to sweep in readers with the widest variety of interests. The promises to subscription agents suggests that potential readers had trouble saying no at the front door. A boy or girl who could sign up thirty subscribers to *Human Life* was due to receive a Boston terrier sent in a crate from the magazine's office. If a subscriber signed up three neighbors for *Success Magazine*, at a dollar each, a 22–caliber rifle arrived as a premium![36]

The Americans who were exposed to muckraking were usually not experienced consumers of political revelations, and there is no sign that the Progressive Era brought an increase in the number of politically sophisticated readers. The circulation of the older, serious political journalism (such as the *Arena* and the *Nation*) remained small. A magazine even modestly successful at muckraking might have ten times the readers of these political journals. In the Progressive Era there was no sign that the public wanted more investigation of social problems than the popular magazines furnished. There is some reason to think that readers wanted less. Book publishers did not have the captive readers represented by a magazine subscription list, and they found no vast public existed for muckraking books. *The Jungle* was a best-seller and Phillips's fiction made respectable sales, but these were exceptions. *The Shame of the Cities* sold 3000 copies. "The Treason of the Senate" did not attract a book publisher in the Progressive Era. The mass taste for exposure was fully met by the magazines, reaching a public much larger than those actively curious and generally informed about political life.[37]

Modern students of communications have measured the effect of critical political reporting on a mass public with the aid of representative samples and control groups. This research has paid close attention to the signs of political malaise that we also seek to explain in the Progressive Era. Methodological disputes still flash between these researchers, but a growing body of evidence points to a connection between negative reporting of political life and the public's trust in government and sense of political efficacy. The crucial point for students of progressivism is the way less sophisticated consumers of political information seem most affected by critical reporting. Conclusions drawn from the response to news documentaries on television need little translation to apply to the public reached by muckraking in popular magazines at the beginning of the century:

> . . . news organizations have been compelled to bombard the American television audience with interpretive, sensational, aggressive, and anti-institutional news items. This content reaches and holds a unique audience, larger and more volatile than that attracted by any other medium. Many of the members of this unique audience are inadvertent to it. These inadvertent viewers tend to lack political sophistication: they cannot cope well with the type of news and information that the networks provide. But because the networks are too credible to be dismissed in their messages, these viewers respond to the content by growing more cynical, more frustrated, more despairing; they become increasingly less enamored of their social and political institutions.[38]

Today, this malaise probably has only a small direct effect on voting for the simple reason that American leadership has adjusted. In modern presidential elections, especially, candidates run against politicians as a class, politics as a profession and Washington as a community. At the beginning of the century neither party knew how to co-opt this diffuse discontent so skillfully. The anti-civics lesson of the popular press was, in its reach and clarity, new. In the Progressive Era the disillusionment with politics affected participation because neither the Plunkitts nor the Roosevelts could connect with a broad new cynicism about how the game was to be played.

Sermons on good citizenship are apt to spring from such discoveries. Serious students of politics—of the Progressive Era or in the 1980s—will not rush to judgment. Is democracy better off if ill-informed citizens feel more comfortable? Are wiser choices made by confident voters who are untouched by controversy? If the electorate shrinks to those who can surmount their frustrations, does the political system suffer? At the end of the Progressive Era, Walter Lippmann cited the lower turnouts for elections as a sign of what he had learned to accept in journalism and politics: there was now a "phantom public." The community to be counted on for informed choice and participation was small, and even these citizens must delegate important decisions to an elite. A recent summary of theories of democracy finds a consensus "that high levels of participation and interest are required from a minority of citizens only and, moreover, the apathy and disinterest of the majority play a valuable role in maintaining the stability of the system as a whole." The value of broad public interest in politics must not be taken for granted.[39]

A history of the press alone cannot fully explain basic changes in political behavior. Patterns of work, family life, and religious belief have much to do with notions of political efficacy and the appeal of elections. But the way political stories are told in the press has special importance in the study of what made citizens willing or unwilling to participate in government. Journalism can change more quickly than the fundamental relationships in

TWELVE MONTHS OF THIS EVERY YEAR. A drawing by H. T. Webster that first appeared in the Chicago Inter-Ocean. (*Literary Digest*, March 31, 1906)

life. In a society in which fundamentals are changing, journalism is common ground, defining and offering agendas for what is important (if anything) about the political process. Muckraking was important not because it was the source of alienation, but rather because it was a rapid transmitter of this anxiety among communities with different reasons to feel lost in the new urban nation. The language for politics in the investigative magazines is one of the few innovations of the Progressive Era pervasive enough to account for the broad withdrawal from elections.

What of the opinion leaders, the men and women with a stock of knowledge about political institutions? Did muckraking in the magazines weaken their faith in traditional politics? Conservatives in the Progressive Era thought this was happening. The "Treason of the Senate" was answered in the *New England Magazine* with the lament that in this slick form "the educated, discriminating element of the populace are prone to accept as gospel truth statements of alleged fact that would be laughed at if published in the ordinary newspaper channels of news."[40] Again, the breadth of the muckraking appeal gave it special power. These glossy magazines were not shunned by serious people, and the celebrity journalists were not quickly dismissed. Walter Lippmann, a college prodigy, was courted by his professors at Harvard, but just before he graduated in 1910 he turned to Lincoln Steffens to define his career. "What I have dreamed of doing is to work under you," Lippmann told Steffens. Unlike antebellum reform, the progressive movement was not hobbled by the reaction of an elite against the breakthroughs in mass publicity.[41] As in all successful periods of reform, there had to be a suspension of disbelief, a granting of some truths, however vaguely stated or wrong in detail. This is what the muckraking magazines brought about. Political reform turned on this consensus, but so too did a new disenchantment with politics.

In life as well as their art, the muckrakers wished to adjourn the traditional politics of party debate and conflict. Sinclair and Russell fled to the Socialist movement, then moved to more idiosyncratic political stands. A host of muckrakers relished their experiences engineering a unified public opinion in Washington during the World War. Lincoln Steffens set a classic model of dreamy, radical-sounding detachment. Disillusionment with the mainstream of American political life obviously owed much to the course of the war, but it was implicit in what the muckrakers had found as political reporters. This was a lesson they had taught well in an age of reform.

AFTERWORD

The American popular press began this century with both firm habits and new ideas about political reporting. It was the habits that proved most valuable to the political culture and the new ideas that were disruptive.

The heritage of political reporting set the course of the profession. Journalists expected to have a responsible position at the center of politics. In large part, reporters defined this role as the detection of the faults and inconsistencies of political leaders. Reporters and editors were not the cynics or detached observers they often claimed to be. They were stewards and moralists in the pattern established in the eighteenth century. The press thought it was its business to study what the government said and to picture how America was governed as vividly as possible. Usually this meant clinging to the narrative forms that were familiar, especially the exposé of lapses from republican virtue. Journalists insisted, on the basis of slender evidence, that the Founding Fathers had envisioned and blessed this reporting.

It is hard to overstate the importance of this outlook. The sense of social responsibility was a vital source of self-esteem and discipline in a profession that had neither an educational requirement nor a license by the state. The marketplace did not require journalists to teach civics. As sociologists such as David Riesman and Michael Schudson have observed, it is impossible to account for the space given to politics and public questions

222

as a business proposition. The traditional idealism in the profession and the acceptance of narrative forms such as the exposé provided the strongest force making journalists the patrons of politics.

The simultaneous drives for greater political influence and success in the marketplace were the source of many new problems in the Progressive Era. The redefinition of politics as a detached search for the truth—no more the ritual connected to a party—helped to bring the mass turnouts for elections to an end. The reach of national magazines into local affairs drew reporters to the center of power and built a dispiriting picture of how Americans were governed. New perspectives on politics, such as the opening to the underworld, made news more exciting; at the same time stories of this type tended to make the process of government seem dull, even pointless. Similarly, the camera that now could catch the politician off guard helped to reduce policy disputes to a clash of personalities. Government in the mass media was becoming a gallery of good and bad office holders, caught up in intrigues, that a citizen was rushed to judge.

The mission of journalism was at odds with its techniques. A profession that loved politics increasingly followed reporting conventions that made the public turn away. Gains in drawing attention to politics were often a loss in comprehension about how the political system worked. That easy vernacular of politics had broken down because the stories that the press now told, meant less to those listening.

ACKNOWLEDGMENTS

I have written this book to answer the questions I could not answer when I began to teach in the Graduate School of Journalism at the University of California, Berkeley. In large measure it has been the students and colleagues in this institution who helped me pose these questions and to understand their importance. I have also had financial support from the University. Barbara Loomis was an excellent Research Assistant. I am very grateful to the people who have offered general editorial advice: Edwin R. Bayley, Tom G. Goldstein, Ann W. Hale, David A. Hollinger, Carol H. Leonard, Barbara Loomis, David Lundberg, Sheldon H. Meyer, and David Nord. Richard Abrams and Ronald G. Walters kindly reviewed chapters in their special fields of interest. At the very end of this project I discovered that Michael E. McGerr was completing a comprehensive study of the decline of voting in the Progressive Era. Prof. McGerr, by sharing his manuscript, allowed me to make that happiest of discoveries among historians: that we agree on many things but have found quite different sources to make our cases.

Conferences held at the American Antiquarian Society and at Indiana University have allowed me to try out some of my ideas in an earlier form. Chapter Two is a revised version of my article in the *Journal of American History*, LXVII (June 1980), 26–40 and is reprinted with permission.

NOTES

Notes for Introduction

[1] Thomas J. Porter to James K. Polk, 23 Dec. 1832, in Herbert Weaver, ed, *The Correspondence of James K. Polk* (4 vols.: to date, Nashville, 1969–77), I, 586. There is a similar request, E. B. Smith to Willie P. Mangum, 8 Apr. 1834, in Henry T. Shanks, ed., *The Papers of Willie Pearson Mangum* (5 vols.: Raleigh, 1950–56), II, 139.

[2] Ronald P. Formisano, "Deferential-Participant Politics: The Early Republic's Political Culture, 1789–1840," *American Political Science Review*, LXVIII (June 1974), 487. Political interest remains a frank puzzle in much social science literature, see for example Thomas A. Kazee, "Television Exposure and Attitude Change: The Impact of Political Interest," *Public Opinion Quarterly*, VL (Winter 1981), 507–18. Other works relevant to the Introduction are discussed in the section For Further Reading.

1. "The Wicked Printer"

1. In 1751–52, the smallpox struck a third of the population of Boston, but no newspaper in the town admitted there was a major epidemic. See John Duffy, *Epidemics in Colonial America* (Baton Rouge, 1953), 1971 reprint, pp. 57–60.

2. Alan Dyer, *A Biography of James Parker, Colonial Printer* (Troy, N.Y., 1982), pp. 4–8, 147 notes the small amount of local news in the New York newspapers in the second quarter of the eighteenth century. John Kern, "Boston Press Coverage of Anglo-Massachusetts Militancy, 1733–1741," in *Newsletters to Newspapers: Eighteenth-Century Journalism*, ed. Donovan H. Bond and W. Reynolds McLeod (Morgantown, W. Va., 1977) makes the plausible claim that reports of mobs in Great Britain played into the thinking of colonial protesters. However, there is remarkably little evidence that colonial newspapers were important in this cultural borrowing.

3. *New-England Courant*, 7 Aug. 1721, no. 1, pp. 1–2. This is a continuation of

a letter by Douglass (signed "W. Philanthropos") that I have quoted from the Boston *News-Letter*, 24 July 1721, no. 912, p. 4.

4. Perry Miller, *The New England Mind: From Colony to Province* (Boston, 1961) [1953], p. 348.

5. *Courant*, 7 Aug. 1721, no. 1, p. 1; Boston *Gazette*, 23–30 Oct. 1721, no. 101, p. 3. Benjamin Colman, *Some Observations on the New Method of Receiving the Small Pox by Ingrafting or Inoculation* (Boston, 1721), p. 6. Zabdiel Boylston invited others to see his patients in July 1721, see his pamphlet, *An Historical Account of the Small Pox Inoculated in New England* (Boston, 1940) [1726], p. 4.

6. *Courant*, 14–21 Aug. 1721, no. 3, p. 1; Olga Elizabeth Winslow, *A Destroying Angel: The Conquest of Small Pox in Colonial Boston* (Boston, 1974), p. 51.

7. *Courant*, 11–18 Dec. 1721, no. 20, pp. 2, 4. *Courant*, 18–25 Dec. 1721, no. 21, p. 2; *Courant*, 25 Dec.- 1 Jan. 1721–22, no. 22, p. 2.

8. *Courant*, 27 Nov.- 4 Dec. 1721, no. 18, pp. 1–2.

9. *Courant*, 14–21 Aug. 1721, no. 3, p. 2; *Courant*, 7 Aug. 1721, no. 1, p. 1; *Courant*, 30 Oct.- 6 Nov. 1721, no. 14, p. 4.

10. *Courant*, 21–28 Aug. 1721, no. 4, p. 2; *Courant*, 30 Oct. - 6 Nov. 1721, no. 14, p. 1.

11. *Courant*, 25 Dec.- 1 Jan. 1721–22, no. 22, p. 1.

12. Increase Mather, letter published in the Boston *Gazette*, 22–29 Jan. 1722, p. 2. J. William T. Youngs, *God's Messengers: Religious Leadership in Colonial New England, 1700–1750* (Baltimore, 1976), pp. 100–102.

13. Cotton Mather, Diary, 1709–1724, in *Collections of the Massachusetts Historical Society*, no. 8, 7th ser. (Boston, 1912), p. 632 (16 July 1721) and p. 663 (9 Dec. 1721).

14. Historians of public opinion who have connected the development of the popular press with a growth of empathy in the eighteenth century usually fail to make this distinction, see for example Daniel Lerner, "Modernization: Social Aspects," *International Encyclopedia of the Social Sciences* (New York, 1968), IX-X, 393. On the elegy and the New England clergy see Gordon E. Geddes, *Welcome Joy: Death in Puritan New England* (Ann Arbor, 1981), pp. 131–33, 159–61.

15. Johan Huizinga, *The Waning of the Middle Ages* (New York, 1954), pp. 144–151, p. 150 quoted. Philippe Aries, *Western Attitudes Toward Death: From the Middle Ages to the Present* (Baltimore and London, 1974), pp. 56–57. David E. Stannard, *The Puritan Way of Death: A Study in Religion, Cultural, and Social Change* (New York, 1977), p. 121, notes some intriguing erotic motifs in Puritan gravestones of the seventeenth century.

16. Stannard, *The Puritan Way of Death*, pp. 108–117.

17. *Courant*, 4–11 Dec. 1721, no. 19, p. 2.

18. J. H. Powell, *Bring Out Your Dead: The Great Plague of Yellow Fever in Philadelphia in 1793* (Philadelphia, 1949), pp. 239–40, 258–59. On the strong impulse to politicize the catastrophe see Martin S. Pernick, "Politics, Parties, and Pestilence: Epidemic Yellow Fever in Philadelphia and the Rise of the First Party System," *William and Mary Quarterly*, 3d. ser., XXIX (Oct. 1972), 559–86.

19. Henry F. May and David Lundberg, in their survey of books in American libraries, 1700–1776, found Trenchard and Gordon in 37 contrasted with Voltaire,

26; Montesquieu, 10; Hobbes, 4; and Rousseau, 3 (Locke led with 41): "The Enlightened Reader in America," *American Quarterly*, XXVIII (Summer 1976). Cato's modern editor has studied the important role of these letters in the colonial press: David L. Jacobson, ed., *The English Libertarian Heritage* (Indianapolis, 1965), pp. li-lvii.

20. The *Courant* published "Reflections upon Libelling" in the sixth and seventh numbers, 4–11 Sept. and 11–18 Sept. 1721 (note, however, that no copy of number 7 survives—this is the only issue of the paper that is missing). "Of Flattery" appeared in the tenth and eleventh numbers, 2–9 Oct. and 9–16 Oct. 1721. "Cautions Against the Natural Encroachments of Power" was printed in the twelfth and thirteenth numbers, 16–23 Oct. and 23–30 Oct. 1721. I have quoted from the standard edition: Jacobson, *The English Libertarian Heritage*, pp. 74–75, 79, 81, 87. "Of Flattery" in *Cato's Letters or, Essays on Liberty . . .* , (4 vols.: London, 1748), II, 10–11, contains the praise of George I missing in the *Courant*, no. 11.

21. *Courant*, 27 Nov.- 4 Dec. 1721, no. 18, pp. 1–2.

22. Arthur Bernon Tourtellot, *Benjamin Franklin, The Shaping of Genius: The Boston Years* (Garden City, 1977), p. 266.

23. The ideals of impartiality and civic responsibility emerged together in the eighteenth century, especially among printers who found themselves cornered. See, for example, [Isaac Thomas] "Proposals for Circulating Thomas's Massachusetts Spy in the Town of Boston and Vicinity," in Mason I. Lowance, Jr., and Georgia B. Bumgardner, eds. *Massachusetts Broadsides of the American Revolution* (Amherst, 1976), p. 105; Wm. David Sloan, "The Journalist as Partisan: Views on American Journalistic Standards, 1789–1816," Paper presented to the History Division at the Association for Education in Journalism and Mass Communications Annual Convention, Corvallis, Ore., August, 1983; William F. Steirer, "Riding 'Everyman's Hobby Horse': Journalists in Philadelphia, 1764–1794," in *Newsletters to Newspapers*, ed. Bond and McLeod.

24. Douglass quoted in John B. Blake, *Public Health in the Town of Boston, 1630–1822* (Cambridge, 1959), p. 62.

25. Tourtellot, *Benjamin Franklin*, p. 438.

26. Clarence S. Brigham, *Journals and Journeymen* (Philadelphia, 1950), p. 80. "Every genealogist soon learns that it is a waste of time to search early newspapers for obituary notices because so little material of this character was printed," Clifford K. Shipton writes in the preface to *Index of Obituaries in Massachusetts Centinel and Columbian Centinel, 1784 to 1840* (5 vols.: Boston, 1961). This paper was an exception and marked the new interest of newspapers at the end of the eighteenth century.

2. News for a Revolution

1. Harbottle Dorr Papers, vol. II, preface (microfilm of original in Massachusetts Historical Society, Boston); for a full description see Bernard Bailyn, "The Indexes and Commentaries of Harbottle Dorr," *Proceedings of the Massachusetts*

Historical Society, LXXXV (1973), 21–35. The careful marking of political developments by reference to newspapers can also be followed in William Duane, ed. *Extracts from the Diary of Christopher Marshall, 1774–1781* (New York, 1969), reprint of 1877 edition.

2. This is the focus of Arthur M. Schlesinger, *Prelude to Independence: The Newspaper War on Britain, 1764–1776* (New York, 1958). Richard L. Merritt's quantitative study of the press, *Symbols of American Community, 1735–1775* (New Haven, 1966), concentrates on 1762–66.

3. The neglect of the community resulting in "newspapers without news" before the Revolution has been noted in passing by many scholars: Elizabeth C. Cook, *Literary Influences in Colonial Newspapers, 1704–1750* (New York, 1912), pp. 3–6; Frank Luther Mott, *American Journalism, A History: 1690–1960* (New York, 1962), pp. 51, 62; Donald H. Stewart, *The Opposition Press of the Federalist Period* (Albany, 1969), p. 4. Stephen Botein argues persuasively that printers "acted in such a way as to retard the development of a public forum where conflicts could be fully and continuously articulated" in "'Meer Mechanics' and an Open Press: The Business and Political Strategies of Colonial American Printers," *Perspectives in American History*, IX (1975), 192, 199. Anna Janney DeArmond, *Andrew Bradford, Colonial Journalist* (Newark, Del., 1949), pp. 117, 160–61, provides additional illustrations of the limited interest in politics before the 1760s. Gary B. Nash, *The Urban Crucible* (Cambridge, 1979) has marshaled the evidence to make the case for a strong political role of the press well before the Revolution, see especially pp. 85, 139–140, 142, 199–204. Jeffery A. Smith, "Impartiality and Revolutionary Ideology: Editorial Politics of the *South-Carolina Gazette*, 1732–1775," *Journal of Southern History*, XLIX (Nov. 1983), 511–26 also argues for continuity. Clearly, the activist press was not born in the 1760s, but I believe this decade was the beginning of newspapers with long-term commitments to controversy and a determination to make distant disputes fit into arguments close to home. Michael Schudson, *Discovering the News: A Social History of American Newspapers* (New York, 1978), finds that "the idea of 'news' itself was invented in the Jacksonian era" (p. 4).

4. William Bradford quoted by Botein, "'Meer Mechanics' and an Open Press," p. 191. In New York, seventeen years after Zenger's vindication, William Livingston attempted to make the *Independent Reflector* a political forum. After a year of political journalism Livingston sent his issues to the bindery with an epitaph for a title page, "Printed (until tyrannically suppressed)." William Livingston et al., *The Independent Reflector . . .*, ed. Milton M. Klein (Cambridge, 1963), p. 54. Alan Dyer, *A Biography of James Parker, Colonial Printer* (Troy, N.Y., 1982), pp. 37–40, 66, notes the timidity of printers in New York.

5. See, for example, Philip Davidson, *Propaganda and the American Revolution, 1763–1783* (Chapel Hill, 1941); Schlesinger, *Prelude to Independence*, pp. 20–47, 85–109; Botein, "Strategies of Colonial Printers," pp. 200–225.

6. *The Writings of John Dickinson*, ed. Paul L. Ford (Philadelphia, 1895), pp. 307, 312, 346; Charles M. Andrews, "The Boston Merchants and the Non-Importation Movement," *Publications of the Colonial Society of Massachusetts*, XIX (1916–17), 201. Carl F. Kaestle, "The Public Reaction to John Dickinson's *Farmer's Letters*," *Proceedings of the American Antiquarian Society*, LXXVIII (1968), 350–51.

Kaestle's total is an estimate; he did not have access to three South Carolina papers. He guessed correctly.

7. *Writings of John Dickinson*, p. 355.

8. *Ibid.*, p. 348.

9. *Ibid.*, pp. 322, 328, 348. Kaestle, "Public Reaction to John Dickinson's *Farmer's Letters*," pp. 352–53, estimates the total circulation to be 75,000 newspaper readers and only 2700 new pamphlet readers. On Dickinson's "simulated spontaneity," see *ibid.*, pp. 339–340. See also "A Citizen" [William Hicks], *Pennsylvania Gazette*, 17 Dec. 1767, p. 2.

10. Dorr Papers, vol. I, 781; *Pennsylvania Gazette*, 7 April 1768, p. 2; *Pennsylvania Chronicle*, 9–16 May 1768, p. 126. Similarly, the town of Lebanon cited the Farmer's "CERTAIN PRESCIENCE," and a newspaper poet sang, "He sees the Chains forg'd for your Infant Race" and does "unmask" the British government. *Pennsylvania Gazette*, 19 May 1768, p. 1, 28 April 1768, p. 3.

11. John Dickinson to James Otis, 5 Dec. 1767, in *Warren-Adams Letters: Being Chiefly a Correspondence among John Adams, Samuel Adams, and James Warren*, ed. Worthington Chauncey Ford (2 vols.: Boston, 1917–25), I, 3.

12. *Boston under Military Rule, 1768–1769, as Revealed in a Journal of the Times*, ed. Oliver M. Dickerson (Boston, 1936), p. 86.

13. *Ibid.*, pp. 37, 71.

14. *Ibid.*, pp. 71, 34, 42, 108.

15. *Ibid.*, pp. 88, 86. J. G. A. Pocock, *Politics, Language and Time: Essays on Political Thought and History* (New York, 1971), pp. 80–103. David J. Rothman, *The Discovery of the Asylum: Social Order and Disorder in the New Republic* (Boston, 1971), p. 8. *New York Weekly Journal*, 12 Nov. 1733, and 21 Jan. 1734.

16. *Boston Under Military Rule*, pp. 40, 34. There have been many attempts to find evidence to verify the reporting and all have been inconclusive: *ibid.*, x, xii; Schlesinger, *Prelude to Independence*, p. 101; Hiller B. Zobel, *The Boston Massacre* (New York, 1970), pp. 109–10. Boston newspapers were as caught up in the question of verification as is this scholarship. "Point out a single Instance of a false or unfair Representation," the Boston *Gazette* thundered against a critic of the journal, or "be content to be looked upon as having attempted to deceive the Public." Boston *Gazette*, 28 Nov. 1768, p. 2. For other defenses of this reporting, see Boston *Gazette*, 5 Dec. 1768, p. 2; Boston *Evening-Post*, 23 Jan. 1769, p. 3. Criticism appeared in the *Massachusetts Gazette*, 24 Nov. 1768, p. 1, 2 Dec. 1768, p. 1; Boston *Weekly News-Letter*, 8 Dec. 1768, p. 2, 29 Dec. 1768, p. 3. Harbottle Dorr studied his copy of the "Journal" and noted "but one mistake in the whole (that I know of)," Dorr Papers, vol. II, 411, 781. In fact propaganda and close questioning about the truth of reports arose together in the Boston papers.

17. Thomas Hutchinson, *The History of the Colony and Province of Massachusetts-Bay*, ed. Lawrence Shaw Mayo (3 vols.: Cambridge, 1936), III, 162. Francis Bernard is quoted in Zobel, *Boston Massacre*, pp. 109–10.

18. On the obsession with misrepresentation, see "Letters of Dennys De Berdt, 1757–1770," *Publications of the Colonial Society of Massachusetts*, XIII (1910–11), 343–44, 348–49, 352, 371, 389, 401. See also the Boston Town Records in *Reports of the Record Commissioners of the City of Boston*, ed. William H. Whitmore et al. (39

vols.: Boston, 1876–1909), XVI, 303–25; *Boston under Military Rule*, pp. 23–24, 31, 66, 82–83, 123. The "Journal" speculated that petty distortions would be found before the correspondence was seen: *ibid.* p. 50.

19. Thomas Hutchinson to Israel Williams, 18 Sept. 1769, Israel Williams Papers (Massachusetts Historical Society, Boston). See also Hutchinson to John Robinson, 24 July 1770, vol. XXVI, Massachusetts Archives (State House, Boston), and Hutchinson to Francis Bernard, 21 Jan. 1772, vol. XXVII, *ibid.* This is a collection of drafts of letters. I have consulted the typescript prepared by Catherine Barton Mayo and Malcolm Freiberg in the Massachusetts Historical Society for the names of recipients.

20. Boston *Gazette*, 14 Aug. 1769, p. 2. This is the language of the merchants' pledge to boycott of Aug. 11th. For similar threats, see *ibid.*, 9 Oct. 1769, p. 1, 20 Nov. 1769, p. 1. *Boston under Military Rule*, p. 100. Self-exposure remained an important form of Revolutionary action. See, for example, *Massachusetts Spy*, 10 Nov. 1774, p.1; Mason I. Lowance, Jr., and Georgia B. Bumgardner, eds. *Massachusetts Broadsides of the American Revolution* (Amherst, 1976), pp. 54–55. On shaming punishments see Michael S. Hindus, *Prison and Plantation: Crime, Justice, and Authority in Massachusetts and South Carolina, 1767–1878* (Chapel Hill, 1980), pp. 100–101.

21. Boston *Gazette*, 30 Oct. 1769, p. 1. Boston *Chronicle*, 14–17 Aug. 1769, p. 261, 21–24 Aug. 1769, pp. 269–70. The lists and commentaries continued through February 1770. See Andrews, "Boston Merchants," pp. 227–29, and Schlesinger, *Prelude to Independence*, pp. 104–8.

22. Boston *Chronicle*, 7–12 Sept. 1769, p. 290. The John Hancock case was explored in Mein's paper and the Boston *Gazette* during the last half of August 1769.

23. Boston *Chronicle*, 14–17 Aug. 1769, p. 261, 21–25 Sept. 1769, p. 306, 22–25 Jan. 1770, p. 32; Boston *Gazette*, 18 Sept. 1769, p. 3, 28 Aug. 1769, p. 3, 2 Oct. 1769, p. 4, 9 Oct. 1769, p. 1.

24. Clarence S. Brigham, *Paul Revere's Engravings* (Worcester, 1954), plates 14, 16. The latter is a broadside that combines Revere's illustration with newspaper commentary that recalled the stories in the "Journal." It has become a tradition, not challenged by recent scholars, to attribute a sketch of the bodies to Revere. See Esther Forbes, *Paul Revere and the World He Lived In* (Boston, 1942). Sinclair Hitchings, "A Broadside View of America," *Lithopinion*, V (Spring 1970), 68–69.

25. Hutchinson to Thomas Pownall 11 Oct. 1767, vol. XXV, Massachusetts Archives; Hutchinson to Bernard, 20 Sept. 1769, vol. XXVI, *ibid.*; Hutchinson to Bernard, 12 Aug. 1770, *ibid.*; Hutchinson, *History of the Colony and Province of Massachusetts-Bay*, III, 283–84.

26. Hutchinson to Bernard, 29 June 1773, vol. XXVIII, Massachusetts Archives; Boston *Gazette*, 14 June 1773, p. 2, 21 June 1773, p. 2, 28 June 1773, p. 2; *Massachusetts Spy*, 24 June 1773, p. 3.

27. "The Hutchinson Letters," *The Papers of Benjamin Franklin*, ed. Leonard W. Labaree et al. (25 vols. to date: New Haven, 1959—), XX, 550.

28. *Works of John Adams*, ed. Charles Francis Adams (10 vols.: Boston, 1850–56), IV, 120.

29. "A." (probably Samuel Adams) put the words in Hutchinson's mouth. Boston *Gazette* 2 Aug. 1773, p. 2. There are many similar verdicts: *ibid.*, 12 July 1773, p. 2, 19 July 1773, p. 3; *Massachusetts Spy*, 24 June 1773, p. 3, 22 July 1773, p. 3.

30. Dorr Papers, vol. IV, 24, 295, 1152, 1157–56. Bernard Bailyn, *The Ordeal of Thomas Hutchinson* (Cambridge, 1974), p. 244.

31. *Diary and Autobiography of John Adams*, ed. Lyman H. Butterfield (4 vols.: Cambridge, 1961), II, 84–85, III, 292.

32. Boston *Gazette*, 21 June 1773, p. 1, 28 June 1773, p. 3, 19 July 1773, p. 3. 2 Aug. 1773, p. 2, 23 Aug. 1773, p. 1.

33. Boston *Gazette*, 2 Aug. 1773, p. 2, 9 Aug. 1773, p. 1. For other critiques of Hutchinson as a reporter, see *ibid.*, 26 July 1773, p. 2; *Massachusetts Spy*, 24 June 1773, p. 3. For the hated words, see "The Hutchinson Letters," p. 546. See also Boston *Gazette*, 28 June 1773, p. 2; *Massachusetts Spy*, Supplement, 31 June 1773, p. 1; *Massachusetts Spy*, 1 July 1773, p. 3.

34. Boston *Gazette*, 2 Aug. 1773, p. 2, 19 July 1773, p. 3, *Massachusetts Gazette*, 15 July 1773, p. 1, 29 July 1773, p. 1, 5 Aug. 1773, pp. 1–3. Hutchinson conceded "there may be some inaccuracies thru inattention to a writing which was designed for one person only and perhaps for one cursory reading only," but he stuck by the "Philalethes" report that it had been a full turpentine barrel. Hutchinson to William Tryon, 6 July 1773, vol. XXVIII, Massachusetts Archives; Hutchinson, *History of the Colony and Province of Massachusetts-Bay*, III, 147, 292–93. The props of civil disobedience, because of their symbolic value, were taken as seriously as fully articulated ideas in English political life, and newspapers were a forum for debate on this important level. See John Brewer, *Party Ideology and Popular Politics at the Accession of George III* (Cambridge, Eng., 1976), pp. 182–84.

35. Soon, the patriots took the rhetorical use of the underworld to its logical conclusion. A single issue of the *New England Chronicle: or the Essex Gazette*, 8–15 June 1775, drew attention to the "armed ruffians" of the Crown and addressed the king as "the greatest CRIMINAL in England." Gen. Gates was compared to a thief, a robber, a murderer, and a pirate. The increased number of secular rituals in colonial society is noted by Robert Middlekauff, "The Ritualization of the American Revolution," in *The National Temper: Readings in American Culture and Society*, ed. Lawrence W. Levine and Robert Middlekauff (New York, 1972), pp. 100–110.

36. On the reversal of the criminal justice system in the rituals of protest see Dirk Hoerder, *Crowd Action in Revolutionary Massachusetts, 1765–1780* (New York, 1977), p. 46, and Peter Shaw, *American Patriots and the Rituals of Revolution* (Cambridge, 1981), p. 10. For the vital role of newspapers in the boycotts see "Extract from the Votes and Proceedings of the American Continental Congress," Boston *Gazette*,. 7 Nov 1774, p. 1; Dorr Papers, vol. IV, 368; Alfred L. Lorenz, *Hugh Gaine, A Colonial Printer-Editor's Odyssey to Loyalism* (Carbondale and Edwardsville, 1972), p. 58.

37. A systematic random sample of the four Boston newspapers published continuously between 1763 and 1773 shows that the percentage of these papers devoted to political news quadrupled. Mary Ann Patricia Yodelis, "Boston's

Second Major Paper War: Economic Politics and the Theory and Practice of Political Expression in the Press, 1763–1775" (Ph.D. diss., Univ. of Wisconsin, 1971), p. 565.

38. John Phillip Reid, *In a Rebellious Spirit: The Argument of Facts, the Liberty Riot, and the Coming of the American Revolution* (Philadelphia, 1979), see especially chaps. 1 and 13.

39. The reluctance of scholars who wish to see the Revolution "from the bottom up" to make imaginative use of newspapers is puzzling. Dirk Hoerder states, for example, "I have purposely refrained from selecting as sources 'important' newspapers. . . ." *Crowd Action in Revolutionary Massachusetts*, p. 14. Hoerder sees grievances of the lower class that the "radical" press did not articulate, but not the habits of mind that the patriot newspapers expressed. The crowds that attacked John Mein are a reminder that newspaper exposés were not over the heads of humble citizens. One way to link the culture of print with folk culture is explored in Robert Darnton, "Writing News and Telling Stories," *Daedalus*, CIV (Spring 1975), 175–94.

40. Bernard Bailyn, *The Ideological Origins of the American Revolution* (Cambridge, 1967); Gordon S. Wood, *The Creation of the American Republic, 1776–1787* (Chapel Hill, 1972), pp. 1–124; Pauline Maier, *From Resistance to Revolution: Colonial Radicals and the Development of American Opposition to Britain, 1765–1776* (New York, 1972), pp. 161–97.

41. Brewer, *Party Ideology and Popular Politics*, pp. 174, 176; G. A. Cranfield, *The Development of the Provincial Newspaper, 1700–1760* (Oxford, 1962), p. 29; Botein, "Strategies of Colonial Printers," p. 197. Benjamin Franklin's "Apology for Printers" (1731), is a representative statement of this modesty before the Revolution. *Papers of Benjamin Franklin*, I, 194–99.

42. Bernard Bailyn, *The Origins of American Politics* (New York, 1968), p. 125. On the tortuous path to a libertarian theory of the press, see Leonard W. Levy, *Emergence of a Free Press* (New York, 1985). For a perceptive account of how polemics nurtured claims to impartiality see William F. Steirer, "Riding 'Everyman's Hobby Horse': Journalists in Philadelphia, 1764–1794," in *Newsletters to Newspapers: Eighteenth-Century Journalism*, ed. Donovan H. Bond and W. Reynolds McLeod (Morgantown, W. Va., 1977), especially pp. 271–73.

Towards the Nineteenth Century

1. Trenton *True American*, 26 July 1802 cited in William David Sloan, "The Party Press: The Newspaper Role in National Politics, 1789–1816" (Ph.D. diss., University of Texas, Austin, 1981). Glyndon G. Van Deusen, *Thurlow Weed: Wizard of the Lobby* (Boston, 1947), p. 20. William H. Hallock, *Life of Gerard Hallock* (New York, 1869), 1970 reprint, p. 15. See also Charles Henry Ambler, *Thomas Ritchie, A Study in Virginia Politics* (Richmond, 1913), pp. 294–95. The editor's view of non-paying subscribers is in [Cyrus Bradley] *Biography of Isaac Hill* (Concord, N.H., 1835), p. 23; for more laments see Clarence S. Brigham, *Journals and Journeymen* (Philadelphia, 1950), pp. 23–26.

2. Joseph Tinker Buckingham to Daniel Webster, 11 May 1832 in Charles M. Wiltse and Harold Moser, eds., *The Papers of Daniel Webster* (ser. 1, 5 vols. to date, Hanover, N.H. and London, 1974–), III, 170.

3. David Hackett Fischer, *The Revolution in American Conservatism* (Chicago, 1965), 1975 ed., p. 131. Allan Nevins, *The Evening Post* (New York, 1922), p. 26; Webster to Nicholas Biddle, 12 May 1835, in Wiltse and Moser, eds., *The Papers of Daniel Webster*, IV, 45; Amos Kendall to Henry Clay, 20 June 1822, in James F. Hopkins and Mary W. M. Hargreaves, eds., *The Papers of Henry Clay* (7 vols. to date: Lexington, Ky., 1959–), III, 236. Beman Brockway, *Fifty Years in Journalism* (Watertown, N.Y., 1891), p. 16.

4. The best guide to this literature is David Paul Nord, "The Evangelical Origins of Mass Media in America, 1815–1835," *Journalism Monographs*, no. 85 (May 1984), pp. 6, 18, 20–21. See also the important essay by Nathan O. Hatch, "Elias Smith and the Rise of Religious Journalism in the Early Republic," in William L. Joyce et al., eds., *Printing and Society in Early America* (Worcester, 1983), pp. 250–77.

3. "Unfeeling Accuracy"

1. Frances Trollope, *Domestic Manners of the Americans* (New York, 1949) [1832], pp. 102–3.

2. "Speeches in Congress," *North American Review*, XXVI (Jan. 1828), 158–63.

3. Frederick S. Siebert, *Freedom of the Press in England, 1476–1776* (Urbana, 1952), pp.346–63; Michael MacDonagh, *The Reporter's Gallery* (London, 1911), Chap. 13; Worthington C. Ford, ed., *Broadsides, Ballads, &c. Printed in Massachusetts, 1639–1800* (Boston, 1922), pp. 6–7. Leonard W. Levy, *Emergence of a Free Press* (New York, 1985), pp. 45, 74. This edition misprints the date the New York Assembly first warned printers. It was in 1745. Franklin was on occasion a broker who brought political speech to readers. His pride and great caution are clear in *The Autobiography of Benjamin Franklin*, Leonard W. Labaree et al., ed. (New Haven and London, 1964), pp. 121, 125, 127.

4. Daniel N. Hoffman, *Governmental Secrecy and the Founding Fathers: A Study in Constitutional Controls* (Westport, 1981), pp. 14–15. J. Edwin Hendricks, *Charles Thomson and the Making of a Nation, 1729–1824* (Rutherford, N.J., 1979), pp. 16, 130; Merrill Jensen, ed., *The Documentary History of the Ratification of the Constitution*, (2 vols. to date: Madison, 1976—) I, *Constitutional Documents and Records, 1776–1787*, pp. 34–35, 322–23; II, *Ratification of the Constitution by the States, Pennsylvania*, pp. 36, 40–42, see pp. 324, 644 for the considerable problems of authenticating what was said in this state. Raymond Walters, Jr., *Alexander James Dallas, Lawyer, Planter, Financier, 1759–1817* (Philadelphia, 1943), pp. 18–20. Jack N. Rakove, *The Beginnings of National Politics: An Interpretive History of the Continental Congress* (New York, 1979), pp. 354–55.

5. Donald H. Stewart, *The Opposition Press of the Federalist Period* (Albany, 1969), pp. 459–60. Elizabeth G. McPherson, "The Southern States and the Reporting of Senate Debates, 1789–1802," *Journal of Southern History*, XII (May 1946), 222–25, 239–40; F. B. Marbut, *News from the Capital, The Story of Washington Reporting*

(Carbondale and Edwardsville, 1971); William E. Ames, *A History of the National Intelligencer* (Chapel Hill, 1972).

6. On the limited knowledge members of the Continental Congresses had of one another see Rakove, *Beginnings of National Politics*, pp. 44, 127–31; for the early congresses see Noble E. Cunningham, Jr., *The Process of Government Under Jefferson* (Princeton, 1978), p. 253.

7. Noble E. Cunningham, Jr., *The Jeffersonian Republicans: The Formation of Party Organization, 1789–1801* (Chapel Hill, 1957), p.193. Clara Hannah Kerr, *The Origin and Development of the United States Senate* (Ithaca, 1895), pp. 175–76. Rhys Isaac, *The Transformation of Virginia, 1740–1790* (Chapel Hill, 1982), has an acute discussion of the oral culture in political life, pp. 121–24, 245–46, 266–69. Charles M. Cooke, *The American Codification Movement: A Study of American Antebellum Legal Reform* (Westport, 1981), pp. 9, 30–31. Michael Kammen has suggested that "the most meaningful generalization one can make about early New York is that this was an aural culture. . . . " *Colonial New York, A History* (New York, 1975), pp. 96–97.

8. Richard Beeman, *Patrick Henry* (New York, 1974), pp. xi, 201n. Computer analysis has deepened doubts about the authenticity of Henry's published speeches, but there is good reason to believe that the oral tradition preserved an important part of his message—see Charles L. Cohen, "The 'Liberty or Death' Speech: A Note on Religion and Revolutionary Rhetoric," *William and Mary Quarterly*, 3d ser., XXXVIII (Oct. 1981), 702–17. Adrienne Koch, ed., *Notes of Debates in the Federal Convention of 1787 Reported by James Madison* (Athens, Ohio, 1966), pp. viii-ix. Irving Brant concluded that Madison held back the notes to increase the value of the literary property for his family and to avoid having his own arguments for broad federal authority during the Convention used against his later defense of state sovereignty. Brant attributed a few mutilations of the manuscript to Madison's embarrassment over the record of what he had said, see *James Madison, Father of the Constitution, 1787–1800* (New York, 1950), pp. 21, 86.

9. On the development of Parliamentary reporting see two excellent essays in George Boyce, James Curran, and Pauline Wingate, eds., *Newspaper History from the Seventeenth Century to the Present Day* (Beverly Hills, 1978): Philip Eliot, "Professional Ideology and Organisational Change: The Journalist Since 1800;" and Anthony Smith, "The Long Road to Objectivity and Back Again: The Kinds of Truth We Get in Journalism." MacDonagh, *Reporter's Gallery*, pp. 136, 139; Thomas Anderson, *History of Shorthand* (London, 1882), p. 221. Robert L. Haig, *The Gazetteer, 1735–1797* (Carbondale and Edwardsville, 1960), pp. 90–92.

10. John Carey, *The System of Short-Hand Practiced by Mr. Thomas Lloyd, in Taking Down the Debates of Congress . . .* (Philadelphia, 1793), Evans no. 25,252, p. 16.

11. Bache spoke out in his *General Advertiser (Aurora)*, 16 Nov. 1792, p. 3; see also 20 Nov. 1792, p. 3, 28 Nov. 1792, p. 3, 19 Dec. 1792, p. 2 and 28 Feb. 1793. On editing and spitting see the *Aurora*, 7 Feb. 1798, pp. 2–3. Eugene Perry Link, *Democratic-Republican Societies, 1790–1800* (New York, 1942), p. 160; Philip S. Foner, ed., *The Democratic-Republican Societies, 1790–1800* (Westport and London, 1976), pp. 10–11, 36, 107, 226, 280, 394. McPherson, "The Southern States and

the Reporting of Senate Debates," pp. 223–46 may give too much credit to the South, see Hoffman, *Secrecy and the Founding Fathers*, p. 278 note 48.

12. In the upper house the failed reporting project was Thomas Carpenter, *The American Senator* (Philadelphia, 1796). The work of the republic's most notorious reporter can be followed in James Thomson Callender, *The History of the United States from 1796* (Philadelphia, 1797); *The Prospect Before Us* (Richmond, 1800).

13. *The Journal of William Maclay, United States Senator from Pennsylvania, 1789–1791* (New York, 1965), pp. 2, 132–33, 177 (quoted); *Annals of Congress*, 1st Cong. 1st Sess. (Philadelphia, 1789–90), I, 952–56, 1095–98. *Columbian Centinel*, 1 March 1794, p. 2 and 8 March 1794, p. 1. As late as 1842 a major New York paper sent an unqualified novice as its only reporter on Capitol Hill, see J. Watson Webb to Willie P. Mangum, 12 Dec. 1842, in Henry T. Shanks, ed., *The Papers of Willie Pearson Mangum* (5 vols.: Raleigh, 1950–56), III, 402.

14. Noble E. Cunningham, Jr., *Circular Letters of Congressmen to Their Constituents, 1789–1829* (3 vols.: Chapel Hill, 1978), marks the discovery of this material. Ames, *National Intelligencer*, pp. 49–50, 59–60, 81; Cunningham, *The Jeffersonian Republicans in Power*, p. 266. William Plumer's *Memorandum of Proceedings in the United States Senate, 1803–1807*, ed. Everett S. Brown (New York, 1923), p. 42.

15. [Cyrus P. Bradley] *Biography of Isaac Hill* (Concord, N. H., 1835), pp. 115–118. Anne C. Lynch, "A Sketch of Washington City," *Harper's New Monthly Magazine*, VI (Dec. 1852), 4. Caleb Atwater, *Mysteries of Washington City* (Washington, 1844), pp. 148–49. George W. Julian, *Political Recollections, 1840 to 1872* (Chicago, 1884), pp. 105–6, 108. James Sterling Young, *The Washington Community, 1800–1828* (New York, 1966), p. 97. T. N. Parmelee, "Memoirs of an Old Stager," *Harper's New Monthly Magazine*, XLIX (Jan. 1874), 255–56. This serialized memoir was published anonymously and Marbut, *News from the Capital*, says the authorship rests on the inferences of specialists (chap. 5, note 13). Apparently these scholars did not have access to the index *Harper's* published for vol. XLIX which named the author of the series.

16. *Plumer's Memorandum*, p. 449; Martin I. J. Griffin, "Thomas Lloyd Reporter ot the First House of Representatives of the United States," *Records of the American Catholic Historical Society of Philadelphia*, III (1888–89), 225; Mathew Carey *Autobiography* (New York, 1942) [1837], p. 12; Callender, *History of the United States from 1796*, p. 279.

17. Joseph T. Buckingham, *Personal Memoirs and Recollections of Editorial Life* (2 vols.: Boston, 1852). Buckingham and Samuel L. Knapp were early Washington reporters and their reports for the *New England Galaxy* are conveniently available here: I, 219 (Knapp quoted). The book Knapp published in 1829 has been reprinted as *American Cultural History, 1607–1829* (Gainesville, 1961), p. 217. Ames, *National Intelligencer*, p. 177. Robert G. Gunderson, "The Southern Whigs," in Waldo W. Braden, ed., *Oratory in the Old South* (Baton Rouge, 1970), pp. 114–15. James A. Shackford, *David Crockett: The Man and the Legend* (Chapel Hill, 1956), pp. 128–31, 134, 156–63, 168, 172–73 and 181–89.

18. Alvin M. Josephy, Jr., *On the Hill: A History of the American Congress from 1789 to the Present* (New York, 1979), p. 155; [J. G. Palfrey] "Congressional

Eloquence," *North American Review*, LII (Jan. 1841), 115; [A. Rhodes] "Speech-Making in Congress," *Scribner's Monthly*, VII (Jan. 1874), 297.

19. Glover Moore, *The Missouri Controversy, 1819–1821* (University of Kentucky, 1953), on non-reported speeches see pp. 32, 41, 46, 55, 97–98, 160, 295, 308; 217 quoted. For additional information on Clay see Frederick Merk, *Fruits of Propaganda in the Tyler Administration* (Cambridge, 1971), p. 26; James F. Hopkins and Mary W. M. Hargreaves, eds., *The Papers of Henry Clay* (7 vols. to date, Lexington, Ky., 1959–), I, 847–48. The published record of the Vesey investigation does not identify the edition of the speech by Senator King that this black leader used, see Robert S. Starobin, ed., *Denmark Vesey, The Slave Conspiracy of 1822* (Englewood Cliffs, 1970), pp. 48, 100; Moore, *The Missouri Controversy*, pp. 55–56, 176–77; Robert Ernst, *Rufus King* (Chapel Hill, 1968), p. 371. Cunningham, *Circular Letters*, I, xxxiv, III, 1045–1126, the letter that reached Jefferson is reprinted pp. 1109–15.

20. "Autobiography of Martin Van Buren," in *Annual Report of the American Historical Association for the Year 1918* (2 vols.: Washington, 1920), II, 215. Andrew Jackson to William Hayden, Jr., 30 March 1824, in John Spencer Bassett, ed., *The Correspondence of Andrew Jackson* (7 vols.: Washington, 1926–35), III, 243. Robert V. Remini, *Andrew Jackson and the Course of American Freedom, 1822–1832* (2 vols.: New York, 1981), II, 234–35.

21. Ben: Perley Poore, *Perley's Reminiscences of Sixty Years in the National Metropolis* (2 vols.: Philadelphia, 1886), I, 215; Dallas C. Dickey, *Sergeant S. Prentiss, Whig Orator of the Old South*, (Baton Rouge, 1945), does much to confirm Poore's judgment (pp. 134, 140–41, 158, 215). On Randolph see Henry A. Wise, *Seven Decades of the Republic* (Philadelphia, 1881), p. 86; McPherson, "The History of Reporting the Debates and Proceedings of Congress," pp. 86, 88. Nathan Sargent, *Public Men and Events* (2 vols.: Philadelphia, 1875) I, 125–26; Ames, *National Intelligencer*, pp. 161–62. George Hoadley to Jeremiah Evarts, Feb. 5, 1807, Virginia Historical Society (photostat) is an acute survey of both houses by the Federalist reporter for the *United States Gazette*. It is noteworthy that this observer equated power with speaking ability in Congress at this time.

22. Hugh McCulloch, *Men and Measures of Half a Century* (New York, 1889), p. 492.

23. "Extracts from the Journal of Henry J. Raymond," *Scribner's Monthly*, XIX (Nov. 1879), 58. Robert C. Winthrop, "Webster's Reply to Hayne, and His General Methods of Preparation, *Scribner's*, XV (Jan. 1894), 118–28. William A. Croffut, *An American Procession, 1855–1914* (Boston, 1931), p. 6. Charles T. Congdon, *Reminiscences of a Journalist* (Boston, 1880), pp. 60–61. See McPherson, "The History of Reporting the Debates and Proceedings of Congress," pp. 104, 107–10, 113–14, 181. Webster's contemporary, George Ticknor Curtis, noted the unprecedented flow of carefully edited speeches to voters in the first biography of the senator: *Life of Daniel Webster* (2 vols.: New York, 1872), I, 366. On the first presidential interview see Charles C. Layton, *Little Mack, Joseph B. McCullagh of the St. Louis Globe-Democrat* (Carbondale and Edwardsville, 1969), pp. 42, 50–55.

24. Charles Francis Adams, ed., *Memoirs of John Quincy Adams, Comprising Portions of his Diary from 1795–1848* (12 vols.: Philadelphia, 1874–77), VIII, 437;

IX, 211–12, 218–19. Allan Nevins, ed., *The Diary of John Quincy Adams, 1794–1845* (New York, 1928), p. 509.

25. Culver H. Smith, *The Press, Politics, and Patronage* (Athens, Ga., 1977), surveys this field. Roy Meredith, *Mathew Brady's Portrait of an Era* (New York, 1982), p. 93.

26. Thomas H. Benton, ed., *Abridgment of the Debates of Congress from 1789 to 1856* [1850] (16 vols.: New York, 1857–61), I, viii-ix, 6; XVI, 522, 541. "Benton's Congressional Debates," *United States Democratic Review*, XL (Nov. 1857), 435; *The Congressional Globe*, 31st Cong., 1st Sess. XXI (1850), 1480–81. Before the *Abridgment* appeared the *Southern Quarterly Review* had examined Benton's memoirs and asked him not "to embalm recriminations," XXVII (April 1855), 291. Giddings to Charles Sumner, 29 April 1861, in George W. Julian, *The Life of Joshua R. Giddings* (Chicago, 1892), p. 384. William Nisbet Chambers, *Old Bullion Benton: Senator from the New West* (Boston and Toronto, 1956), pp. 425, 431, 436, 438. George Alfred Townsend, *Washington, Outside and Inside* (Cincinnati, 1873), pp. 364–66. Oliver Dyer commented on Benton's earlier efforts to control reporting in *Great Senators of the United States Forty Years Ago* (New York, 1889), pp. 206–7. Benton's exchange with Foote seems to have been the first piece of congressional business witnessed by a woman with an assigned place in the reporters' gallery, see Jane Grey Swisshelm, *Half a Century* (Chicago, 1880), pp. 130–31.

27. Sargent, *Public Men and Events*, II, 46–49; Poore, *Reminiscences*, I, 161–62, 301–2. Sargent said there was a rule against reading speeches in Parliament and he urged Americans to adopt this practice. James Parton, "The Pressure Upon Congress," *Atlantic*, XXV (Feb. 1870), 148–49. T. N. Parmelee, a correspondent for the New York *Herald*, also noted this change in debate with sadness— see "Recollections of an Old Stager," *Harper's New Monthly Magazine*, XXXXVII (July 1873), 254.

28. Poore, *Reminiscences*, I, 400, II, 525. Poore, "The Place of Charles Sumner in History," *The International Review*, V (Jan. 1878), 64–74, is a cool view of this "writer of parliamentary orations" (p. 70). The only comprehensive study is Joseph Patrick McKerns, "Benjamin Perley Poore of the Boston Journal: His Life and Times as a Washington Correspondent, 1850–1887" (Ph.D. diss., Univ. of Minn., 1979). Lambert A. Wilmer, *Our Press Gang* (Philadelphia, 1859), most often indicts papers in New York and Philadelphia, but Wilmer learned his first lessons in Washington working for Duff Green. In his "boyish simplicity" Wilmer imagined "that *correct moral deportment* was one of the necessary qualifications of the political journalist!" (p. 22).

29. David Donald, *Charles Sumner and the Coming of the Civil War* (New York, 1960), pp. 214–17, 282, 287, 290–94, 354 (quoted).

30. *Plumer's Memorandum*, pp. 448–50. Donald, *Charles Sumner and the Coming of the Civil War*, pp. 356–57, and *Charles Sumner and the Rights of Man* (New York, 1970), pp. 547–48. Beeman Brockway of the New York *Tribune* recalled an instance when the senator seemed indifferent to republication: *Fifty Years in Journalism* (Watertown, N.Y., 1891), pp. 174–75. There is evidence of Sumner's keen interest in shepardling his speeches into the party press, see his letter to John Bigelow [Aug. 1852] in John Bigelow, *Retrospections of an Active Life* (5 vols.: New

238 *Notes to pages 86–90*

York, 1909–13), I, 126–29. Sumner's Republican colleague John P. Hale similarly discounted the Senate as an audience in 1858, see Allan Nevins, *Ordeal of the Union* (2 vols.: New York, 1947), I, 96. Eric Foner has pointed out that this was also the plan of the Republican senator William H. Seward in the debates on slavery: *Free Soil, Free Labor, Free Men: The Ideology of the Republican Party before the Civil War* (New York, 1971), p. 7. At times Seward seems to have matched Webster's energy in editing reports of his speeches, see John W. Forney, *Anecdotes of Public Men*, (2 vols.: New York, 1891), I, 424.

31. The South had begun to fear full reporting soon after their congressmen won this reform, see *Plumer's Memorandum*, p. 128. Dwight L. Dumond, "William Lowndes Yancey," *Dictionary of American Biography*, Dumas Malone, ed. (21 vols.: New York, 1928–36), XX, 592–95; Robert T. Oliver, *History of Public Speaking in America* (Boston, 1965), pp. 205–6; John Witherspoon Dubose, *The Life and Times of William Lowndes Yancey* (2 vols.: New York, 1942) [1892], I, 91–92, 134, 266, 310–11. Other prominent secessionists were print-shy, see H. Hardy Perritt, "The Fire-Eaters," in *Oratory in the Old South*, Waldo W. Braden, ed. (Baton Rouge, 1970), pp. 238, 241. Clement Eaton, *Freedom of Thought in the Old South* (Durham, 1940), p. 78, on circulation figures.

32. Philip Kinsley, *The Chicago Tribune, Its First Hundred Years* (2 vols.: New York, 1943), I, 56–58, 84, 86; *The Collected Works of Abraham Lincoln*, Roy P. Basler et al., eds. (9 vols.: New Brunswick, 1953–55), II, 544; III, 144, 365. Robert S. Harper, *Lincoln and the Press* (New York, 1951), p. 20. Don E. Fehrenbacher has noted the unusual behavior of the press in his invaluable discussion of this campaign in *Prelude to Greatness: Lincoln in the 1850s* (Stanford, 1962). Donald W. Riddle, *Congressman Abraham Lincoln* (Urbana, 1957), p. 49.

33. Saul Sigelschiffer, *The American Conscience, The Drama of the Lincoln-Douglas Debates* (New York, 1973), p. 177. *Collected Works of Abraham Lincoln*, III, 144, 365. Kingsley, *The Chicago Tribune*, I, 57. Horace White, *The Lincoln and Douglas Debates* (Chicago, 1914), p. 16. White had some distance on the Lincoln legend. He had said earlier, and repeated in this book (p. 31), that a speech by Douglas on the eve of the Civil War impressed him more than any address he had heard Lincoln make.

34. *Collected Works of Abraham Lincoln*, III, 116, 221, 280, 300, 327–28. J. McCann Davis, *Abraham Lincoln: His Book, A Facsimile Reproduction* (New York, 1901) is the first of his two campaign scrapbooks.

35. Lincoln's second scrapbook has been published: *The Illinois Political Campaign in 1858* [Washington, 1958], pp. 2–3, 5–7, 9. Robert Gerald McMurtry, "The Different Editions of the 'Debates of Lincoln and Douglas'," *Illinois State Historical Society Journal*, XXVII (April 1934), p. 95. William H. Herndon and Jesse W. Weik, *Abraham Lincoln, The True Story of a Great Life* (2 vols.: New York, 1893) II, 302 is one source for the belief that Lincoln did not read books thoroughly.

Another sign of the new interest in verbatim records of political activities was the reports of the party conventions of 1860. *Caucuses of 1860* (Columbus, 1860) was published by the same firm that did the Lincoln-Douglas debates, and used by the Republicans during the campaign. This volume was the work of the rising young reporter Murat Halstead. Robert W. Johannsen, *Stephen A. Douglas* (New York, 1973), p. 783.

36. George W. Julian, *Speeches on Political Questions*, L. Maria Child, ed. (New York, 1872), p. 144. Julian, *Political Recollections*, p. 161. The New York *Tribune*, 23 June 1860, also welcomed the publication of speeches by hated Democrats, see the reprint in James S. Pike, *First Blows of the Civil War* (New York, 1879), p. 523.

37. The quoted phrase is from the perceptive discussion in Young, *The Washington Community*, pp. 149–50, 252. Alexis de Tocqueville, *Democracy in America* (New York, 1956) vol. I, chap. XI, esp. p. 193. Joel H. Silbey, *The Shrine of Party: Congressional Voting Behavior 1841–1852* (Pittsburgh, 1967). In the course of his quantitative analysis, Allan G. Bogue has noted the importance of the comprehensive reporting at mid-century, *The Earnest Men, Republicans of the Civil War Senate* (Ithaca and London, 1981), p. 296.

38. Michael F. Holt, *The Political Crisis of the 1850s* (New York, 1978), p. 15. The role of editors in restricting information about their political allies can be studied in Thurlow Weed, *Autobiography of Thurlow Weed* (2 vols.: Boston, 1884), I, 372–73. Similarly, in 1844 Henry Clay, the Whig candidate for president, had great difficulty getting his "Raleigh letters" published in the fiercely Whig *National Intelligencer*, see Ames, *National Intelligencer*, p. 270.

39. Charles T. Congdon, *Tribune Essays* (New York, 1869), p. 85. New York *Weekly Tribune*, May 22, 1858; Glyndon G. Van Deusen, *William Henry Seward* (New York, 1967), p. 127. Nevins, *Ordeal of the Union*, I, 95–96. Wayne E. Fuller, *The American Mail, Enlarger of the Common Life* (Chicago and London, 1972), p. 290.

40. Cunningham, *Circular Letters*, I, xix–xx, xxix–xxx. Riddle, *Congressman Abraham Lincoln* p. 74. Hoffman, *Governmental Secrecy and the Founding Fathers*, pp. 92, 123, 125, 194–97. The 'XYZ' Affair of 1798, taken up by angry Federalists, did result in a circulation above 10,000.

41. On the 1970s see Norman J. Ornstein, "The Open Congress Meets the President" in Anthony King, ed., *Both Ends of the Avenue, the Presidency, the Executive Branch, and Congress in the 1980s* (Washington, 1983), pp. 185–211, especially 200–202. Pike, *First Blows of the Civil War*, pp. 506–7 reprints the dispatch from Washington of 6 April 1860. The first stories of the speech were published in the *Tribune*, 7 April 1860, p. 7 and 9 April 1860, p. 4. George V. Bohman, "Owen Lovejoy on 'The Barbarism of Slavery,' April 5, 1860," in J. Jeffery Auer, ed., *Antislavery and Disunion, 1858–1861, Studies in the Rhetoric of Compromise and Conflict* (New York, 1963), pp. 121–22.

42. Nevins, *Ordeal of the Union*, I, 292, 295–96. Robert F. Dalzell, Jr., *Daniel Webster and the Trial of American Nationalism, 1843–1852* (Boston, 1973), p. 185. Charles Sumner to John Bigelow, 25 May 1850, in Bigelow, *Retrospections*, I, 101.

43. Two valuable studies of this maturing process are Douglas Price, "Careers and Committees in the American Congress: The Problem of Structural Change," in William O. Aydelotte, ed, *The History of Parliamentary Behavior* (Princeton, 1977), and Nelson Polsby, "The Institutionalization of the U. S. House of Representatives," *American Political Science Review*, LXII (March 1968), 144–68.

44. Perhaps the most cultured despiser of efficient reporting was James Russell Lowell: *The Writings of James Russell Lowell* (10 vols.: Boston, 1892), V, 18–19, 265–66.

4. Visual Thinking: The Tammany Tiger Loose

1. Frank Luther Mott, *A History of American Magazines* (5 vols.: Cambridge, 1966–68), I, 36–37, 87; William Murrell, *A History of American Graphic Humor* (2 vols.: New York, 1933), I, 28. Mason Jackson, *The Pictorial Press, Its Origin and Progress* (London, 1885), p. 279. Celina Fox, "The Development of Social Reportage in English Periodical Illustration During the 1840s and early 1850s," *Past and Present*, no. 74 (Feb. 1977) pp. 90–111, esp. p. 98.

2. *Early Vermont Broadsides*, John Duffy, ed. (Hanover, N.H., 1975) pp. xvi, 28–29. Elizabeth Carroll Reilly, *A Dictionary of American Printers' Ornaments and Illustrations* (Worcester, 1975), pp. xxi, 367, plate 1563. American weakness in the graphic arts was widely recognized and bewailed, see Frank Weitenkampf, *American Graphic Art*, (New York, 1924), pp. 48–50, 54–55, on imaginary portraits. Harry T. Peters, *America on Stone* (New York, 1931), plate 33 is the Crockett portrait and comment. Harold Holzer, Gabor S. Boritt, and Mark E. Neely, Jr., *The Lincoln Image, Abraham Lincoln and the Popular Print* (New York, 1984), pp. 73–78. On the recycling of pictures as late as the 1880s see the autobiography in manuscript of Louis F. Post at the Library of Congress (p. 284) Post Papers, box 4.

3. Roy Meredith, *Mathew Brady's Portrait of an Era* (New York, 1982), pp. 134–36. Robert S. Kahan, "The Antecedents of American Photojournalism" (Ph.D. diss., Univ. of Wisc., 1969), p. 78. The enormous appeal of studio portraits is documented in William C. Dannah, *Cartes de Visites in Nineteenth Century Photography* (Gettysburg, 1981).

4. There is one cartoon in the pack-rat accumulation of Samuel Lyman, see his scrapbook in the William L. Clements Library, the University of Michigan. Lincoln's scrapbooks (see Chapter 3) have no pictures. Holzer, Boritt, and Neely, *The Lincoln Image*, p. 9. At the Republican convention of 1860, Lincoln supporters in the balcony showered woodcuts of their candidate upon the delegates. Few Republicans saved the pictures and today they are very rare. Beaumont Newhall, *The Daguerreotype in America*, 3d ed. rev. (New York, 1976), p. 109, suggests that scrapbooks with pictures first became popular in the 1860s.

Between the 1830s and 1890s more than 7000 illustrations fall into the Currier & Ives canon. (The name of the firm and the origin of the prints varied.) *Currier & Ives, A Catalogue Raisonné* (2 vols.: Detroit, 1984) lists only about 250 of these scenes in political categories. See also Frederick A. Conningham, *Currier & Ives Prints, An Illustrated Check List* [updated by Colin Simkin] (New York, 1970) pp. vi, xiii. These lithographers were responsible for more than half of the work in this medium in nineteenth-century America. Peters, *America on Stone*, surveys other printmakers. Of the 154 illustrations in the volume perhaps a dozen bring in political matters before the Civil War. Two ante-bellum catalogues of prints reproduced here have no political entries (pp. 16–17). Georgianne McVay, "Yankee Fanatics Unmasked: Cartoons on the Burning of a Convent," *Records of the American Catholic Historical Society of Philadelphia*, LXXXIII (Sept.-Dec. 1972), 160. On strike pictures I am indebted to the study by Josh Brown, Director, Visual Research and Graphic Art of the American Social History Project, Graduate Center of the City University of New York. Some conclusions of this study appear in "Visualizing Nineteenth-Century American Social History" delivered at the convention of the American Historical Association, Dec. 1985.

5. The figures of separately published cartoons come from the checklist, Frank Weitenkampf, *Political Caricature in the United States* (New York, 1953). On the decline of newspaper illustration see Roger Butterfield, "Pictures in the Papers," *American Heritage,* XIII (June 1962), 97. Raymond Smith Schuneman, "The Photograph in Print: An Examination of New York Daily Newspapers, 1890–1937" (Ph.D. diss., Univ. of Minn., 1966), also notes this backsliding.

6. Weitenkampf, *American Graphic Arts,* pp. 76–78. William M. Ivins, *Prints and Visual Communication* (Cambridge, 1953), p. 107 and p. 114, on the hierarchy of values that made the mass production of pictures suspect in many quarters through the nineteenth century. Daniel Webster to [Isaac P. Davis] 29 March 1830, in Charles M. Wiltse and Harold Moser, eds., *The Papers of Daniel Webster* (1st ser., 5 vols. to date: Hanover, N.H. and London, 1974–), III, 49. In his fourth decade of work with early American newspapers, Clarence S. Brigham still found the paucity of illustrations "strange"—see *Journals and Journeymen* (Philadelphia, 1950), pp. 49–50. Charles T. Congdon, *Reminiscences of a Journalist* (Boston, 1880), pp. 10–11; Valerian Gribayedoff, "Pictorial Journalism," *Cosmopolitan Magazine,* XI (Aug. 1891), 471–81. Charles F. Wingate, ed., *Views and Interviews on Journalism* (New York, 1875), p. 317. There is valuable information on the making of illustrations for *Harper's Weekly,* in W. A. Rogers, *A World Worth While* (New York, 1922), pp. 12–15.

7. Albert Boime, "Thomas Nast and French Art," *American Art Journal,* IV (Spring 1972), 43–65 has carefully traced this cultural transmission. One reason for the homages to Jean-Léon Gérôme was that the artist married into the Goupil family, art publishers with a New York office. In addition to the models for Nast cited here, compare Gérôme's "Reception of the Siamese Ambassadors at Fountainbleau" (1864) with "The Economical Council, Albany, New York," *Harper's Weekly,* 25 Dec. 1869. Peter C. Marzio, *The Democratic Art, Pictures for a 19th-Century America* (Boston, 1979) is very informative on this unheralded spread of art.

8. Nast's first assignment was to draw a holiday crowd at the moment a ferry captain called, "All aboard!" *Harper's Weekly* called Nast's work "pictorial analyses" of New York, and when the Civil War came his editor asked him, "How does a field look after a battle? Can you draw that? Suppose you make it night." Albert B. Paine, *Th. Nast, His Period and His Pictures* (New York, 1904), p. 18; *Harper's Weekly,* 19 May 1859, p. 180; *Harper's Weekly,* 5 Jan. 1907, p. 14.

9. Gribayedoff, "Pictorial Journalism," p. 479.

10. Michael Wolff and Celina Fox, "Pictures from the Magazines," in *The Victorian City, Images and Reality,* H. J. Dyos and Michael Wolff, eds. (2 vols.: London and Boston, 1973), II. See Fox, "The Development of Social Reportage in English Periodical Illustration" on the many varieties of "tasteful neutrality" (p.93). The first two chapters of Peter B Hales, *Silver Cities: The Photography of American Urbanization, 1839–1915* (Philadelphia, 1984) is a perceptive discussion of the idealization of the city.

11. *Frank Leslie's Illustrated Newspaper,* 21 Jan. 1871, pp. 309, 313, achieved the same effect with its coverage of the ball.

12. "The Charter and Bye-Laws of Tammany Society or Columbian Order in the City of New-York," ca. 1860, p. 43 in Edwin Patrick Kilro Collection, Special Collections, Columbia University Library.

13. New York *Times*, 29 July 1871, p. 1, notes the lithograph in an office. Meredith, *Mathew Brady's Portrait of an Era*, pp. 155–56. The imprinted checks can be found in William M. Tweed, Miscellaneous Manuscripts, New-York Historical Society. Mott, *A History of American Magazines*, III, 440–42. The earliest version of the Tweed quote I have found is a paraphrase in *Harper's Weekly*, 26 Aug. 1871, p. 803. Historians seem to have followed Charles F. Wingate, "An Episode of Municipal Government," *North American Review*, CXX (Jan. 1875), 124, the version given here. The judgment that Nast's drawings mobilized "suppressed opinion" was made in the first historical treatment of the Ring, William L. Stone, *History of New York City* (New York, 1872), p. 635n.

14. In addition to standard works cited in the bibliography section I am indebted to Arthur Sweeney, Jr., to this author, 10 Oct. 1978. Leo Hershkowitz, "P.B.S., The Squire of New York," NAHO (Sp.-Summer 1981).

15. Matthew P. Breen, *Thirty Years of New York Politics Up-to-Date* (New York, 1899), pp. 51–52; Allan Nevins and Milton H. Thomas, eds., *The Diary of George Templeton Strong* (4 vols.: New York, 1952), IV, 394–95.

16. *Harper's Weekly*, 12 Aug. 1871, p. 738.

17. *Harper's Weekly*, 13 March 1869, p. 163; 18 March 1871, p. 235; 11 Nov. 1871, p. 1051.

18. L. Perry Curtis, Jr., *Apes and Angels, The Irishman in Victorian Caricature* (Washington, 1971), pp. 26, 29, 35, 58–59. Curtis suggests that in London and in New York the tenuous connection of cartoonists themselves to the Anglo-Saxon tradition led them to create this picture of the Irish (p. 96).

19. Alexander Alland, Sr., *Jacob Riis, Photographer and Citizen* (Millerton, N.Y, 1974), pp. 97, 163.

20. *Harper's Weekly* 22 Jan. 1870, p. 50. Leo Hershkowitz, *Tweed's New York: Another Look* (Garden City, 1977) comes to the rescue of the boss.

21. *Harper's Weekly* 8 Oct. 1870, p. 642. The cartoon was published on 29 Oct. 1870.

22. In 1857 the phrase was already a saying attributed by Republicans to Democrats, see New York *Tribune*, 23 March 1857, in James S. Pike, *First Blows of the Civil War* (New York, 1879), pp. 370–74.

23. New York *Times*, 8 April 1870, p. 6; 13 April 1870, p. 4; 1 May 1870, p. 4. George T. McJimsey, *Genteel Partisan: Manton Marble, 1834–1917* (Ames, 1971), explains how an old antagonist of Tweed, the New York *World*, was persuaded to keep quiet during the 1870–71 exposé.

24. New York *Times*, 24 Sept. 1870, p. 1; 29 Sept. 1870, p. 5; 11 Oct. 1870, p. 5.

25. Alexander B. Callow, Jr., *The Tweed Ring* (New York, 1966), p. 257; New York *Times*, 25 Sept. 1870, p. 2.

26. New York *Times*, 1 Oct. 1870, p. 4; 8 Oct. 1870, p. 4; 1 July 1871, p. 4.

27. Meyer Berger, *The Story of the New York Times* (New York, 1951), p. 42. There is a slightly different version of the meeting in Paine, *Th. Nast, His Period and His Pictures*, p. 168. Jennings's recollection dates from 1887 according to

Paine. The earliest published account that I have found of O'Brien's visit to the *Times* is Charles F. Wingate, "An Episode of Municipal Government," *North American Review*, CXX (Jan. 1875), 154. Wingate was a respected reporter writing for editors who had great knowledge of the subject. He quoted no dialogue and found that George Jones had taken O'Brien's information on July 18th. If this is so, the *Times* began the exposé ten days before this evidence was at hand. O'Brien himself did not mention Jennings, only Jones, in his recollections of bringing the Secret Accounts to the *Times*. This politico did not make clear how much evidence he shared with the *Times* early in 1871, but he recalled that Jones had the key figures for more than a month before publishing them: "Jas. O'Brien's Story," New York *World*, 16 Aug. 1891, pp. 1–2.

28. New York *Times* (Supplement), 29 July 1871; 27 July 1871, p. 4. Hershkowitz, *Tweed's New York*, pp. 173–74 and 213–14. The *Nation* called attention to this early period of abuse as it "prepared the public mind to be greatly stirred up by the revelations when made," XIII (23 Nov. 1871), 334.

29. New York *Times*, 8 Oct. 1870, p. 4. George Juergens, *Joseph Pulitzer and the New York World* (Princeton, 1966), p. 100 has noted the strong tendency for "verbal drawing" in the popular press of the late nineteenth century.

30. John Foord, *The Life and Public Services of Andrew Haswell Green* (Garden City, 1913), p. 94. Foord made this observation in 1872. See the typescript, "A Year's Record of a Reformer as Comptroller of New York City," p. 3 (1872), in the A. H. Green Papers, The New-York Historical Society.

31. George C. D. Odell, *Annals of the New York Stage* (15 vols.: New York, 1927–49) IX, 196. David Grimsted, *Melodrama Unveiled: American Theater and Culture, 1800–1850* (Chicago, 1968), pp. 160–62, James Hackett writing in 1834 quoted by Grimsted, p. 161. The stage versions of *Uncle Tom's Cabin* are the exceptions that prove the rule. This was one of very few stage vehicles to come from national political debate. In the theater, however, the political message was evaded and finally dropped altogether. Mark Twain's play, "Colonel Sellers" was a hit, but has never been published. An amanuensis manuscript is in the Mark Twain Papers, University of California, Berkeley. See also Charles Dudley Warner to Samuel Clemens, 30 April 1874 in MTP. Politics rarely engaged American dramatists before the Progressive Era according to Arthur H. Quinn, *A History of the American Drama* (New York, 1936), I, 104.

32. New York *Times*, 20 July 1871, p. 4, and the paper's Supplement, 29 July 1871. Figures and quotes refer to this supplement unless otherwise attributed.

33. New York *Times*, 8 July 1871, p. 5

34. New York *Times*, 29 July 1871, p. 1. Soon the paper learned more about the men it accused and put this information in a pamphlet with the Secret Accounts: *How New York Is Governed. Frauds of the Tammany Democrats* (New York, 1871). Still, the *Times* referred to September 1871 as the "eve of our investigation" into specific transactions (p. 2).

35. *Harper's Weekly*, 4 Nov. 1871, p. 1026. Wingate, "An Episode in Municipal Government," p. 150.

36. Gordon W. Allport and Leo Postman, *The Psychology of Rumor* (New York, 1947), see especially pp. 100–105.

37. *Harper's Weekly*, 26 Aug. 1871 (Supplement), p. 803

38. *Harper's Weekly*, 13 Jan. 1872, p. 27.

39. Juergens, *Joseph Pulitzer and the New York World*, pp. 29–30, 93–95.

Towards the Twentieth Century

1. Michael Schudson, *Discovering the News, A Social History of American Newspapers* (New York, 1978) documents the emergence of "objectivity" as an ideal peculiar to the post WWI era, see especially pp. 120–59.

5. Reporting From the Bottom

1. For broadside verse that joined leaders to the criminal class see Elizabeth Winslow, *American Broadside Verse* (New Haven, 1930), no. 64; Mason I. Lowance, Jr. and Georgia B. Bumgardner, eds., *Massachusetts Broadsides of the American Revolution* (Amherst, 1976), no. 5. William Eben Schultz, *Gay's Beggar's Opera, Its Content, History, and Influence* (New Haven, 1923), pp. 108–9. James Alexander, *A Brief Narrative of the Case of John Peter Zenger, Printer of the New York Weekly Journal*, Stanley Nider Katz, ed. (Cambridge, 1972), 2nd ed., p. 43. Alice M. Earle, *Curious Punishments of Bygone Days* (New York, 1907), p. 69. William Duane, ed., *Extracts from the Diary of Christopher Marshall . . . 1774–1781* (Albany, 1877), 1969 reprint, p. 16.

2. Lawrence M. Friedman, *A History of American Law* (New York, 1974), p. 63 (the phrase is Harold Garfinkel's). Thomas M. McDade, *The Annals of Murder, A Bibliography of Books and Pamphlets on American Murders from Colonial Times to 1900* (Norman, 1961), also has a valuable discussion of the legal system.

3. Olive Woolley Burt, ed., *American Murder Ballads and Their Stories* (New York, 1958), see especially pp. 6, 37, 108. Winslow, *American Broadside Verse*, no. 40. On ministers as reporters see Wayne C. Minnick, "The New England Execution Sermon, 1639–1800," *Speech Monographs*, XXXV (March 1968), 77–89; Ronald A. Bosco, "Lectures at the Pillory: The Early American Execution Sermon," *American Quarterly*, XXX (Summer 1978), 156–76. Gordon E. Geddes, *Welcome Joy: Death in Puritan New England* (Ann Arbor, 1981), pp. 89–95. Broadsides had a much lower survival rate than pamphlets, but the imperfect modern record shows they were more numerous than the sermons. Bosco found 62 printed sermons, 1674–1798. Clifford K. Shipton and James E. Mooney, *The National Index of American Imprints Through 1800: The Short-Title Evans* (Worcester, 1969) lists more than twice that many non-sermons reporting on the lives of criminals.

4. Winslow, *American Broadside Verse*, no. 38. Lowance and Bumgardner, eds., *Massachusetts Broadsides* nos. 26 and 28.

5. Rachel Wall, *Life, Last Words and Dying Confession . . .* (Boston, 1789), Evans no. 22,235. Samuel Frost, *The Confession and Dying Words . . .* (Worcester, 1793), Evans no. 25,521. John Stewart, *The Confession, Last Words, and Dying Speech . . .* (Boston, 1797), Evans no. 32,879. For examples of the detailed accounting of

past crimes see Levi Ames, *The Last Words and Dying Speech* . . . (Boston, 1773), Evans no. 42,401; Johnson Green, *The Life and Confession of Johnson Green* . . . (Worcester, 1786),Evans no. 19,693.

6. William Smith, *The Convict's Visitor: Or Penitential Offices* . . . (Newport, 1791), Evans no. 23,775. On p. 16 Smith called on others to report the criminal vernacular. Herman Mann, the printer, issued *The Last Words of Ebenezer Mason* . . . (Dedham, 1802), pp. iv, 15. I am indebted to Robert B. Hanson, president of the Dedham Historical Society for checking coverage of the case in Mann's newspaper, the *Columbian Minerva*.

7. On the far richer European response to crime see Douglas Hay et al., eds., *Albion's Fatal Tree: Crime and Society in Eighteenth-Century England* (New York, 1975). Robert Darnton, "Trade in the Taboo: The Life of a Clandestine Book Dealer in Prerevolutionary France," in *The Widening Circle: Essays on the Circulation of Literature in Eighteenth-Century Europe*, ed. Paul J. Korshin (Philadelphia, 1976). William E. Nelson, "Emerging Notions of Modern Criminal Law in the Revolutionary Era: An Historical Perspective," in Lawrence M. Friedman and Harry N. Scheiber, eds., *American Law and the Constitutional Order, Historical Perspectives* (Cambridge, 1978).

8. The insults in the press are quoted in Donald H. Stewart, *The Opposition Press of the Federalist Period* (Albany, 1969), p. 531; Fawn Brodie, *Thomas Jefferson, An Intimate History* (New York, 1974), pp. 321–22. On songs and criminals see David Hackett Fischer, *The Revolution of American Conservatism* (Chicago, 1965), 1975 ed., pp. 146–47.

9. Dagobert D. Runes, ed., *The Selected Writings of Benjamin Rush* (New York, 1947), p. 396. In Boynton Merrill Jr.'s painstaking research on the Jefferson crime, contemporary newspapers were little help in reconstructing the killing. No doubt, the race of the victim contributed to the failure of the press to take note—*Jefferson's Nephews, A Frontier Tragedy* (Princeton, 1976), pp. 263, 300.

10. Hezekiah Niles in *Niles' Register*, XXVI (27 March 1824) 52. Duane quoted in Jerry W. Knudson, "The Jefferson Years: Response by the Press, 1801–1809" (Ph.D. diss., Univ. of Va., 1962), 54. Allan Nevins, *The Evening Post: A Century of Journalism* (New York, 1922), pp. 72, 180.

11. On the labor press and crime see Dan Schiller, *Objectivity and the News: The Public and the Rise of Commercial Journalism* (Philadelphia, 1981), p. 55. [Thomas Gill] *Selections from the Court Reports Originally Published in the Boston Morning Post, from 1834 to 1837* (Boston, 1837). Crime reports from the New Orleans *Picayune*, 1840–42, have been collected by E. Merton Coulter in *The Other Half of Old New Orleans* (Baton Rouge, 1939). Pelig W. Chandler's "experiment" in court reporting, *American Criminal Trials* (Boston, 1841), also marks the new attention to lawlessness.

12. New York *Herald*, 14 Sept. 1836, p. 2; cf. *Herald*, 27 April 1836, p. 1. Paul Boyer, *Urban Masses and Moral Order in America, 1820–1920* (Cambridge and London, 1978), pp. 31–33, 55–56.

13. On shaming punishments see Michael S. Hindus, *Prison and Plantation: Crime, Justice, and Authority in South Carolina, 1767–1878* (Chapel Hill, 1980), pp. 100–101.

14. New York *Herald*,. 31 Aug 1835, p. 3.

15. Philadelphia *Public Ledger*, 31 March 1836, p. 2; see also 8 April 1836, p. 2 and 11 April 1836, p. 2.

16. New York *Herald*, 12 April 1836, p. 4. This passage is half torn away in the microfilm record of the paper. I have used the text reprinted in Oliver Carlson, *The Man Who Made News, James Gordon Bennett* (New York, 1942), p. 160.

17. Nils Gunnar Nilsson, "The Origin of the Interview," *Journalism Quarterly*, XXXXVIII (Winter 1971), 707–13.

18. New York *Herald*, 12 April 1836, p. 12. John E. Walsh, *Poe the Detective: The Curious Circumstances Behind the Mystery of Marie Roget* (New Brunswick, 1968). The other penny papers in New York gave equal attention to the killing and the businessmen's papers finally entered the competition by printing the transcript of Robinson's trial. During the next eight years, James L. Crouthamel has found, the *Herald* provided equal or greater coverage of at least eight murder cases, see "James Gordon Bennett, the *New York Herald*, and the Development of Newspaper Sensationalism," *New York History*, LIV (July 1973), 308–9. Bennett had found no calling to be a detective in earlier reporting, see Wallace B. Eberhard, "Mr. Bennett Covers a Murder Trial," *Journalism Quarterly*, XXXXVII (Autumn 1970), 457–63.

19. New York *Herald*, 13 April 1836, p. 1; *Herald*, 15 April 1836, p. 1; *Herald*, 25 April 1836, p. 1.

20. Philadelphia *Public Ledger*, 15 April 1836, p. 2; *Public Ledger*, 26 April 1836, p. 2.

21. New York *Herald*, 30 April 1836, p. 2. Philadelphia *Public Ledger*, 29 April 1836, p. 2.

22. Philadelphia *Public Ledger*, 18 July 1836, p. 4; 25 July 1836, p. 2; 8 Aug. 1836, p. 2; and 10 Oct. 1836, p. 2. New York *Herald*, 23 Aug. 1836, p. 2. 27 Aug. 1836, p. 1; and 23 Sept. 1836, p. 2. Michael Schudson, *Discovering the News: A Social History of the American Newspaper* (New York, 1978), notes the indifference of the early penny press to formal political events, pp. 21–31. Daniel J. Czitrom, *Media and the American Mind: From Morse to McLuhan* (Chapel Hill, 1982), pp. 15–16.

23. New York *Herald*, 24 Aug. 1836, p. 2; *Herald*, 9 June 1836, p. 1; *Herald*, 21 June 1836, p. 1; *Herald*, 19 Aug. 1836, p. 2; *Herald*, 29 Aug. 1836, p. 2; *Herald*, 29 Nov. 1836, p. 2; *Herald*, 5 Dec. 1836, p. 2; Philadelphia *Public Ledger*, 26 Oct. 1836, p. 2.

24. Doris A. Graber, *Crime News and the Public* (New York, 1980), p. 37.

25. Carol Smith-Rosenberg, "Beauty and the Beast and the Militant Woman: A Case Study in Sex Roles and Social Stress in Jacksonian America," *American Quarterly*, XXIII (Oct. 1971), 562–84; *The Liberator*, 10 May 1934, p. 75. Garrison made the case for thorough reporting of vice in a review that commended a clergyman for citing the Jewett-Robinson case, *The Liberator*, 17 Sept. 1836, p. 151. I owe these references to Ronald G. Walters, *The Antislavery Appeal: American Abolitionism After 1830* (Baltimore, 1976), chap. 5. John Allen Krout, *The Origins of Prohibition* (New York, 1925), pp. 184–89. Leonard L. Richards, *"Gentlemen of Property and Standing," Anti-Abolition Mobs in Jacksonian America* (New York, 1970),

makes discerning observations on the effects of this literature of exposure, see pp. 71–73, 162, 167.

26. Neil Harris, *Humbug: The Art of P. T. Barnum* (Boston and Toronto, 1973). Alexander Saxton, "George Wilkes: The Transformation of a Radical Ideology, *American Quarterly*, XXXIII (Fall 1981), 437–58. See also Schiller, *Objectivity and the News*. Jay Monaghan, *The Great Rascal, The Life and Adventures of Ned Buntline* (Boston, 1952), pp. 132–47.

27. Melville E. Stone, *Fifty Years a Journalist* (Garden City and Toronto, 1921), p. 179. See also Russell A. Mann, "Investigative Reporting in the Gilded Age: A Study of the Detective Journalism of Melville E. Stone and the *Chicago Morning News*, 1881–1888" (Ph.D. diss., Southern Illinois University at Carbondale, 1972).

28. George W. Alger, *Moral Overstrain* (Boston and New York, 1906), p. 29.

29. All of the photographs are reproduced in Alexander Alland, Sr., *Jacob A. Riis, Photographer & Citizen* (Millerton, N.Y., 1974), pp. 51, 95, 107, 151, 153, 157, 159, 161. Peter B. Hales, *Silver Cities: The Photography of American Urbanization, 1839–1915* (Philadelphia, 1984), p. 171; the chapter on Riis is excellent.

30. Mark Sullivan, *The Education of an American* (New York, 1938), p. 125; Alfred Henry Lewis, "Confessions of a Newspaper Man," *Human Life*, III (June 1906), 7.

31. Charles E. Russell, *Bare Hands and Stone Walls:Some Reflections of a Side-Line Reformer* (New York, 1933), p. 79; *These Shifting Scenes* (New York, 1914), pp. 15–16, 18.

32. Russell, *Bare Hands and Stone Walls*, p. 115. He had endorsed the same view earlier in "Forward, Citizens, to the Firing Line!" *Everybody's Magazine* XIX (Nov. 1908), 702. Harvey J. O'Higgins, "The Reformer," *Success Magazine*, XIV (June 1911), 12–14, 48–9, is a detective story of political despair in which the underworld proves too strong for conventional reform.

33. Ella Winter and Granville Hicks, eds., *The Letters of Lincoln Steffens* (2 vols.: New York, 1938), I, 86, 98, 108. Nevins, *The Evening Post*, pp. 72, 180.

34. *The Autobiography of Lincoln Steffens* (2 vols.: New York, 1958) [1931], I, 229–30; II, 380–84, on Minneapolis. Lincoln Steffens, "William J. Burns, Intriguer," *American Magazine*, LXV (April 1908), 614–25, 625 quoted. In Boston, Steffens sought out "the worst man in town," Martin M. Lomasney. Their affection for each other is documented in Leslie G. Ainley, *Boston Mahatma* (Boston, 1949), pp. 181–86.

35. Upton Sinclair, *The Jungle* (New York, 1906), pp. 196–97, 298–99, 302–3, 308.

36. The picture of the Whitechapel Club is in John T. McPhaul, *Deadlines & Monkeyshines: The Fabled World of Chicago Journalism* (Englewood Cliffs, 1962). The young reporters' scrapbooks, heavy with coverage of crime, are in box 50 of the Russell Papers and box 103 of the Whitlock Papers, both in the Library of Congress. "What Good Does It Do?" *Everybody's*, XVI (May 1907), p. 586. *Forty Years of It* (New York, 1925) [1914].

37. *The Anamosa Prison Press*, 16 March 1907, in Whitlock Papers, box 98. Steffens to BW, 9 Sept. 1907, in *The Letters of Lincoln Steffens*, I, 184–85. Whitlock to LS, 17 Sept. 1907, in Allan Nevins, ed., *The Letters and Journal of Brand Whitlock* (New York, 1936), p. 79.

38. Josiah Flynt [Willard] and Francis Walton [Alfred Hodder], *The Powers That Prey* (New York, 1900), p. vii. *McClure's* had published this as the series, "True Stories from the Underworld" beginning in August 1900. Josiah Flynt, *My Life* (New York, 1908), pp. 297–99. This autobiography was a serial in *Success*, beginning December 1906, the height of the magazine's work for reform. Josiah Flynt, *Notes of an Itinerant Policeman* (Boston. 1900), pp. 79–82. On the importance of the lawlessness theme to a leading muckraker, see S.S. McClure, "Advertising Magazine and Books," typescript (carbon) ca. 1903 pp. 13–14 in Houghton Library, Harvard University. S.S. McClure to Lincoln Steffens, 25 May 1903, and 20 Jan. 1903, in Lincoln Steffens Papers, Columbia University. George Kibbe Turner, "Tammany's Control of New York by Professional Criminals," *McClure's* (June 1909). This article was praised and supplemented in *Current Literature*, XXXXVII (Aug. 1909), 120–27. On the reaction to reporting see Harold S. Wilson, *McClure's Magazine and the Muckrakers* (Princeton, 1970), pp. 123–25, 136, 151–52.

39. William Traves Jerome was the crusading D.A. and his candidacy was also an awakening for Upton Sinclair: *The Autobiography of Upton Sinclair* (New York, 1962), pp. 62–63, 103.

40. Hutchins Hapgood, *A Victorian in the Modern World* (New York, 1939), p. 168. Ellery Sedgwick, *The Happy Profession* (Boston, 1946), pp. 126–35.

41. Alfred Henry Lewis, "The Chief, A Novel of the New York Police," was announced in *Human Life*, XII (Jan. 1911), 4. The series ran during the next four months in this magazine.

Muckrakers also were lawmen who, like Whitlock, saw society indicted by its treatment of the criminal. For George Creel (who took the night sticks away from cops when he was police commissioner of Denver) this was a major discovery in his investigation of American cities. He argued that crime was caused by the same injustices that progressives protested. A warden whom Creel interviewed cited Whitlock's *Turn of the Balance* to illustrate how political reform could solve the crime problem. Creel, like his associates Ben Lindsey and Harvey J. O'Higgins, came into the reform magazines with this message. See George Creel, *Rebel at Large* (New York, 1947), pp. 62–63. Creel, "Mending Broken Men," *Success*, XIV (June 1911), 18–19, 38–40.

42. Phillips to Whitlock, [1907] copy in box 98, Whitlock Papers.

43. The editorial announcement, "The Riddle of the Negro," by Baker appeared in *American Magazine*, LXIII (March 1907), pp. 517–21; the first installment is in this volume: "Following the Color Line, A Race Riot, and After" (April 1907), pp. 563–79, quoted p. 564. "The Negro in Southern City Life," *American Magazine*, LXIII (June 1907), 135–48, also makes it clear that Baker headed straight for the police courts.

6. The Provincial Scandal

1. Stephen Vaughn, *Holding Fast the Inner Lines, Democracy, Nationalism, and the Committee on Public Information* (Chapel Hill, 1980), treats the CPI as "above

all a nationalizing agent," pp. xi, 197, 201. George Juergens, *News from the White House* (Chicago and London, 1981), p. 175. Ray Stannard Baker, *Woodrow Wilson, Life and Letters, Youth, 1856–1890* (Garden City, 1927), pp. 6–11. David H. Burton, ed., *Progressive Masks, Letters of Oliver Wendell Holmes, Jr. and Franklin Ford* (Newark, Del., 1982), charts the interest in a visionary plan for changing news gathering.

2. Beeman Brockway, *Fifty Years in Journalism* (Watertown, N.Y., 1891), p. 425. *Autobiography of Amos Kendall*, William Stickney, ed. (Boston, 1872), p. 164. Robert Stewart, "The Exchange System and the Development of a Political Movement in the 1820s," paper presented to the History Division of the Association for Education in Journalism and Mass Communications, 23–24 Feb. 1985, is a valuable quantitative study of the national reach of political news.

3. Francis P. Weisenburger, "The Mid Western Antecedents of Woodrow Wilson," *Mississippi Valley Historical Review*, XXIII (Dec. 1936), 375–90, quoted p. 382.

4. L. U. Reavis was the author. On the young Pulitzer's city see John A. Kouwenhoven, "Eads Bridge: The Celebration," and "Downtown St. Louis as James B. Eads Knew it When the Bridge was Opened a Century Ago," *Bulletin, The Missouri Historical Society*, XXX (April 1974), 159–95; [Works Progress Administration] *Missouri: A Guide to the 'Show Me' State* (New York, 1941).

5. Wyatt W. Belcher, *The Economic Rivalry Between Chicago and St. Louis, 1850–1880* (New York, 1947).

6. James Creelman, "Joseph Pulitzer—Master Journalist," *Pearson's Magazine*, XXI (March 1909), 238–39.

7. John J. Jennings, *Theatrical and Circus Life; or, Secrets of the Stage, Green-Room and Sawdust Arena* (St. Louis, 1882), pp. 3–4, 315. Cockerill was the first to publish Lafcadio Hearn. As much as a quarter of the paper Cockerill edited in Cincinnati was given over to the work of this early naturalist. See Malcolm Cowley's introduction to *The Selected Writings of Lafcadio Hearn*, Henry Goodman, ed. (New York, 1959), p. 3.

8. St. Louis *Post and Dispatch*, 31 Jan. 1879, p. 1; 11 Feb. 1879, p. 4; 15 Feb. 1879, p. 2; 18 Feb. 1879, p. 1; 19 Feb. 1879, p. 2.

9. *Post and Dispatch*, 18 Feb. 1879, pp. 1–2; 31 Jan. 1879, p. 1; 12 Feb. 1879, p. 4. On the pretensions of St. Louis see also the editorials 14 Feb. 1879, p. 2, and 20 Feb. 1879, p. 2.

10. *Post and Dispatch*, 31 Jan. 1879, p. 1; 18 Feb. 1879, p. 1; 5 March 1879, p. 2.

11. Julian S. Rammelkamp, *Pulitzer's Post-Dispatch, 1878–1883* (Princeton, 1967), pp. 134–35. Pulitzer made early pledges of non-partisanship, see, for example, the issue of the paper on 13 Dec. 1878.

12. Whitelaw Reid, "Schools of Journalism," *Scribner's Monthly*, IV (June 1872), 204. The best accounts of the underlying causes of independence are Daniel J. Boorstin, *The Americans: The Democratic Experience* (New York, 1973), Part Two, and Frank Luther Mott, *American Journalism: A History: 1690–1960*, 3d ed. (New York, 1960), chaps. XXV–XXX.

13. St. Louis *Post-Dispatch*, 3 Jan. 1881, pp. 1–2.

14. St. Louis *Post-Dispatch*, 12 April 1882, p. 8.

15. Rammelkamp, *Pulitzer's Post-Dispatch*, pp. 151–55; *Post-Dispatch*, 27 Sept. 1880, p. 4.

16. St. Louis *Post-Dispatch*, 28 Sept. 1880, p. 5; 29 Sept. 1880, pp. 4–5; 12 Oct. 1880, p. 8; 20 Oct. 1880, p. 4; 27 Dec. 1880, p. 1. The wider picture of corruption is given 8 Feb. 1881, p. 3; 17 March 1881, p. 4; 28 March 1881, p. 4; 4 April 1881, p. 6.

17. St. Louis *Post-Dispatch*, 4 April 1883, p. 3; 5 April 1883, p. 3; 9 April 1883, p. 2.

18. J. J. McAuliffe, "Fighting the Good Fight in Missouri," *Leslie's Monthly Magazine*, LVIII (June 1904), 204.

19. St. Louis *Post-Dispatch*, 12 March 1881, p. 8; 9 April 1883, p. 2.

20. Marshall S. Snow, "The Government of Saint Louis," *Johns Hopkins University Studies in Historical and Political Science*, Herbert B. Adams, ed., 5th ser., IV (Baltimore, 1887), 20–21, 39. Lord Bryce's *American Commonwealth* (1888) relied on this account and gave scant notice to the corruption of this city. Frederick W. Dewart, *Proceedings of the Louisville Conference for Good City Government and of the Third Annual Meeting of the National Municipal League* (Philadelphia, 1897), pp. 227, 231; Charles Nagel, *Proceedings of the Rochester Conference for Good Government and the Seventh Annual Meeting of the National Municipal League* (Philadelphia, 1901), p. 106.

21. W. H. Bishop, "St. Louis," *Harper's New Monthly Magazine*, LXVIII (March 1884), 497–517; Charles Dudley Warner, "Studies of the Great West, VIII—St. Louis and Kansas City," *Harper's New Monthly Magazine*, LXXVII (Oct. 1888), 752 (quoted); C. M. Woodward, "The City of St. Louis," *New England Magazine*, V (Jan. 1892), 608. Julian Ralph, "The New Growth of St. Louis," *Harper's New Monthly Magazine*, LXXXV (Nov. 1892), 920, 922; Albert Shaw, "Notes on City Government in St. Louis," *Century Magazine*, LII (June 1896), 255 (quoted), 262; John Snyder, "The Higher Life of St. Louis," *Outlook*, LIV (29 Aug. 1896), 373. James L. Blair, a Democrat, celebrated his party's victories in the elections of 1900 and 1901 but said little about the sins of Republican rule in St. Louis: "Novel Municipal Conditions in St. Louis," *Harper's Weekly*, XLV, 13 July 1901, 695.

22. *The Autobiography of Lincoln Steffens* (2 vols.: New York, 1958) [1931], II, 364, 368. There is, however, evidence that Steffens had picked up the scent earlier—see Brand Whitlock, *Forty Years of It* (New York, 1925), p. 158. Steffens may have been drawn to the city by stories of the Folk investigation that circulated in New York early in 1902. The New York press played down the story until *McClure's* took it up: see the two stories in *Outlook*, LXX (8 Feb. 1902). When Steffens examined Rhode Island he acknowledged his dependence on newspapers in New York and Springfield, making clear how little of this muckraking was a release of new information: Lincoln Steffens, "Rhode Island: A State for Sale," *McClure's*, XXIV (Feb. 1905), 341.

23. *Grandeur of the Universal Exposition at St. Louis* (St. Louis, 1904), no page. Claude H. Wetmore and Lincoln Steffens, "Tweed Days in St. Louis, Joseph W. Folk's Single-handed Exposure of Corruption, High and Low," *McClure's*, XIX (Oct. 1902), 577–86; Lincoln Steffens, "The Shamelessness of St. Louis, Something New in the History of American Municipal Democracy," *McClure's*, XX (March 1903), 539–60, 553 (quoted); Lincoln Steffens, "Enemies of the Republic,

The Political Leaders Who Are Selling Out the State of Missouri, and the Leading Business Men Who Are Buying It— Business as Treason— Corruption as Revolution," *McClure's*, XXII (March 1904), 587–99.

24. Wetmore and Steffens, "Tweed Days," p. 580; Steffens, "The Shamelessness of St. Louis," p. 553; "Enemies of the Republic," pp. 587–88. "The system" was new coinage but had precedents, see, for example, Lambert A. Wilmer, *Our Press Gang* (Philadelphia, 1859) 1970 reprint, p. 186. The phrase became a Steffens refrain and was echoed by other muckrakers, see, for example, Thomas W. Lawson, "Frenzied Finance: The Story of Amalgamated," *Everybody's Magazine*, XI (July 1904), pp. 1–2. In 1908 TR told Steffens that the phrase was striking and misleading: TR to LS 5 June 1908 in Elting E. Morison et al., eds., *The Letters of Theodore Roosevelt* (8 vols.: Cambridge, 1951–54), VI, 1052.

25. Samuel S. McClure to LS, 20 Jan. 1903 and to Robert McClure, 12 June 1903, in Lincoln Steffens Papers, Columbia University. LS to John S. Phillips, 14 July 1902 in John S. Phillips Papers, Lilly Library, Indiana University. *The Autobiography of Lincoln Steffens*, II, 394.

26. Wetmore and Steffens, "Tweed Days," pp. 577, 581, 586.

27. Steffens only acknowledged Wetmore in his autobiography but another St. Louis journalist helped him, see Orrick Johns, *Time of Our Lives: The Story of My Father and Myself* (New York, 1973), p. 156.

28. Ray Stannard Baker, *American Chronicle* (New York, 1945), p. 113.

29. Theodore Dreiser, "Out of My Newspaper Days—III: "Red" Galvin," *Bookman*, LIIII (1901–2), 542. Max Putzel, *The Man in the Mirror: William Marion Reedy and His Magazine* (Cambridge, 1963), pp. 49–51. On the treacherous local market for exposés before 1902 in St. Louis, see Claude H. Wetmore, *The Battle Against Bribery* (St. Louis, 1904), p. 9; James W. Markham, *Bovard of the Post-Dispatch* (Baton Rouge, 1954), pp. 1–2.

30. B.O. Flower, *Progressive Men, Women, and Movements of the Past Twenty-five Years* (Boston, 1914), p. 56. The *McClure's* survey of tramps is reprinted in Josiah Flynt (Willard), *The World of Graft* (New York, 1901), p. 31. "The Power of the Magazines," *Success*, IX (March 1906), 175. See in Will Irwin's "The American Newspaper" the eleventh, thirteenth, and fourteenth article: *Collier's*, XXXXVIII 17 June 1911, p. 18; 10 July 1911, pp. 15 ff.; and 22 July 1911, pp. 13 ff. Robert V. Hudson, *The Writing Game, A Biography of Will Irwin* (Ames, 1982), has found that the revelations had great impact in Pittsburgh, especially on the young reporter George Seldes, p. 72. See also, "Criticizing Collier's," *Collier's*, XXXVI, 24 March 1906, 8; "Freedom of the Press" *Survey*, XXIV, 4 June 1910, 365–68. "Our Newspaper Critics," *Hampton's Magazine*, XXIV (Jan. 1910), 152; "Newspaper Criticism," *ibid.* (May 1910), 733–34. *Success*, XI (May 1909), 327–28, reprinted a terminal diagnosis of newspapers made by a leading Philadelphia paper: " . . . the period of the daily newspaper as the exponent of enlightened public opinion had closed, as they became localized. . . . "

31. *The Autobiography of Lincoln Steffens*, II, 368. Letter signed "St. Louis" to LS, 30 March 1903 in Lincoln Steffens Papers, Columbia University; letter to the editor of *McClure's* dated 10 April 1904 with confession and letter signed "Jos. S. Dinwoody." In editing her husband's papers Ella Winter found the author to be Charles F. Kelly, writing in 1903 (Steffens Papers, Columbia). See also

Steffens, "The Shamelessness of St. Louis," p. 559. Mark Sullivan, *The Education of an American* (New York, 1938), pp. 202–3 testifies to the mood in the *McClure's* office. George Creel and Sloane Gordon, "What Are You Going To Do About It?" *Cosmopolitan*, LI (Oct. 1911), 599–610, notes the crucial importance of national publication of corruption long known to local citizens (p. 600).

Minneapolis is another city in which Steffens's exposé amounted to catching up with old news in the community. Albert Shaw, editor of a favorite progressive journal the *Review of Reviews*, began his career in Minneapolis writing editorials against the machine of Albert "Doc" Ames for the *Tribune*. Steffens exposed this colorful boss almost twenty years later. The Minneapolis papers had helped to drive Ames from office six months before the *McClure's* article was published. Still, the effect of national exposure was dramatic. *McClure's* revived interest in prosecuting this forgotten figure. See Lloyd J. Graybar, *Albert Shaw of the Review of Reviews: An Intellectual Biography* (Lexington, Ky., 1974), pp. 35–36, and Richard B. Kielbowicz, "The Limits of the Press as an Agent of Reform: Minneapolis, 1900–1905," *Journalism Quarterly*, LVIIII (Spring 1982), pp. 21–27, 170.

32. Morton Keller has noted this decline of provincialism in the press of the late nineteenth century in *Affairs of State, Public Life in Late Nineteenth Century America* (Cambridge and London, 1977), p. 566.

33. "Inside with the Editor," *Pearson's*, XV (May 1906) p. 539. *Pearson's* was "unfettered" in ways that must have been puzzling to progressives. It posed as a enemy of sensational exposés at the same time it featured the very writers close to Hearst who had produced these works.

34. Sullivan, *The Education of an American*, pp. 252–55. Hartley Davis, "Reporters of Today," *Everybody's Magazine*, XIV (Feb. 1906), 206–7. Joel W. Eastman, "Claude L'Engle, Florida Muckraker," *Florida Historical Quarterly*, VL (Jan. 1967), 243–52, is a state study of journalism that was patterned after the progressive magazines and contemptuous of local newspapers.

In Wisconsin, Steffens's judgment in *McClure's* was of great importance to the reform governor. David P. Thelen has found that "La Follette became more comfortable and effective raising issues with muckrakers than he was with the politicians in his own legislature." *Robert M. La Follette and the Insurgent Spirit* (Boston, 1976), pp. 44, 50.

35. LS to Joseph Steffens, 17 Oct. 1903 in *The Letters of Lincoln Steffens*, Ella Winter and Granville Hicks, eds. (2 vols.: New York, 1938) I, 158; Peter Lyon, *Success Story: The Life and Times of S. S. McClure* (New York, 1963), p. 222.

36. Walter Johnson, *William Allen White's America* (New York, 1947), pp. 63–64, 78–79. See John DeWitt McKee, *William Allen White, Maverick on Main Street* (Westport, 1975), for bibliography.

37. David Graham Phillips, "Secretary Root and His Plea for Centralization," *Arena* (Feb. 1907), reprinted in Louis Filler, ed., *Contemporaries: Portraits in the Progressive Era of David Graham Phillips* (Westport, 1981), p. 140. In Judson A. Grenier's sample of 40 muckrakers, 17 held newspaper jobs in Western cities early in their careers. This does not include journalists such as Steffens and McClure who drew on experiences in the West. The great majority of muckrakers, Grenier shows, migrated to New York and Washington: "The Origins and Nature of Progressive Muckraking" (Ph.D. diss.,U.C.L.A., 1965). Theodore

Francke's valuable study also touches on this: "Investigative Exposure in the Nineteenth Century: The Journalistic Heritage of the Muckrakers," (Ph.D. diss., Univ. of Minn., 1974), p. 358. As might be expected, if one includes minor figures in the muckraking movement the Western element is less prominent, but the migration I have described is still a common pattern— see Peter N. Barry, "The Decline of Muckraking: A View from the Magazines" (Ph.D. diss., Wayne State University, 1973), pp. 50, 52.

38. Vaughn, *Holding Fast the Inner Lines*, pp. 25–26 on O'Higgins; p. 29 on Sisson; William L. Chenery also fits this pattern, see his memoir, *So It Seemed* (New York, 1952); William MacLeod Raine was another reporter Creel brought in from Denver, see also p. 64. Thomas C. Leonard, "George Creel," *Dictionary of American Biography* Supplement V (New York, 1977), 141–43.

39. Vaughn, *Holding Fast the Inner Lines*, has reproduced these posters, pp. 165, 167; see pp. 130–31 on Russell. James R. Mock and Cedric Larson, *Words that Won the War: The Story of the Committee on Public Information, 1917–1919* (New York, 1939) remains useful. Cleveland Moffett, "The Conquest of America in 1921," and "Saving the Nation" ran in *McClure's*, XXXXV–XXXXVI (1915–16). For a wider view of the place of muckrakers in war-time appeals see David M. Kennedy, *Over Here: The First World War and American Society* (New York, 1980), chap. 1, and Thomas C. Leonard, *Above the Battle: War-Making in America from Appomattox to Versailles* (New York, 1978) chap. 9.

40. Vaughn, *Holding Fast the Inner Lines*, pp. 194–97.

7. The Civics and Anti-Civics of Muckraking

1. There are two quantitative studies of this reporting: Judson A. Grenier, Jr., "The Origins and Nature of Progressive Muckraking" (Ph.D. diss., U.C.L.A., 1965), and Peter N. Barry, "The Decline of Muckraking: A View from the Magazines" (Ph.D. diss., Wayne State University, 1973). In Barry's sample between a quarter and a third of the muckrakers held jobs in government in the course of their careers (p. 57).

2. I have relied on the voting analysis in Walter Dean Burnham, "The Changing Shape of the American Political Universe," *The American Political Science Review*, LIX (March 1965), 7–28; Burnham, *Critical Elections and the Mainsprings of American Politics* (New York, 1970), chap. 4, see especially p. 84; and Paul Kleppner, *Who Voted?: The Dynamics of Electoral Turnout, 1870–1980* (New York, 1982). Richard L. McCormick, *From Realignment to Reform, Political Change in New York State, 1893–1910* (Ithaca and London, 1981), confirms this trend and shows that in New York lower turnout was not an artifact of changed voting procedures (see pp. 187–89, 241–42, 252–53, 262, 269). See also Michael Paul Rogin and John L. Shover, *Political Change in California, Critical Elections and Social Movements, 1890–1966* (Westport, 1970), pp. 26–28; and John Francis Reynolds, "Testing Democracy: Electoral Participation and Progressive Reform in New Jersey, 1888–1919" (Ph. D. diss., Rutgers University, 1980).

Puzzlement about the decline of voting began during the Progressive Era, see, for example, William G. Brown, "The Changing Character of National Elections," *Independent*, LVIII (19 Jan. 1905), 121–26, Charles E. Russell, "The Break-Up of the Parties," *Success*, XII (Jan. 1909), 9; and "New Anxieties about Voting," *Century Magazine*, LXXXV (Dec. 1912), 311–12. Recognition of this problem by historians is remarkably recent, see Daniel T. Rodgers, "In Search of Progressives," *Reviews in American History*, X (Dec. 1982), 113–32, especially 115–17, and Thomas C. Leonard, "The 'Bully Pulpit': Who Listened?" *ibid.*, XI (March 1983), 104–7.

3. Raymond E. Wolfinger and Stephen J. Rosenstone, *Who Votes?* (New Haven, 1980), p. 100.

4. Burnham, *Critical Elections*, p. 73. Richard Jensen, *The Winning of the Midwest, Social and Political Conflict, 1888–1896* (Chicago and London, 1971), p. 13. Warren E. Miller, "Disinterest, Disaffection, and Participation in Presidential Politics," *Political Behavior*, II (1980), 12, 14, suggests that voter turnout by itself may not be an adequate measure of political interest. In the past two decades, for example, citizens have reported a stronger habit of writing letters to representatives in government at the same time turnout for elections has declined. No one has data from the Progressive Era to permit fine distinctions, but I know of no evidence of broader participation in politics by males in this period.

5. The most sophisticated and comprehensive study of this matter is Michael E. McGerr, *The Decline of Popular Politics: The American North, 1865–1928*, (New York, 1986).

6. Jacob Citrin, "The Alienated Voter," *Taxing & Spending*, I (Oct.-Nov. 1978), 10–11. For a more ambiguous reading of the evidence see Richard Brody, "The Puzzle of Political Participation in America," in Anthony King, ed., *The New American Political System* (Washington, 1978), pp. 287–324, especially pp. 308–10.

7. Jensen's extensive discussion of campaign styles in *The Winning of the Midwest* should be supplemented with Jean H. Baker, *Affairs of Party: The Political Culture of Northern Democrats in the Mid-Nineteenth Century* (Ithaca and London, 1983), pp. 288–97 on martial forms in political life.

8. "Cheerful Vanity," *Hampton's Magazine*, XIV (Jan. 1910), 152–53. "Political Duty," *Independent*, LV (14 May 1903), 1159. See also "The Revolt of the Plain Citizen," *World To-Day*, VIII (April 1905), 345–46.

9. On the varied causes of anti-partyism in the 1890s see, in addition to McGerr cited above, Jensen, *The Winning of the Midwest*, pp. 164, 174–75, 306–7. Paul Kleppner, *The Cross of Culture: A Social Analysis of Midwestern Politics, 1850–1900* (New York, 1970), is another convincing demonstration of the primacy of religious and ethnic factors in elections and the importance of ritual in political participation.

That a more complex presentation of issues hurts turnout is axiomatic in social science literature, see for example Miller, "Disinterest, Disaffection, and Participation . . . ," pp. 30–31. Both historians and students of contemporary political behavior have good reason to be modest in speculation. Rodgers, "In Search of Progressivism," observed that "no one really knows" why a complex withdrawal from politics occurred early in this century (p. 116). In *Who Votes?* (1980) Wolfinger and Rosenstone cautioned that "research on this topic has not progressed much beyond a few very broad (and sometimes false) propositions. . . ." (p. 2). *Who Votes* makes a major advance in our understanding of participation with the aid of the Current Population Survey of the Bureau of the Census and the National Election Studies from the University of Michigan. We still lack clear answers to many questions, however. Do parents, siblings or spouses influence the participation of family members? Does the form of political discourse in society affect the mobilization of voters? Historians will not find much guidance in the current interpretations of the survey data.

10. William L. Riordon, *Plunkitt of Tammany Hall* (New York, 1963) [1905], pp. 36, 81–83. *McClure's Magazine*, XXIV (March 1905), 525 has this cartoon by Dan Beard. Steffens filed a concise plea against party loyalty in "Enemies of the Republic," *McClure's*, XXIII (Aug. 1904), 395–408.

11. Charles E. Russell, "At the Throat of the Republic" *Cosmopolitan*, XXXXIV (Dec. 1907, Jan. 1908, Feb. 1908, April 1908), 146–57, 259–71, 361–69, 475–80 (p. 150 quoted).

12. Lincoln Steffens, "Rhode Island: A State for Sale," *McClure's*, XXIV (Feb. 1905), 342. Ray Stannard Baker, "What Is Lynching?" *ibid*. 422. David Graham Phillips, *The Plum Tree* (Indianapolis, 1905), pp. 12–13. Brand Whitlock, *The Thirteenth District, The Story of A Candidate* (Indianapolis, 1902), pp. 116–17, see also 236–37; Whitlock, "The City and Civilization," *Scribner's Magazine*, LII (Nov. 1912), 628. The wide attention to rural Ohio in the reform press is fully documented in Genevieve B. Gist, "Progressive Reform in a Rural Community: The Adams County Vote-Fraud Case," *Mississippi Valley Historical Review*, XLVIII (June 1961), 60–78.

13. David Grayson, "Adventures in Contentment, The Politician," *American Magazine*, LXIV (Oct. 1907), 646–50. For a discussion of the anti-urban theme in the later Grayson stories see John F. Semonche, *Ray Stannard Baker: A Quest for Democracy in Modern America, 1870–1918* (Chapel Hill, 1969) 168–71. Similar sentiments in muckraking magazines: "Confessions of a Country Mouse in the City" and "The Call of the Tame," *Independent*, LVI (11 Feb. 1904), 310–11 and 339–40. George Creel, "Mending Broken Men," *Success*, XIV (June 1911), 18–19, 38–40, esp. 39. In light of the analogy I shall make between muckraking and the mass media of contemporary America, it is significant that Herbert J. Gans found "small-town provincialism" a basic value shaping coverage, in *Deciding What's News, A Study of CBS Evening News, NBC Nightly News, Newsweek, and Time* (New York, 1979), pp. 48–50.

14. White, *Gazette*, Feb. 1, 1912, and June 20, 1912, cited in Jean B. Quandt, *From the Small Town to the Great Community: The Social Thought of Progressive Intellectuals* (New Brunswick, 1970). "Emporia and New York," *American Magazine*, LXIII (Jan. 1907), 258–64. Helen O. Mahin, ed., *The Editor and His People, Editorials by William Allen White* (New York, 1924), pp. 252–53, 309–11.

15. Quandt, *From the Small Town to the Great Community*, chap. 10, is an illuminating discussion, see especially pp. 66, 70. See Kleppner, *The Cross of Culture*, p. 304, on Bryan's campaign of 1896.

16. David P. Thelen, *The New Citizenship: Origins of Progressivism in Wisconsin, 1885–1900* (Columbia, 1972), p. 288. There is a vast literature on ethnic tensions

within progressivism. Some of the most valuable discussions are John Higham, *Strangers in the Land: Patterns of American Nativism, 1860–1925* (New York, 1963), pp. 116–22, 174–79; John D. Buenker, *Urban Liberalism and Progressive Reform* (New York, 1973), pp. 163–97. David H. Hollinger, "Ethnic Diversity, Cosmopolitanism and the Emergence of the American Liberal Intelligentsia," *American Quarterly*, XXVII (May 1975), 133–51.

17. The definitive study of the changed focus of reporting in the capital is George Juergens, *News from the White House, The Presidential-Press Relationship in the Progressive Era* (Chicago and London, 1981). The press corps moved camp from Capitol Hill to the White House, a building not routinely covered before the end of the 1890s.

18. The photo of Phillips is in Isaac F. Marcosson, *David Graham Phillips and His Times* (New York, 1932). Bailey Millard, "David Graham Phillips, His Work and His Clothes," *Human Life*, VIII (June 1909), 9–23.

19. *Leslie's Weekly*, C, 30 March 1905, 304. All of the photographs save one are reproduced in the reprint edition published in New York in 1953.

20. The only precedent I have found for the snap shots of senators appeared in a story favorable to the upper house: Walter Wellman, "Operating the United States Senate," *Success*, VII (Oct. 1904), 559–61. What the New York *Times* called "promiscuous photographing" (snap shots of the Democratic presidential candidate) arose in the 1904 campaign, 16 July 1904, p. 2.

"The Shame of California-Photographed," appeared in *American Magazine*, LXV (Dec. 1907), 144 as part of Lincoln Steffens, "The Mote and the Beam." George E. Mowry, *The California Progressives* (Berkeley and Los Angeles, 1951), pp. 60, 174.

Charles E. Russell's series, "What Are You Going To Do About It?" *Cosmopolitan*, XLIX-L (July-Oct. & Dec. 1910) is a striking example of how composite photos brought a new element to the work of a veteran muckraker. In his earlier, celebrated work on the Beef Trust and the tenements owned by Trinity Church, documentary photographs had come without theatrical effects.

James Creelman, "The Romance and Tragedy of Wood Engraving," *Pearson's Magazine*, XVII (March 1907), 293, called the half-tone process a "revolution" in illustration and emphasized the economy. A master engraver fetched $150 to $200 for a picture that could now be made ready for the press for $6 to $30. The savings in time was just as dramatic. See also Neil Harris, "Iconography and Intellectual History: The Half-Tone Effect," in *New Directions in American Intellectual History*, ed., John Higham and Paul K. Conkin (Baltimore, 1979).

21. David Graham Phillips, *The Treason of the Senate*, George E. Mowry and Judson A. Grenier, eds. (Chicago, 1964) pp. 59, 85, 92, 99, 114–15, 121, 126, 146; "orators of the treason" appeared in a conclusion at the end of the third installment in *Cosmopolitan*, the phrase is not reproduced in this edition. Phillips also dismissed speeches in the Senate writing in *Appleton's Magazine* (April 1906). David J. Rothman, *Politics and Power: The United States Senate, 1869–1901* (Cambridge, 1966), is the best single demonstration of how little of his subject Phillips understood.

"The Treason of the Senate" was longer, but not more extreme than other exposés of Congress in these magazines. Alfred Henry Lewis said that his political reporting was modeled after the rattlesnake's approach to intruders, and Lewis was frequently as good as his word. See, for example, "Confessions of a Newspaper Man," *Human Life*, II (Nov. 1905), 4; "Some Presidential Candidates," *ibid.*, VII (April 1908), 9–10, 32–33; "What Is 'Joe' Cannon?" *Cosmopolitan*, XLVIII (April 1910), 569–75. Samuel Merwin, "Taking the Hoe to Congress," *Success*, IX (Sept. 1906), 604–5, 647–48. Hearst's long-drawn-out release of the "Archbold Letters" was an assault on the integrity of the Senate, see *Hearst's Magazine, The World To-Day*, XXI (May 1912), 2201–16, and *ibid.* (June 1912) 2362–2776h.

22. Phillips, *The Treason of the Senate*, pp. 60, 69, 92, 99, 104, 194, 214. Upton Sinclair, *The Jungle* (New York, 1906), see especially pp. 110, 308. Virtually all of the fiction I use first appeared in muckraking publications. I cite the books as a convenience. There was much taunting of the reader in Russell, "At the Throat of the Republic," pp. 150, 260, 475. Alfred Henry Lewis spoke of "a numskull public" in "The Revolution at Washington," *Cosmopolitan*, XLIX (July 1910), 245.

23. John Graham (David Graham Phillips), *The Great God Success, A Novel* (New York, 1901), p. 173; Phillips, *The Cost*, p. 241; Phillips, *The Plum Tree*, pp. 220, 252. For dispiriting testimony about how politics worked see, for example, Eltweed Pomeroy, "An Outsider's Experiences with Inside Politics" and the editorial "Popular Government; 1904," *Independent*, LVI, 5 May 1904, 1006–10 and 1039–40; William Hemstreet, "The New Primary Law," *Arena*, XXVIII (Dec. 1902), 585–95.

24. Alfred Henry Lewis, "Mr. Lewis' Editorial Comment," *Human Life*, IV (Nov. 1906), 17. Charles E. Russell, "The Break-Up of the Parties," *Success*, XII (Jan. 1909), 6. Phillips, *The Cost*, p. 252. Similarly, the posthumously published *George Helm* (New York, 1912) treated politics as a black art whose deceptions corrupted the best citizens. This novel ran as a serial in Hearst's *The World To-Day*, XXI-XXII, during the presidential campaign of 1912.

25. Sinclair, *The Jungle*, pp. 339–41, 366–67.

26. "Albert J. Beveridge: A Character Sketch," *Success* (Aug. 1905), reprinted in Louis Filler, ed., *Contemporaries, Portraits in the Progressive Era by David Graham Phillips* (Westport, 1981), p. 125 (quoted).

27. I have quoted from the Roosevelt text in the Mowry and Grenier edition of *The Treason of the Senate*, pp. 218, 223. For a full account of the Roosevelt-Sinclair exchange and each man's role in the reform legislation see Robert M. Crunden, *Ministers of Reform* (New York, 1982), pp. 163–99.

28. Mowry and Grenier, *The Treason of the Senate*, p. 220. Elting E. Morison et al., eds., *The Letters of Theodore Roosevelt* (8 vols.: Cambridge, 1951–54), V, TR to Alfred Henry Lewis, 17 Feb. 1906, pp. 156–57; TR to William H. Taft, 15 March 1906, p. 184. TR to George H. Lorimer, 12 May 1906, pp. 264–5. George W. Alger had made similar points earlier in the *Atlantic* about the depressing and isolating effects of exposure for the ordinary reader, see his *Moral Overstrain* (Boston and New York, 1906), pp. 124–27.

29. Morison, ed., *The Letters of Theodore Roosevelt*, V, TR to George H. Lorimer, 12 May 1906, 269.

30. Robert M. Crunden, *A Hero in Spite of Himself: Brand Whitlock in Art, Politics, and War* (New York, 1969), p. 107.

31. *Ibid.*, p. 74.

32. On Whitlock's disgust with the political process see Crunden, *A Hero in Spite of Himself*, p. 36; Whitlock, *Forty Years of It* (New York, 1925) pp. 94–95. This autobiography was published in book form in 1914; it had reached the public through magazines a year earlier. Whitlock, *The Thirteenth District*, p. 433.

33. Barry, "The Decline of Muckraking" has the most comprehensive and carefully qualified circulation figures, see pp. 26–27 and Appendix II.

34. David H. Chalmers estimated that 12 million monthly readers, encompassing 20 million families were reached by periodicals with muckraking themes, "The Muckrakers and the Growth of Corporate Power: A Study in Constructive Journalism," *American Journal of Economics and Society*, XVIII (April 1959), 297. Beveridge quoted by David P. Thelen, *Robert M. LaFollette and the Insurgent Spirit* (Boston, 1976), p. 76.

35. Finley Peter Dunne, "National Housecleaning," *Collier's*, XXXVI, 16 Dec 1905, 12.

36. "The Publishers' Outlook," *Success Magazine*, XII (Oct. 1909), 613, reviews clubbing schemes. The editors said that there had been a five-fold increase in the circulation of subscription agency catalogues since 1900. *Ibid.*, VI (Oct. 1903), 621.

37. Richard Hofstadter, *The Age of Reform: From Bryan to F. D. R.* (New York, 1955), pp. 186–98. According to the letter to Lincoln Steffens from Doubleday, Page & Co., 25 Jan. 1909, *The Shame of the Cities* sold 29 copies from 1 July 1908 to 24 Nov. 1908. A letter from this publisher on 1 Aug. 1909, reported that 39 copies had been sold in the preceding six months (both in Lincoln Steffens Papers, Columbia University). For the total sales figures of this book and others see Barry, "The Decline of Muckraking," pp. 215–17.

38. Michael J. Robinson, "Public Affairs Television and the Growth of Political Malaise: The Case of 'The Selling of the Pentagon'," *American Political Science Review*, LXX (June 1976), 426. Thomas A. Kazee, "Television Exposure and Attitude Change": The Impact of Political Interest," *Public Opinion Quarterly*, VL (Winter 1981), 507–18, is a confirming study of the Watergate era with a valuable review of the literature on the ways reporting may decrease the public's sense of its political efficacy. Austin Ranney, *Channels of Power: The Impact of Television on American Politics* (New York, 1983), is a particularly lucid consideration of the implications of this research. Ranney follows Herbert Gans in drawing attention to similarities between progressivism before WWI and TV newspeople in the 1980s (pp. 53–54). Gans, *Deciding What's News*, pp. 203–6. Arthur H. Miller, Edie N. Goldenberg, and Lutz Erbring, "Type-Set Politics: Impact of Newspapers on Public Confidence," *American Political Science Review* LXXIII (March 1979), 67–84 shows that the effects of political criticism was greatest on those whose education has not prepared them to take account of complexity. The authors take issue with earlier methods of studying this problem.

During the Progressive Era some editors of the older magazines made a dark prognosis of the new exposés, see, for example, "The Cheap Magazines in Politics," *Harper's Weekly*, LVII, 25 Jan 1913, 5.

39. Walter Lippmann, *Public Opinion* (New York, 1922) and *The Phantom Public* (New York, 1927). Carole Pateman, *Participation and Democratic Theory* (New York, 1980) [1970], p. 7. This book is a careful examination of the inadequacies of contemporary democratic theory.

40. David S. Barry, "The Loyalty of the Senate," *New England Magazine*, XXXV (Oct. 1906), 141. *McClure's* itself published letters of its elite, appreciative readers, see vol. XXII (June 1904), 221–24.

41. Ronald Steel, *Walter Lippmann and the American Century* (New York, 1981), p. 34. Even Hearst's editors had an appetite for theoretical work by progressives, see for example Walter E. Weyl, "The New Democracy," *Hearst's Magazine, The World To-Day*, XXI (June 1912), 2489–94. Leonard L. Richards, *"Gentlemen of Property and Standing," Anti-Abolition Mobs in Jacksonian America* (New York, 1971), see especially pp. 71–73, 162–70.

For Further Reading

This is a book about the birth of political reporting, not about its full development or about related forms of journalism. The distinction saves me (and the reader) from the "break down" Allan Nevins warned about in his acute observations "American Journalism and Its Historical Treatment," *Journalism Quarterly*, XXXVI (Fall 1959). For a well-organized bibliography of the broad field see Edwin Emery and Michael Emery, *The Press and America: An Interpretive History of the Mass Media*, 5th ed. (Englewood Cliffs, 1984).

The Notes contain the evidence that bears on specific parts of my argument and there I have included information on manuscript sources. Here I wish to acknowledge works that have played a more general role in determining my approach. I hope this will help readers to answer their own questions about the course of political reporting.

The Eighteenth Century

In the Introduction I am indebted to the recent scholarship collected in Bernard Bailyn and John B. Hench, eds., *The Press & the American Revolution* (Worcester, 1980), especially the essays by Stephen Botein and Robert M. Weir; also William L. Joyce et al., eds., *Printing and Society in Early America*,(Worcester, 1983), especially the essays by Donald M. Scott and Rhys Isaac; Michael Zuckerman, *Peaceable Kingdoms; New England Towns in the Eighteenth Century* (New York, 1970).

For the social basis of printing, see Stephen Botein, " 'Meer Mechanics' and an Open Press: The Business and Political Strategies of Colonial American Printers," *Perspectives in American History*, IX (1975), and Charles W. Wetherell, " 'Brokers of the Word': An Essay in the Social History of the American Press, 1639–1783" (Ph.D. diss., Univ.

of New Hampshire, 1980). Lawrence C. Wroth, *The Colonial Printer* (New York, 1931) remains valuable.

Leonard W. Levy has documented the record of restraints and coercion in eighteenth-century journalism in *Emergence of A Free Press* (New York, 1985). The major texts are readily available. *The English Libertarian Heritage* (Indianapolis, 1965) edited by David L. Jacobson presents some of the most important of Cato's Letters. Stanley N. Katz has edited James Alexander, *A Brief Narrative of the Case and Trial of John Peter Zenger, Printer of the New York "Weekly Journal"* (Cambridge, 1963). See also Leonard W. Levy, ed., *Freedom of the Press from Zenger to Jefferson* (Indianapolis, 1966).

Boston

The best overview of this city is G. B. Warden, *Boston, 1689–1776* (Boston, 1970). The most detailed account of the life of the town that swirled around James Franklin's print shop is Arthur Bernon Tourtellot, *Benjamin Franklin, The Shaping of Genius, The Boston Years* (Garden City, 1977). Tourtellot adds something to each of the three standard treatments of the smallpox crisis: Perry Miller, *The New England Mind: From Colony to Province* (Boston, 1961) [1953], chap. 21; John B. Blake, *Public Health in the Town of Boston, 1630–1832* (Cambridge, 1959), chap. 4; Ola Elizabeth Winslow, *A Destroying Angel: The Conquest of Smallpox in Colonial Boston* (Boston, 1974). The skill as observers of the inoculators is well displayed in their pamphlets: Zabdiel Boylston, *Some Account of What Is Said of Inoculation . . .* (Boston, 1721) and *An Historical Account of the Small Pox Inoculated in New England* (London, 1726, reprinted Boston, 1730); Benjamin Colman, *Some Observations on the New Method of Receiving the Smallpox by Ingrafting or Inoculation, In New England* (Boston, 1721).

The Revolution

Isaiah Thomas, *The History of Printing in America*, ed., Marcus A. McCorison (New York, 1970), is a unique storehouse of research and personal observation. Thomas published the *Massachusetts Spy* in the 1770s and brought out this volume in 1810. No scholarship in the nineteenth century was superior. There is much to be learned from Philip Davidson, *Propaganda and the American Revolution, 1763–1783* (Chapel Hill, 1941), but in my view this notion of "propaganda" does not grasp all that these partisan writers let loose. Arthur M. Schlesinger, *Prelude to Independence: The Newspaper War on Britain, 1764–1776* (New York,

1958), gracefully sums up a lifetime of reading of the colonial press. Schlesinger's earlier articles on eighteenth-century journalism contain more detail. I have often been guided by Schlesinger's work.

Of the exposés I discuss, only the "Farmer's Letters" and the "Journal of Occurrences" have been republished in a modern edition (see Notes). John Mein, *A State of the Importations from Great Britain into the Port of Boston . . .* (Boston, 1769), brings together the Tory critique of the patriots that appeared in the Boston *Chronicle*. *The Writings of Samuel Adams*, ed., Harry A. Cushing (4 vols.: New York, 1904–08), is a great convenience in the study of this busy radical (Adams used more than twenty pseudonyms in newspapers). *The American Colonial Crisis, The Daniel Leonard-John Adams Letters to the Press, 1774–1775*, ed., Bernard Mason (New York, 1972), includes Adams's "Novanglus" essays and shows that polemics did come to display the learning used earlier in the newspaper war against Britain by John Dickinson.

The political complexion of the English press can be studied in the excellent work by Geoffrey A. Cranfield, *The Development of the Provincial Newspaper, 1700–1760* (Oxford, 1962). Roy M. Wiles has valuable information in *Freshest Advices: Early Provincial Newspapers in England* (Ohio State University Press, 1965). For the London press see John Brewer's superb *Party Ideology and Popular Politics at the Accession of George III* (Cambridge, 1976).

The passions of Massachusetts politics were not fully expressed in newspapers. Richard D. Brown has studied an important new form of communication, *Revolutionary Politics in Massachusetts: The Boston Committee of Correspondence and the Towns, 1772–1774* (Cambridge, 1974). Dirk Hoerder has shown that the "radical" press, when viewed from the bottom of society, may not have articulated pressing issues: *Crowd Action in Revolutionary Massachusetts, 1765–1780* (New York, 1977). The most valuable works on the ideas and institutions in conflict before 1776 are: Bernard Bailyn, *The Ideological Origins of the American Revolution* (Cambridge, 1967) and *The Ordeal of Thomas Hutchinson* (Cambridge, 1974); Pauline Maier, *From Resistance to Revolution; Colonial Radicals and the Development of American Opposition to Britain, 1765–1776* (New York, 1972); Gary B. Nash, *The Urban Crucible: Social Change, Political Consciousness, and the Origins of the American Revolution* (Cambridge, 1974); Peter Shaw, *American Patriots and the Rituals of Revolution* (Cambridge, 1981); John Shy, *Toward Lexington: The Role of the British Army in the Coming of the American Revolution* (Princeton, 1965). This scholarship does not mean that the fights begun by colonial journalists have been settled; some historians carry them on with the same attention to the minutia and props of revolution. Hiller B. Zobel discounted many of the patriots' claims against royal officials in *The Boston Massacre* (New

York, 1970), and was challenged, as Sam Adams would have challenged him, by another vision of street life in Boston— see Jesse Lemisch, "Radical Plot: Boston," *Harvard Law Review*, LXXXIV (1970–71), 485–504.

Donald H. Stewart, *The Opposition Press of the Federalist Period* (Albany, 1969), is an encyclopedic survey of the first years of self-government.

The Nineteenth Century

Much work remains to be done in explaining how politics became so popular and how the press became so enmeshed in political life in the first decades of this century. I am grateful to recent scholars who have helped me see these are open questions: William E. Gienapp, "'Politics Seem To Enter into Everything': Political Culture in the North, 1840–1860," in Stephen E. Maizlish and John J. Kushma, eds., *Essays on American Antebellum Politics, 1840–1860* (College Station, Tx., 1982); Alexander Saxton, "Problems of Class and Race in the Origins of the Mass Circulation Press," *American Quarterly*, XXXVI (Summer 1984), 211–34; Dan Schiller, *Objectivity and the News: The Public and the Rise of Commercial Journalism* (Philadelphia, 1981); Michael Schudson, *Discovering the News: A Social History of American Newspapers* (New York, 1978); William E. Ames, *A History of the National Intelligencer* (Chapel Hill, 1972).

My picture of political reporting in the nineteenth century has been drawn from these accounts:

Joseph Tinker Buckingham, *Personal Memoirs and Recollections of Editorial Life* (2 vols.: Boston, 1852).

Charles T. Congdon, *Recollections of a Journalist* (Boston, 1880).

Fred A Emery, "Washington Newspaper Correspondents," *Records of the Columbia Historical Society*, XXXV-XXXVI (1935), pp. 248–88.

L. A. Gobright, *Recollection of Men and Things at Washington* (Philadelphia, 1869).

Charles Lanman, "The National Intelligencer and Its Editors," *The Atlantic Monthly*, VI (Oct. 1860), 470–81.

"The 'National Intelligencer' and Its Editors," *Harper's Weekly*, II (Jan. 1858), 45.

[T. N. Parmelee] "Recollections of an Old Stager," *Harper's New Monthly Magazine*, XXXXV-XLIX (Aug. 1872–June 1874)

Ben Perley Poore, "Washington News," *Harper's New Monthly Magazine*, XXXXVIII (Jan. 1874), 225–36.

————, *Perley's Reminiscences of Sixty Years in the National Metropolis* (2 vols.: Philadelphia, 1886).

Francis A. Richardson, "Recollections of a Washington Correspondent," *Records of the Columbia Historical Society*, VI (1903), pp. 24–42.

Nathan Sargent, *Public Men and Events from the Commencement of Mr. Monroe's Administration, in 1817 to the Close of Mr. Fillmore's Administration in 1853* (2 vols.: Philadelphia, 1875).

Jane Grey Swisshelm, *Half a Century* (Chicago, 1880).

George Alfred Townsend ("Gath"), *Washington, Outside and Inside* (Hartford and Chicago, 1873).

Henry Villard, *Memoirs of Henry Villard, Journalist and Financier* (2 vols.: Boston and New York, 1904).

Franc B. Willkie, *Personal Reminisces of 35 Years of Journalism* (Chicago, 1891).

Henry A. Wise, *Seven Decades of the Republic* (Richmond, 1881).

Tweed's New York

The best single work on this period is Alexander B. Callow, Jr., *The Tweed Ring* (New York, 1966). Callow republished key chapters of this book along with wide-ranging views of the political machine in *The City Boss in America: An Interpretive Reader* (New York, 1976). The full complexity of the Democratic party is described by Jerome Mushkat, *The Reconstruction of the New York Democracy, 1861–1874* (Rutherford, N.J., 1981). Only one of Tweed's associates has attracted a modern biographer: Croswell Bowen, *The Elegant Oakey* (New York, 1956). Leo Hershkowitz, *Tweed's New York: Another Look* (Garden City, 1977), corrects and fills in the record and makes a dogged plea for the defense. Seymour Mandelbaum wrote a perceptive book without attempting to re-open the case but instead showing how Tweed's special virtues as a communicator were rewarded in the metropolis: *Boss Tweed's New York* (New York, 1965). The following older histories continue to throw light on the subtleties of machine government: Gustavus Myers, *The History of Tammany Hall* (New York, 1901); Denis T. Lynch, *"Boss" Tweed, the Story of a Grim Generation* (New York, 1927); and Edwin Kilroe, *Tammany, A Patriotic History* (New York, 1924). Jon C. Teaford, *Unheralded Triumph: City Government in America, 1870–1900* (Baltimore and London, 1984) marks the rejection of the tradition of fretting about how American cities were governed in the Gilded Age.

The role of the press in shaping urban life is illuminated by two excellent books: Gunther Barth, *City People: The Rise of Modern City Culture in Nineteenth-Century America* (New York, 1980), and Paul Boyer, *Urban Masses and Moral Order in America, 1820–1920* (Cambridge, 1978). Meyer Berger, *The Story of the New York Times* (New York, 1951), is lively and informed, but Berger wrote with a reporter's caution to not ask questions past the point they might hurt the story. The earlier official history of the paper by Elmer Davis is less helpful. Morton Keller, *The Art and Politics of Thomas Nast* (New York, 1968) is the best collection and commentary. However, the Tweed section must be used with caution—some of the cartoon captions have been transposed. There is much new information in Albert Boime, "Thomas Nast and French Art," *American Art Journal*, IV (Spring 1972), 43–65. Albert B. Paine, *Th. Nast: His Period and His Pictures* (New York, 1904), is still useful and has many cartoons that Keller does not reproduce. Paine's book resurrected Nast for progressives and gave them courage in the new struggles for urban reform—see the review by B. O. Flower in *Arena*, XXXIII (March 1905), 270–88.

The "picture-hungry" society of the 1860s is the theme of a superb work: Harold Holzer, Gabor S. Boritt, and Mark E. Neely, Jr., *The Lincoln Image, Abraham Lincoln and the Popular Print* (New York, 1984). New ground is also covered in Peter C. Marzio, *The Democratic Art, Pictures for a 19th-Century America* (New York, 1979). Neil Harris has important insights on the role of photographs on the eve of progressivism: "Iconography and Intellectual History: The Half-Tone Effect," in *New Directions in American Intellectual History*, John Higham and Paul K. Conkin, eds. (Baltimore, 1979).

There is no single definitive work on American political cartoons. Stephen Hess and Milton Kaplan, eds., *The Ungentlemanly Art: A History of American Political Cartoons*, rev. ed. (New York & London, 1975) is particularly useful for its bibliography. See also David Kunzle, *The Early Comic Strip: Narrative Strips and Picture Stories in the European Broadsheet from c. 1450 to 1825* (Berkeley, 1973), and Randall P. Harrison, *The Cartoon, Communication to the Quick* (Beverly Hills & London, 1981).

Crime

Thomas M. McDade, *The Annals of Murder, A Bibliography of Books and Pamphlets on American Murders from Colonial Times to 1900* (Norman, Ok., 1961), is very helpful. David Brion Davis, *Homicide in American Fiction, 1798–1860* (Ithaca, 1957), remains valuable. On the far richer European response to crime see Douglas Hay et al., eds., *Albion's Fatal Tree: Crime and Society in Eighteenth-Century England* (New York, 1975). Schiller's *Objectivity and the News* treats some of the material I have taken up from a different point of view. David R. Johnson, *Policing the Urban Underworld: The Impact of Crime on the Development of American Police, 1800–1887* (Philadelphia, 1979), and Roger Lane, *Violent Death in the City, Suicide, Accident, and Murder in Nineteenth Century Philadelphia* (Cam-

bridge, 1979) make extensive use of crime reports in the Philadelphia
Public Ledger.

Hoaxing and "sleuthing" in the press are major themes in Neil Harris,
Humbug: The Art of P. T. Barnum (Boston and Toronto, 1973); Melville
E. Stone, *Fifty Years a Journalist* (Garden City, N.Y. and Toronto, 1921),
p. 179.

St. Louis & Provincial Journalism

Daniel J. Boorstin, *The Americas: The National Experience* (New York,
1965) has written with perception about the strong local roots of the
daily press. Several scholars have given the regional literature of exposure the careful attention and broad perspective it deserves: David
Paul Nord, *Newspapers and New Politics: Midwestern Municipal Reform,
1890-1900* (Ann Arbor, 1981), Julian S. Rammelkamp, *Pulitzer's Post-
Dispatch, 1878–1883* (Princeton, 1967), and Max Putzel, *The Man in the
Mirror, William Marion Reedy and His Magazine* (Cambridge, 1963). Orrick
Johns, *Times of Our Lives, the Story of My Father and Myself* (New York,
1973), has much to say about Pulitzer's St. Louis days and the course
of crusading journalism. Like Lincoln Steffens's *Autobiography*, the Johns
memoir was first published in the 1930s and gave an elegant and im-
passioned critique of American journalism from the left. There is a good
biography of Steffens's source: Louis Geiger, *Joseph W. Folk of Missouri*
(University of Missouri Studies, XXV, No. 2) [Columbia, 1953]. Ernest
Kirschten's popular history of St. Louis, *Catfish and Crystal* (Garden
City, 1960), has a full discussion of machine politics. I have also used
William H. Taft, *Missouri Newspapers* (Columbia, 1964), and Homer W.
King, *Pulitzer's Prize Editor: A Biography of John A. Cockerill, 1845–1896*
(Durham, 1965).

The Twentieth Century

The combined efforts of W. A. Swanberg, Julian Rammelkamp, and
George Juergens have produced a clearer picture of Joseph Pulitzer
than exists for any other major figure in journalism at the turn of the
century. Pulitzer's personal papers have long been available to scholars;
William Randolph Hearst's remain inaccessible, except for some early
materials in the Bancroft Library at the University of California, Berkeley. This has severely limited serious appraisal. George Juergens gives
an excellent account of the working press in the capital in *News from
the White House: The Presidential-Press Relationship in the Progressive Era*
(Chicago and London, 1981).

Richard Hofstadter's brief discussion of the muckrakers in *The Age of Reform* (New York, 1955) remains an admirable essay on these journalists. However, the standard published works provide a good deal of information that does not fit Hofstadter's picture: Louis Filler, *The Muckrakers* (University Part, Pa., 1976), an enlarged edition of his *Crusaders for American Liberalism* (1939); David M. Chalmers, *The Social and Political Ideas of the Muckrakers* (New York, 1964); Harold S. Wilson, *McClure's Magazine and the Muckrakers* (Princeton, 1970); Richard L. McCormick, "The Discovery that Business Corrupts Politics: A Reappraisal of the Origins of Progressivism," *American Historical Review*, LXXXVI (April 1981), 247–74. Michael D. Marcaccio, "Did a Business Conspiracy End Muckraking? A Reexamination," *Historian*, XLVII (Nov. 1984), 58–71 presents the evidence that makes it very difficult to believe that muckraking was stopped by an economic conspiracy. Harvey Swados and Arthur and Lila Weinberg have edited anthologies of the muckrakers' work.

Some of the best memoirs of reform journalism early in this century are: Ray Stannard Baker, *American Chronicle* (New York, 1945); Charles E. Russell, *Bare Hands and Stone Walls: Some Reflections of a Side-Line Reformer* (New York, 1933); *The Autobiography of Lincoln Steffens* (2 vols.: New York, 1958) [1931]; Mark Sullivan, *The Education of an American* (New York, 1938); William Allen White, *The Autobiography of William Allen White* (New York, 1946); Brand Whitlock, *Forty Years of It* (New York, 1914).

There is a growing list of sophisticated biographies: Justin Kaplan *Lincoln Steffens* (New York, 1974); Robert M. Crunden, *A Hero in Spite of Himself: Brand Whitlock in Art, Politics, & War* (New York, 1969); Robert C. Bannister, Jr., *Ray Stannard Baker, The Mind and Heart of a Progressive* (New Haven, 1966). John E. Semonche, *Ray Stannard Baker: A Quest for Democracy in Modern America, 1870–1918* (Chapel Hill, 1969). Ronald Steel, *Walter Lippmann and the American Century* (New York, 1981).

Daniel J. Czitrom, *Media and the American Mind, From Morse to McLuhan* (Chapel Hill, 1982), covers the central period of this book, but with quite different interests. Czitrom's references are particularly useful.

The classic descriptions of the press corps fully document the way journalists have placed themselves as the patrons of politics: see, for example, Leo C. Rosten, *The Washington Correspondents* (New York, 1937); David Halberstam, *The Powers That Be* (New York, 1979). I am also indebted to Michael Schudson, "The Politics of Narrative Form: The Emergence of News Conventions in Print and Television," *Daedalus*, CXI (Fall 1982), 97–111.

Index

269